THE CAMPAIGN OF ADOWA AND THE RISE OF MENELIK

THE
CAMPAIGN OF ADOWA
AND
THE RISE OF MENELIK

BY

G. F-H. BERKELEY

WITH MAPS

The Naval & Military Press Ltd

Published and © by the
The Naval & Military Press

Unit 10 Ridgewood Industrial Park,
Uckfield, East Sussex, TN22 5QE
Tel: +44 (0) 1825 749494
Fax: +44 (0) 1825 765701

MILITARY HISTORY AT YOUR FINGERTIPS
www.naval-military-press.com
ONLINE GENEALOGY RESEARCH
www.military-genealogy.com
ONLINE MILITARY CARTOGRAPHY
www.militarymaproom.com

Printed and bound in Great Britain by
CPI Antony Rowe, Chippenham and Eastbourne

TO MY MOTHER

PREFACE

The battle of Adowa, and the campaign that preceded it, are important from many points of view, though as yet they have received but little attention in the British Isles.

In the first place it may rank as a peculiar phenomenon,—for it amounts to nothing less,—that a European army of about twenty thousand men should be annihilated by a native African race. To the best of my belief there is no parallel case in modern history.

The casualties during that one day's fighting amounted to over 25,000 in killed and wounded alone; but it is not merely these high numbers that give it a claim to attention. The whole war should be considered as one completed episode in the history of our Italian allies and of African colonization—an episode with many sides. To those, for instance, who make a study of campaigns, it offers a singularly suitable subject, as it lies (so to speak) "in a nutshell." Instead of there being several armies in the field, several lines of communication and several widely distant theatres of war, each of which influences the action in the other, there are here only two hostile forces confronting one another at the end of their lines of communication like two dogs fighting at the end of their chains. The element of chance is eliminated, as far as it is possible to eliminate it in war. Each move brings its inevitable result, which is often foreseen by the leaders with complete accuracy. It becomes easy, in fact, to enter into the feelings of the opposing generals.

For Britons it should have a special interest, as being the first important campaign in which a nation with a conscript army has had to face serious colonial difficulties; and one of the first wherein modern long-range weapons come into play on both sides.

Here also is a campaign in which, owing to the nature of the ground, the Italians decided to employ *no mounted troops whatsoever*,—a fact that proves how singularly their experience differs from our own during the last six years.

Finally, from the broader standpoint of politics and history, it seems possible that it heralds the rise of a new power in Africa—we are reminded that the natives of that continent may yet become a military factor worthy of our closest attention. The suggestion has even been made—absurd as it appears at present—that this is the first revolt of the Dark Continent against domineering Europe. And what a series of anomalies does Abyssinia represent! A nation chiefly of Semitic blood, of dark skin, and of feudal institutions. A nation that is young to-day, though it was powerful when the book of Genesis was written, and was Christian when our ancestors still worshipped Thor and Odin.

It is in these considerations and not in the actual story of the fighting—though the Italo-Abyssinian war abounds in dramatic incidents—that lies the true interest of the Campaign of Adowa.

There were no British or Americans with either the Italian or Shoan armies, so that in our language there can be no first-hand narrative of the events; any account of them must be drawn from the memoirs and conversation of survivors. As regards the memoirs etc. consulted, I give a list of the best that I was able to discover during a search of some months in Italy. More especially must I acknowledge a debt to the work of Signor Vico Mantegazza, for his description of the war-preparation at Massowah, which it would have been impossible for anyone to describe merely from official returns without having seen it.

The spelling of Abyssinian names is a matter of difficulty. I have spelt, as far as possible, phonetically, according to English pronunciation, giving also in many places the Italian spelling for the benefit of those who prefer the more detailed Italian maps.

George F-H. Berkeley.

CONTENTS

THE CAMPAIGN OF ADOWA; AND THE RISE OF MENELIK

PART I.—MENELIK BECOMES NEGUS NAGASTI OF ABYSSINIA.

PART II.—THE WAR BETWEEN ITALY AND ABYSSINIA.

LIST OF PRINCIPAL AUTHORITIES CONSULTED

ITALIAN

Baratieri, O.	Memorie d'Africa.
Bourelly, G.	La battaglia di Abba Garima.
Cecchi, A.	Da Zeila alle frontière del Caffa.
	L'Abissinia Settentrionale.
Chiala, V.	Il Generale Da Bormida nella giornata del 1° Marzo 1896.
Gamerra, G.	Ricorde di un prigionero allo Scioa.
	Fra gli Ascari.
Mantegazza, V.	La Guerra d'Africa.
	L'Assedio di Macalle.
Melli.	La Colonia Eritrea.
Menarini, G.	La brigata Dabormida alla battaglia d'Adua.
Moltedo, G.	L'Assedio di Maccale.
Münzinger, W.	Studi sull'Africa Orientale.
N. N.	I nostri errori in Africa.
Pianavia Vivaldi (Signora).	Tre Anni in Eritrea.
Sambon, L.	L'esercito abissino.
Sapeto.	Etiopia.
Toselli, P. (Un Eritreo).	Pro Africa Italica.
Ximenes, E.	Sul Campo d'Adua.

Comitato di Soccorso delle dame Romane per i prigioneri in Africa diario della missione e documenti.

Italian green books, official reports, narratives, newspapers, etc. Martini's report on Erythrea, etc.

FRENCH

Combes, P.	L'Abyssinie.
De la Jonquière.	Les Italiens en Erythrée.
Lamberti.	Rapport du General Lamberti sur la bataille d'Adoua.
Raffray, A.	Afrique Orientale — Abyssinie.
Le Roux, Hugues.	Menelik et Nous.
Luzeux, General.	L'Italie et L'Abyssinie.
Simon, G.	Voyage en Abyssinie et chez les Gallas Raias.

ENGLISH

Bruce (James) of Kinnaird.	Travels.
Holland & Hozier.	Expedition to Abyssinia.
Portal, Sir Gerald, K.C.B.	By Mission to Abyssinia.
Wilkins, Col. H. St. C.	Reconnoitring in Abyssinia.
Wingate, Sir F. R., K.C.B.	Mahdiism and the Egyptian Soudan.
Wylde.	Abyssinia.

ERRATA.

Page 77, fifteenth line from bottom: *For* "branches broken" *read* "branches were broken," etc.

Page 79, eleventh line from bottom: *For* "January 20th" *read* "January 30th."

Page 123, ninth line from top: *For* "1900" *read* "2100."

Page 332, twelfth line from top: *For* "Villafranca" *read* "San Martino."

PART I

MENELIK BECOMES NEGUS NAGASTI OF ABYSSINIA

CHAPTER I

THE EVENTS THAT LED TO THE TREATY OF UCCIALLI BETWEEN ITALY AND MENELIK

Results of the battle of Metemmeh (Gallabat)—The Italians seize three Abyssinian provinces—Menelik also extends his frontiers—Ras Alula checks their action—The Abyssinian army—Ras Alula's personality—Menelik's character—His friendship with Count Antonelli—They draw up the Treaty of Uccialli—Article III (the frontiers)—Article XVII (the Italian protectorate)—Maconnen's visit to Rome—The Convention of Uccialli—Italy formally announces her protectorate over Abyssinia—Baldissera resigns.

When, during the early hours of March 10th, 1889, the Emperor John of Abyssinia lay dying on the field of Metemmeh, near Gallabat, where he had that day gloriously defeated and almost annihilated the Dervish army, he called the greatest of his chiefs to him, and in their presence solemnly acknowledged young Ras Mangasha as his natural son by the wife of his own brother. As Ras Arya Selassie, his only legitimate offspring, had died a few months before, there was no direct successor to the throne; but now, in moving terms, he commended Mangasha to the care of all his followers and especially to that of Ras Alula, his old campanion-in-arms. Such a recommendation was tantamount to appointing him his heir; but the imperial throne of Abyssinia is not lightly given to a boy of twenty-five; the chiefs required time to deliberate. On the morning after the battle the Emperor died while as yet no agreement had been concluded amongst them, and no oath of allegiance sworn. As the Abyssinian army wended its way homewards, of all the greater chiefs who had followed John, only one remained with his son,—the old Ras Alula.

Abyssinia,[1] or Ethiopia as it is more correctly termed, is divided into five provinces; Tigré in the North, Amhara in the centre, Gojjam in the West, Shoa in the South and Harrar in the South East. John, before ascending the imperial throne, had been the ruler of Tigré, so it was to this province that Mangasha and Alula turned their steps; here, at all events, it seemed likely that the young man would reap the benefit of the respect and admiration that his father had so justly earned.

It had been a fitting end for the Emperor to die at the moment of victory; but it was a terrible misfortune for his country. At that time Abyssinia was surrounded by enemies; the Dervishes had been disposed of by John, but there remained the Italians[2] at Massowah, on the north-east

[1] Ethiopia is the name by which its inhabitants have known it since the days before the book on Genesis was written; the word Abyssinia is merely a corruption of Abeschi, "the people of mixed blood," *i.e.* "the mongrels"—a term of abuse fixed on it by its Mohammedan invaders and introduced into Europe by the Portuguese. To be called "an Abyssinian" is still resented by the Ethiopians, unless it is a European who is speaking to them; in his case they know that no insult is intended.

[2] During the previous four years (since January 25th, 1885,) the Italians had been endeavouring to establish a colony at Massowah and on the surrounding territories, to all of which the Abyssinians laid claim.

frontier, and, in the South, Menelik of Shoa, who, a traitor to his race, had allied himself with the invaders.

The want of the strong arm was soon perceptible. The Italians, under General Baldissera, dashed down from the North, occupying the towns of Asmara and Keren, and seizing the three outlying provinces of Hamacen, Serae and Okule-Kusai. There Baldissera halted and established his boundary along the line of the rivers Mareb, Belesa and Muna, and to this day the Mareb-Belesa-Muna frontier is the basis of negotiations with Abyssinia.

In the South, Menelik had not been idle; he had sent his representative, a man named Seium, into Tigré to make what capital he could out of the situation.

At this moment, just as the Italians were seizing his province of Hamacen, Ras Alula himself returned from the slaughter of Metemmeh, accompanying the young Ras Mangasha, to whom, in the words of a celebrated Italian officer,[1] "he was both mind and arm." With the arrival of the old warrior matters soon took a different turn. He hunted Seium out of Tigré, and although unable to make head against the Italians, he captured and imprisoned one of their most important native allies.

These little successes restored some semblance of order into that distracted country. Menelik was no longer one of the invaders; the three Northern provinces were irrevocably in the grasp of Italy; but throughout the remainder of Tigré Mangasha and Alula were gradually able to obtain the acknowledgment of their authority.

Before proceeding with the history of the many struggles

[1] Major Toselli.

between Italy and the various peoples of Ethiopia, it may be as well to give a short description of the numbers, armament, and leaders of the latter; for since their success at Adowa it has become the fashion in certain quarters to speak of them as almost European in organization. They have even been compared to the Japanese by some writers; but such comparisons are absurd, as every man who has taken an interest in the question knows.

* * *

Some years ago, at a schoolboy debating club, the rather unprofitable question was raised as to whether the heroes of the Middle Ages could, even if armed with modern weapons, have withstood for a moment the scientific generals of this century: whether, for instance, the generalship at the battle of Hastings was very greatly inferior to that at Waterloo. The query of course is absurd, but it leads one to a fairly accurate illustration of what has actually taken place in the Italian-Abyssinian wars. In that struggle we have seen a feudal army, with hardly an attempt at modern organization,—that is to say, without brigades, regiments or battalions, without any knowledge of scientific warfare, an army in which each chief served out rifles and cartridges to his own followers on the declaration of war, and in which each follower fought loyally for his lord, his nation, and his own honour—pitted against a European field-force led by generals of no mean ability: the arms in the hands of the Ethiopians were modern, but the organization was, in many respects, very similar to that of the English at the battle of Agincourt.

The Negûs Nagasti is supreme general of the Abyssinian Army; under his orders are the Ras or governors of provinces; under them the Dedjazmatches (often shortened to Dejatches) or commanders of the rear-guard; next in rank is the Cagnasmatch (commander of the right wing), and then the Guerasmatch (commander of the left wing); after him, curiously enough, ranks the Fitaurari or leader of the advanced guard. These are the highest military ranks, but below them, of course, are many of lesser importance, as, for instance, a Balambaras or commandant of a fortress.

There are a certain number of professional soldiers in Abyssinia, followers of the chiefs; but the great strength of their army lies in the fact that every man is a warrior, trained from childhood to the use of the sword, shield and spear, and on every man lies the obligation to serve when called upon by his chief.

The method of raising an army is very simple. On the declaration of war, the Negûs orders a proclamation to be read out in the market and other public places, while the long rolls are beaten on the Negarit or great war-drums;[1] the date and place of assembly are also given out by the crier of the King, who can be seen by all, standing high on the up-turned drum, with the lance and mantle, insignia of his office, held at his side by a slave. The call to arms is usually well obeyed; partly from fear of the ruler, partly from love of fighting, and partly from custom, it comes about that very few of the male population are absent on the day of assembly. The chief then serves out rifles to those whom he selects as best able to use them; many, of course, bring their own fire-arms with them; the result is a

[1] This is known as beating the kitet; and levies *en masse* are called the kitet, corresponding to the ancient fyrd of England.

motley collection of infantry armed with every conceivable weapon from a Lebel to a flintlock.[1] Before 1880 the majority of the rank and file relied on their lance,—"a terrible weapon," says the Italian traveller Cecchi, "in the hands of an Abyssinian," about six feet long with a sharp steel or iron head shaped like an olive leaf,—and on the heavy sword, often curved back so as to hit a man behind his round shield; but since then they have been rapidly procuring European weapons. During the great war with Italy it was said that four out of five men carried a fire-arm of some sort, many of which were magazine rifles.

So much for the infantry; and the cavalry differ little from them, except for the fact that they are on horseback; they bear the same weapons and their tactics are more or less identical. Until of late years it did not always follow that the mounted men were separated from the infantry; the whole line would often charge indiscriminately, horse and foot intermingled. The greater part of Abyssinia is mountainous, therefore infantry preponderates; but from the plains come splendid contingents of irregular cavalry, men and horses vying with each other in hardihood and courage; Italian officers bear witness to having seen them cross ravines and ambas that seemed quite impassable.

Artillery is of course in its infancy in Abyssinia, but it is by no means unknown. In 1868 the Emperor Theodore had about 40 guns, but they were of little or no use against the English. At Adowa, in 1896, Menelik had 42, but

[1] This acount of the Abyssinian army is not up to date, as Menelik is now adopting European ideas; but it is a true account of the fighting organization with which the Italians had to deal.

although some of them were modern, his gunners were not sufficiently trained to cope with the Italian mountain batteries.

The commissariat and transport are the most easily described of all departments,—they don't exist.[1] Every man brings his own food for a certain number of days,—usually four: he requires only a handful or two of meal per day to make himself a few little cakes. Beyond this scanty provision, all trust to living on the country through which they are marching; in a friendly district they help themselves as sparingly as possible, but in the enemy's country they consider it a virtue to take everything. As an Abyssinian army often numbers about 80,000 men accompanied by 30,000 women, slaves, and camp-followers with mules bearing private stores for the chiefs, it will be understood that it leaves a desert wherever it goes. Another result of this lack of organization is that it can only fight in a fertile territory, otherwise the warriors starve; it can never remain halted for more than two or three weeks in the same place, and, even for so short a period as this, is obliged to send out marauding parties to collect food.[2]

[1] It is said that for the Adowa campaign Menelik made some efforts to organize supplies for his army, but this was unusual.

[2] The following numbers of the Abyssinian army are given by the Italian traveller Cecchi, whose book was published in 1887.

Province	Total number of troops	How many are mounted	Firearms	Breechloaders
Amhara . .	35,000	10,000	20,000	10,000
Tigré . . .	20,000	4,000	15,000	8,000
Gojjam . .	20,000	8,000	11,000	2,000
Shoa. . . .	70,000	35,000	25,000	8,000
	145,000	57,000	71,000	28,000

According to this estimate, more than half the troops would be without firearms, whereas in 1895 about 4 out of 5 men

The method of encamping is primitive; the Negûs first pitches his red tent which is surrounded by a palisade,[1] and his followers arrange themselves as comfortably as possible. Women, slaves and children are plentiful, and if any stay is made, a market is set up; but cleanliness and order hardly exist except about the tents of the more important chieftains.

The following is an account by an eye-witness of Menelik's army on the march on January 31st, 1896. "While marching I made my observations: the columns were now to be seen winding along in the depths of the valleys, now on the sides of the mountains, now on their summits, mounting up and getting down again with the facility of squirrels. They did not consist of fighting men only; there were women, grandfathers, lame people, babies, priests, lepers: every kind of individual. 'It is not an army,' said Paoletti to me at one moment, 'it is an invasion,—the transplanting of a whole people.'

"They were all crowded one on to the other, amidst donkeys, mules and horses on the same track. And when the road was not wide enough, or when, owing to the arrival of some important chief, or of a Ras, or of the Negûs himself, they were obliged to make way, they threw themselves indifferently to the right or to the left; if on to the plain, then every trace of vegetation vanished under those hundreds

possessed them. These numbers are the utmost that Abyssinia could put into the field; he estimates her usual army at 87,000 men, of whom Amhara sent 25,000, Tigré 15,000, Gojjam 12,000 and Shoa 35,000.

[1] Except that the four great chiefs Dedjazmatch, Fitaurari etc. are ranged round him in order of march,—Fitaurari in front, Dedjazmatch in rear etc.

of thousands of feet; if on to the mountain, they went a little more slowly; those who were bolder or more active set the example, the others followed. The mules and donkeys, climbing amidst the shouts and imprecations and whacks of their drivers, sometimes rolled over when the ascent was impossible, and, rebounding from rock to rock and projection to projection, usually ended by falling, crushed, to the bottom of a valley, and sometimes on to the good road that was below them."[1]

The same eye-witness, Captain Moltedo of the Italian Artillery, describes elsewhere the Royal Engineers of the Negûs. "We found a detachment of the Abyssinian military engineers at work (making a road). A few thousands of individuals whom I saw, were cutting furiously with their swords at the branches of trees; others, with small hoes, were toiling patiently at the stems of large plants in order to make their levelling more easy; others were cutting grass; others carrying stones; others clearing away little plants. It was a continuous noise caused by branches being torn off and thrown away; a continuous deafening sound of beating. All were working,—it was for the Negûs."

It will be understood from this description that the Abyssinian army is not more civilized than were the Highland followers of Dundee. It has the characteristic weaknesses of a feudal institution; the men often think more of their chief than of the Negûs, and the leaders are disposed to quarrel with one another. But, on the other

[1] Moltedo, G.: *L'Assedio di Maccalé.* His observations are of special value, having been made while the war was actually in progress, when he was kept as a hostage by Menelik.

hand, the rank and file are animated by a splendid courage that almost redeems the defects of organization; to be a man is to be a soldier, and to be a soldier is to be a warrior. Their usual custom is to advance in the half-moon formation common to all savage races, but they do not, like the Dervishes, hurl themselves recklessly across the open; on the contrary, each man fights more or less as a separate unit, and with great skill. "We fight man for man," say the Ethiopians, "but you fight like a herd of slaves" (referring to European drill). The officers are good, for they are selected by the chiefs from amongst their best men, and the safety of the chief will often depend on his skill in selecting. In attacking a position every man makes the best use of each vestige of cover, and as cartridges are precious, seldom throws away a shot; he has received no training in musketry, but being possessed of a splendid eye is a very fair marksman. When he has advanced as far as possible towards the enemy, then at length, by command of the chief, the final combined rush begins; then sword and lance come into play, and each warrior charges home, raising the war-cry of his tribe. "Together! together!" is that of Shoa; "God pardon us, Christ!" is that of Gojjam; while the wild Galla [1] horsemen shout "Slay! slay!"

War is their pastime, and almost their only profession; the veteran dreams of rich plunder, and the young chief seeks glory either on the field of battle or in the tournament,—for they hold tourneys not unlike those of our own days of chivalry. The Azmari, or troubadours, not only

[1] The Gallas are Mohammedan tribes of the South, subject to Ethiopia.

compose verses in praise of the chiefs, but often go with them into the fight, encouraging the men by their chants, through many of which there runs an undeniable vein of poetry. Take, for instance, the following song of an Azmari who led a small band of tired and famished warriors to victory.

"Brothers, are ye hungry? are ye thirsty? Oh true sons of my mother, are ye not birds of prey? Forward! behold the flesh of your enemy!

"And I will be the carver of your feast; forward! If ye lack mead I will give ye my blood to drink!"

The greatest leader that Abyssinia has produced since the death of the Emperor Theodore in 1868, is undoubtedly Ras Alula; a chief whose honourable and fearless character stands out in bold relief against the background of intrigue and fraud that fills every picture of Abyssinian political life. Though the son of a yeoman farmer entirely destitute of hereditary influence or wealth, by sheer hard service he rose to be the right-hand man of the Emperor John. His list of successes was almost unbroken. In the two great victories of 1875 and 1876 over the Egyptian invading armies,—whose weapons were modern and whose superior officers were European,—he played a prominent part; at Kufit he routed the Mahdiists under Osman Digna; and at Dogali he crushed the Italians. It was, in fact, only during his absence that the latter had been able to occupy the Abyssinian provinces,—a proceeding for which he never forgave them. From the day when they seized his stronghold of Asmara, Ras Alula left no stone unturned in working for his revenge, until the day, seven years later, when he sent his mounted men after the fugitives from Adowa, in a desperate endeavour to capture his personal enemy General Baratieri.

He has now been dead for several years, but there is at least one photograph of him extant, which portrays him as a weather-beaten, bearded, old man with a wonderfully powerful face; his whole attitude is one of command. As to the descriptions of him, the best is that of Sir Gerald Portal, who was his prisoner for some time, and has left a graphic picture of the chief, by whose personality he was evidently impressed.

"He was dressed," said Sir Gerald Portal, "in a long dark robe of purple silk, with, I think, some gold embroidery work on it; his head was uncovered save by his own curly but now somewhat grizzled hair, which he wore rather longer than was usual with Abyssinians, and not plaited in rows according to the general custom. His complexion was darker than that of most men of the Tigré mountains, being of a rich chocolate colour; but, whatever the colour, the owner of that powerful, cruel[1] and intelligent face would be bound to make his name known in any country, whether as a leader or a destroyer of men. But, although all these details may be afterwards observed and recalled, attention at first was riveted to one striking peculiarity,—a pair of gleaming tawny eyes of much lighter colour than the skin of the face. To these flashing yellow orbs whose effect was aided by a

[1] Mr. Wylde, who tells us that he knew Ras Alula for 20 years, says that he never persecuted any man for his religion,—a remarkable record in Abyssinia; Mr. Wylde in another place describes him as being "like an English gentleman."—Wylde's *Abyssinia*.

brilliant row of white regular teeth, was no doubt due much of the terror with which Ras Alula was generally regarded. I had seen such eyes in the head of a tiger (at the 'Zoo' only), and of a leopard, but never in that of a human being. On one side of the Ras, on the divan, lay his curved sword, and within reach of the other hand was a Martini-Henry carbine."

Never, probably, has there been a greater contrast between two men whose fortunes eventually bring them together with one great patriotic aim in view, than that between Ras Alula and Menelik. They are as different as the sons of Rebecca, to whom, in character, they bear some resemblance, except that Alula is perhaps not quite so reckless as Esau: he was never the man to sell his birthright for a mess of potage. But Menelik is a typical Jacob; he will work seven years or twice that time to accomplish an object. The most remarkable fact about his career is that although he has dominated a fighting nation like Abyssinia, he is himself by no means a warrior; some Italian writers have even called him a coward, but his own description of himself is probably more accurate—namely, that he is a man of peace who has several times been compelled to fight. It is in organization and in the diplomatic arts that he excels; he is careful, crafty, and persevering, the very type of man to succeed in this world; and he is said to believe in his destiny.

Anent this last trait a curious story was told to the Italian traveller Cecchi[1] about Menelik's christening. Ailu,

[1] It should be noted that this story appears in Cecchi's book "Da Zeila alle frontiere del Caffa," vol. I., p. 250, published by the Italian Geographical Society in 1886—some years before Menelik became Emperor. It cannot therefore be called a

his father, came of the old royal stock that traced its descent to Menelik I., son of Solomon by the Queen of Sheba. Ailu was eldest son of a great chief named Sella-Selassie, under whom Shoa attained to its highest pitch of power. Now Sella-Selassie's own name had formerly been Menelik, but he had been warned by a monk to change it, or he would suffer great misfortune; he should, however, said the monk, call the son of his first-born by the name of Menelik, and the child so christened would one day be the conqueror of all Ethiopia and the greatest of her rulers since the days of Menelik I. son of Solomon. As soon, therefore, as the slave-girl gave birth to a boy he was named Menelik.

Throughout his life Menelik has been attended by a good fortune that at times appeared miraculous; it seems, therefore, that this prophecy possessed at all events the cardinal virtue—so rare nowadays—of being completely fulfilled. It may of course be that the prophecy, working on the imagination of a naturally astute man, has caused its own fulfilment, by bringing self-confidence and perseverance to the support of his unusually high abilities. This is a point that we cannot here decide. But for those who are interested in his character, no description will give a better idea of it than the history of the events that centre round the Treaty of Uccialli,—events to which, after this long digression, it may be advisable to return without further delay.

* * *

prophecy after the event; it may, of course, have been invented by Menelik to pave the way for his schemes, but this is unlikely, for some of the details which I suppress are exceedingly unflattering to his mother.

No sooner did the news of John's death at Metemmeh reach Shoa than Menelik caused himself to be proclaimed Emperor (March 26th, 1889). With customary prudence, however, he determined not to act alone, and at once turned for support to his Italian allies; here, obviously, was an opportunity for negotiation.

The man to whom Menelik would naturally look was Count Antonelli. This ambitious Italian had been at his court for many years and had entirely won (or flattered himself that he had won) the confidence of the Shoan monarch. Although a nephew of the celebrated Cardinal Antonelli, he had in his youth deserted the "black" or Papal party at Rome, and had consequently been welcomed with open arms by the Royalists, who were delighted to receive into their fold a man of his family traditions and influence. He had foreseen, from the moment he arrived as resident at Shoa, the future possibilities for that little kingdom; with a keen grasp of the situation he had made himself the friend of the Queen Taitu, a woman of great character, niece of John and wife of Menelik; while bringing the more tangible products of civilization for Menelik he did not forget to provide Parisian shoes and stockings for Her Majesty. He believed firmly in an alliance with Shoa; and the advance of that nation in power and prosperity was largely due to him; it was he who had negotiated the first treaty, by which Menelik had been given rifles and ammunition and encouraged to defy John; he was therefore a person who stood in high favour with both governments,—Italian and Shoan; it seemed as if his efforts were at length about to be rewarded.

One man only, of those in power, disapproved of Antonelli's philo-Shoan policy,—this was Baldissera, who had directed the Italian advance with such wisdom and success. Now that John was dead, he saw plainly that Menelik was the most dangerous of the Abyssinian chiefs; he already regarded Shoa as a possible enemy of Italy and was opposed to any further assistance being offered to her.

The situation, therefore, in 1889, when the first permanent differences arose between Italy and Abyssinia stood as follows: Ras Alula and Ras Mangasha were defending their territory of Tigré against the Italian field-force on the North, and against Menelik's Shoans on the South. Of the Italians, Count Antonelli was in favour of a joint action with Menelik, but Baldissera preferred an independent policy.

Count Antonelli at once gave Menelik to understand that he could not ask the Italians to assist him on to the Imperial throne unless he was ready to allow them some tangible advantage in return. The whole question now resolved itself into an arrangement of terms that would satisfy both parties, and at the end of a week the famous Treaty of Uccialli was drawn up by Antonelli and signed by Menelik, who agreed to send his first cousin Dejatch Maconnen with an embassy to Rome in order to obtain the necessary ratification from the Italian Ministers.

On the terms of the Treaty of Uccialli depends the whole history of the period; its chief provisions may be roughly summarised as follows. Menelik was referred to as the King of the Kings of Ethiopia, and a perpetual peace and friendship were established between him and Italy.

By *Article 3*, the line of the high plateau[1] was to mark the Italian-Ethiopian boundary: starting from the region of Arafali, the villages of Halai, Saganeiti and Asmara were to be considered within the Italian boundary; in the province of Bogos, Adi Nefas and Adi Johannes were to be under the Italian rule; from Adi Johannes a straight line East and West was to mark the Italian-Ethiopian boundary.

By *Article 17*, that afterwards led to innumerable disputes, it was agreed that "His Majesty the King of the Kings of Ethiopia *consents* to employ the government of His Majesty the King of Italy in treating of all matters that may arise with other Powers and Governments."

The remaining clauses have no great historical importance.

As regards the boundaries. It will be seen, by a glance at the map, that those indicated are absurdly narrow as compared with the territory that the Italians seized before the end of 1889,—that is during the course of the negotiations and before the treaty was ratified. These boundaries did not include Hamacen, Okule-Kusai, or Serae, all of which provinces the Italians occupied in the autumn of 1889. This restriction of their frontiers was due to the fact that the treaty had been drawn up and signed by Menelik on May 2nd, five or six months before Baldissera's advance began, and at that time it probably represented the height of Italian desires, but they must have regretted its limitations long before it arrived at Rome for ratification; hence arose the Additional Convention that will presently be described.

As regards the political relation of the two nations. In

[1] *I.e.* The Italians were barely allowed to enter the ancient territories of Ethiopia.

Article 17 there was an attempt of the Italian Government to obtain the suzerainty over all Ethiopia; it was represented by them to the other European Powers as being an acknowledgment of their protectorate. But Menelik, if he ever understood it in this light, had no intention of observing the treaty. The use of the word "consents" is unfortunate, as in all the other clauses it is stipulated that a thing "shall be" or "shall not be" done; but owing to the use here of a less absolute term, Menelik apparently did not consider himself irrevocably bound by the clause. The Amharic version may have been a bad one; but it is curious that in this one clause whose avowed intention was to set up an Italian protectorate, the word "protectorate" is not even suggested, and the diplomatic formality taken as its equivalent is less strongly insisted on than many trifling affairs in other clauses.

On August 28th, 1889, Dejatch Maconnen,—he has since been promoted to the rank of Ras,—arrived at Rome, together with his guide and philosopher, Count Antonelli, and proceeded to conclude the treaty of alliance. He was received with great pomp, and every effort was made to impress him with the power of Italy. This young Dejatch, who had never before strayed beyond the high plain of Ethiopia, was suddenly brought into one of the great town-centres of civilization, and the experiences of that short visit have left an indelible mark on his character; he realizes the power of the white men, but does not altogether trust them. During his stay in Italy of four and a half months, he must have learnt enough to exhaust the brain of any ordinary man; from one sight to another he was led by his hosts, taking quiet observation of all his surroundings, but especially of any details connected with the Italian army, many of which he doubtless afterwards suggested to his cousin and sovereign.

On October 1st an additional convention was signed by Signor Crispi and by Maconnen, modifying the Treaty of Uccialli in certain important points, but not in any way touching on the Protectorate question. As regards boundaries, it provided that: "in virtue of the preceding articles, a rectification of the two territories will be made, taking as a basis the actual possession *de facto*." This, of course, entirely changed the frontiers named in the original treaty; since the date of the first treaty (May 2nd) Italy had made some notable acquisitions,[1] and she was in the very act of preparing for her great advance. This was, therefore, a bad arrangement, because the possession *de facto* was liable to vary from day to day.

In return for the concessions implied by this alteration, Menelik was to be allowed to borrow four million lire (£150,000) from an Italian bank, the government agreeing to guarantee the loan. In case of his failing to pay the interest (a fraction over five per cent),[2] the customs of the southern province of Harrar would pass into the hands of Italy; this was the security he gave them.

The loan also plays an important part in the history of

[1] She had already occupied Asmara and Keren since May 2nd (the date when Menelik signed the first treaty), and before this second treaty reached Menelik for ratification the Italians had seized the large provinces of Okule-Kasai, Serae and Hamacen; the "possession *de facto*" clause thus represented an immense gain to them.

[2] De la Jonquière: *Les Italiens en Erythrée.*

Ethiopia. It was stipulated that half of it (two million lire) should be paid in silver; the other two millions to lie in the Italian treasury, and to be used as payment for the various purchases that Menelik hoped to make in Europe. But some heated discussions took place when it eventually transpired that Menelik was stipulating for the payment of these two millions chiefly in the form of rifle-cartridges.

It is plain that the Convention made essential alterations in the original Treaty of Uccialli, so it still remained to be seen whether Menelik would ratify it or not; on December 4th, 1889, Maconnen started from Italy to return to Shoa.

Meanwhile, on October 11th, the Italian Government communicated to all the European Powers, in a formal manner, the establishment of her protectorate over Abyssinia.

But on December 14th a very different piece of news awaited her—namely, the resignation of General Baldissera. In spite of his great successes the general no longer cared to remain in the colony; he disapproved of the philo-Shoan policy of Antonelli, whose advice was followed in everything by the Government; he saw plainly that the only true course for Italy to pursue was "Divide et Impera," namely, to play off the Tigréan chiefs of the North, against the Shoan chief of the South. Now as long as Tigré, under the leadership of the Emperor John, was the dominating power of Ethiopia, so long had Antonelli's support of Menelik and his Shoans been justifiable, because it was necessary to raise an adequate opposition to Tigré. But since Tigré had become weak, to continue to support Menelik was merely to render him all-powerful and independent. The Italian Government did not either then, or for some time afterwards, realize that the centre of political supremacy had been shifted (at the death of the Emperor John) from Tigré to Shoa; these ministers continued to support Menelik until he was powerful enough to turn and rend them.

Baldissera had shown considerable powers of organization during his two years in the colony; in every branch the results of his thought were apparent. The town of Massowah had been immensely improved by the addition of new buildings; it had been in every way rendered more suitable for inhabitation by Europeans; a conduit had been constructed to bring drinking water from Monkullo, the lighting of the streets had been improved, and fresh roads made. In agricultural matters numerous experiments had been begun; in governmental matters the administrative machinery itself had been systematized, and the first battalions of a native African corps enlisted. The results of his work had been good; and he had even found himself in a position to raise a small municipal tax in Massowah to pay for the improvements.

It was therefore a singularly evil portent that so careful and earnest a man should consider it necessary to resign, at the very height of his success. Ostensibly he asked to be recalled because he was suffering from ophthalmia, but in Italy it was diagnosed as Ophthalmia Antonelliana.

CHAPTER II

THE BREAKDOWN OF COUNT ANTONELLI'S PHILO-SHOAN POLICY

I. The Frontier. General Orero governor—"The Colony of Erythrea"—Orero and Menelik invade Tigré from opposite sides—Orero ordered back—Antonelli endeavours to arrange matters—Duped by Menelik—Disagreement as regards frontiers between Shoans and Italians—Famine.

II. The Protectorate. September 27th, 1890, Menelik protests against the Treaty of Uccialli—Antonelli again sent to Addis Abeba—Reasons for preserving the alliance with Menelik—Results of Menelik's letter to the European powers—He writes to King Humbert denouncing the Treaty of Uccialli—Asserts mistranslation of the Treaty—Repudiates Article 17—Deceives Antonelli—Italy turns to alliance with Magasha—Convention of the Mareb, December 6th, 1891—The demeanour of Ras Alula.

I. DISAGREEMENTS WITH MENELIK OVER THE FRONTIERS.

On January 1st, 1890, the Italian possessions on the Red Sea were united by royal decree into one province under a governor; the name given to the new dependency was "The Colony of Erythrea."

Never, probably, had Italian affairs in Africa been progressing more favourably; General Orero, who succeeded Baldissera, found himself ruling over a territory extending as far as the Mareb-Belesa-Muna boundary:[1] all this had

[1] A natural boundary formed by the rivers Mareb, Belesa, and Muna, which run south of the three annexed provinces.

been won in four years, with comparatively little bloodshed. Nor was there any hostile chief powerful enough to occasion real anxiety to the Italians; Menelik was their ally, having ratified the additional convention to the Treaty of Uccialli.

In Tigré,—or at least in those provinces that were not occupied by the Italians,—Mangasha had succeeded in establishing himself as an entirely independent ruler; he acknowledged as suzerain neither the Erythrean Government nor the Negûs. And in this position it should have been the aim of the Italians to maintain him; but Count Antonelli thought otherwise.

No sooner had Antonelli's policy attained to the summit of its success, than it begins to show signs of underlying weakness, and gradually the edifice that he had built up crumbles away and falls to the ground piecemeal, until there is not one stone left on another. It rested on several insecure bases. In the first place, it assumed that Menelik would be contented with the name of Negûs Nagasti and a somewhat reduced territory,—as compared with that of previous Emperors. In this respect the Italians were very widely mistaken; no sooner had Menelik ascended the Imperial throne than he showed plainly that he intended to be in fact, as well as in name, Negûs Nagasti of Ethiopia. Secondly, the success of Antonelli's policy depended on the observance of the Treaty and the Convention, whereas treaties of this kind are in reality of little value unless backed by mutual interest, or by force, or by the guarantee of some third party. The Treaty of Uccialli was soon found to have no more value than so much waste-paper.

At this moment Tigré lay like a carcase between the two

eagles—namely, Menelik on the South, and the Italians on the North. It would, one cannot help thinking, have been to the interest of the latter to have turned it into a buffer state, and this would perhaps have been the aim of General Baldissera had he been allowed a free hand. Both he and General Orero perceived that Menelik was merely using Italy for his own purposes; they believed in dealing directly with the Tigréan chiefs,—in bringing them under the immediate suzerainty of the Roman Government, and thereby weakening Menelik. They did not care so much for the existence of the protectorate, provided that Italy obtained the immediate and substantial advantages.

But opposite ideas prevailed; the ministers persistently followed the policy of Count Antonelli, which consisted in supporting the Shoans. Menelik, according to Antonelli's view, had placed himself under the Italian protectorate, therefore (the Count argued) they should support him until the whole country was brought under his rule, and consequently under their suzerainty. This might have been a suitable and cheap arrangement had the Negûs intended to deal honestly with them.

In January 1890 Menelik advanced northwards against Tigré in order to obtain the submission of Mangasha, while General Orero advanced southwards to support him. Both invasions were at first successful; Orero reached Adowa, the capital of Tigré, and Menelik, after waiting until his allies had done all the work, penetrated as far as Macalle, the former capital of Ethiopia (in John's reign); but here the eagles, as is usually the case, began to quarrel. Orero, to his disgust, received orders from Rome to evacuate Adowa;

it now appeared that his rapid advance had given offence to Menelik, whose feelings Count Antonelli was anxious to respect; Orero was therefore obliged to retire, but he left his ally, Ras Sebath, in occupation of Adowa.[1]

Menelik now began to feel that his own position was far from agreeable; he had come with the intention of having himself crowned, after the custom of Ethiopian Emperors, in the holy city of Axum; but everywhere he found his Shoans received with hatred and contempt by the inhabitants of Tigré. The latter had not yet forgotten that they were the true leaders of the Ethiopian race, and when the Tigréan chiefs heard that Menelik intended being crowned at Axum, they swore that if he dared to enter their sacred place he would never go back to Shoa alive. Menelik therefore concluded that it was better to leave them for a few more months to be humiliated by Italian aggression, and to experience the joys of anarchy; he prepared to retire from the country at the earliest opportunity.

Now was the moment of triumph for Antonelli; all competitors would soon have vanished from the field; it only remained for him, as the representative of Italy and the friend of Shoa, to make any dispositions that might seem advisable. He and his friend Ras Sebath advanced towards Hausien, where Menelik was still halted, in order to hold an interview with him and with the Italian and Shoan commissioners (appointed under the Treaty of Uccialli,

[1] As Signor Vico Mantegazza says, the history of Orero's period of command is simply a record of quarrels with Antonelli; such is the effect of having two captains in the ship,—a policy almost invariably pursued in the colony.

for the purpose of marking out the exact frontiers). At this meeting they were to settle once and for all, two questions; the first was the defining of the frontiers, the second was the disposal of Tigré amongst the various contending chiefs.

A peculiar surprise awaited Antonelli. Menelik was far too clever to allow his allies, the Italians, to have the deciding voice in the matter; during the previous weeks he had come to secret terms with Mangasha, to whom Alula and nearly all the Tigréans remained faithful, and had arranged that Seium, his Shoan follower, should have the eastern portion of Tigré (including Sebath's province of Agamé), that Mangasha himself should have the West, and that another supporter of Menelik's, named Meshasha Workiè, should have a third division of Tigré, including a considerable slice of the Italian territory.[1] In this manner Menelik hoped to leave two representatives behind him to hold Mangasha in check, and at the same time to set back the Italian frontier. In fact, when Antonelli arrived at Hausien to arrange matters, he found the whole country already divided up amongst Tigréans and Shoans; from Menelik's point of view the situation was not without humour.

Such, however, was not the opinion of Sebath when he

[1] There is a story that Menelik in the presence of his chiefs stretched out both arms, and laying his right hand on Seium, said: "This my son shall have the East," then laying his left hand on Mangasha, said: "This my son shall have the West," after which, addressing Meshasha Workiè, he said: "You shall stand between them and the Italians." If this story is true, it was indeed a patriarchal way of dividing up another man's territory.

heard that his province of Agamé was given to Seium; he at once left the meeting and hastened away to organize its defence. As for Antonelli, he had to swallow the pill as best he might.[1] On March 19th Menelik started from Hausien, leaving two Shoan commissioners behind him to settle with the Italians the question of frontiers.

Menelik, we have said, retired on March 19th; on March 22nd all discussions were broken off between the Italian and Shoan commissioners. The Shoans suggested a ridiculous line of boundary from Skiket (It. Schichet), that would have left Okule-Kusai and Serae to Abyssinia;[2] the Italians, of whom Major Toselli was one, refused to treat except on the basis of the Mareb-Belesa-Muna frontier. So far their affairs were in exactly the same position in which they stood before Baldissera resigned.

As regards the Protectorate, (Article 17) it is true, one point had been gained. Menelik had been persuaded while in Tigré to be represented at the Conference of Brussels[3] by Italy; but he did so chiefly because in case of his refusal

[1] According to one story, Antonelli was never even informed of the secret treaty, but Sebath having discovered its existence hastened away privately to Agamé and sent a messenger back to bring the news to Antonelli.

[2] Menelik argued that the Additional Convention dated from October 1st, the day when it was signed by Signor Crispi and Maconnen at Naples; this was slightly before the Italian advance, so that the "territories in their possession" would not have extended to the Mareb: they would have included Asmara and Keren, but not the provinces since occupied. *Vide* note, Ch. I, p. 21.

[3] At the Conference of Brussels the questions of the commerce in arms and alcohol with barbarous nations, and also the slave trade, were under discussion.

Italy would have tried to prevent the importation of arms into Ethiopia: and when one considers how easily his chances might have been cut off for ever by such a measure, his ultimate success appears the more truly wonderful.

Meanwhile Seium had resigned all claims to Agamé,—having been defeated by Sebath. But any further political action was put an end to for some months by famine; the constant state of war and anarchy had done its work; the whole country lay at the feet of Italy; had she desired to annex Tigré it would not have been difficult, but she preferred her Mareb-Belesa-Muna frontier.

Only one more event deserves to be chronicled; General Orero, disgusted by Antonelli's philo-Shoan policy that constantly paralysed his own action, sent in his resignation and was succeeded by General Gandolfi.

On the whole, the results of these campaigns were very small; Italy had gained practically nothing during Orero's governorship, and Menelik was represented in Tigré only by Meshasha Workiè, a poor paralytic old man who was practically a nonentity,—he was apparently only meant to be used as a buffer. The Tigréans had emerged with a greater share of independence than might have been expected. Ras Sebath, for instance, having reconquered Agamé for himself owed allegiance to nobody. Mangasha had acknowledged the suzerainty of Menelik, but he was still the most powerful chief in Tigré,—strong in the national pride and loyalty of his people; had he been a man of more ability he might have remained a formidable factor in Abyssinian politics.

Between Italy and Menelik the first disagreements had

arisen, that afterwards culminated in their great war; disagreements primarily as to frontiers, but soon to be supplemented by those concerning the Protectorate.

II. DISAGREEMENTS WITH MENELIK OVER THE PROTECTORATE.

On September 27th, 1890, the Abyssinian question was re-opened by a letter from Menelik, protesting against the Protectorate established by Article 17 of the Treaty of Uccialli. In October an embassy under Count Antonelli was again sent to Addis Abeba[1] for the purpose of satisfying him.

Why, in the face of constant rebuffs, did the Italians cling with such desperate earnestness to their alliance with Menelik? There is only one reason that can account for it; they were, at that moment, afraid of making him an enemy. The schemes for the general partitioning of Africa were in the air; by the year 1890 the various European nations had been for some time turning their thoughts towards a division of the Dark Continent into "spheres of influence," according to the interests that each Power had created for herself; and Italy was anxious to obtain a satisfactory share. Now the eastern shoulder of Africa was the sphere on which she had fixed her eyes, and the Ministers were not slow to perceive how greatly it would strengthen the claims of their diplomats, if they could appear at

[1] The new capital of Abyssinia founded by Menelik; the name signifies "New Flower," which, Major Gamerra remarks, is a singularly inapplicable name, as neither in beauty nor in scent does it in the least resemble a flower.

the European congresses bearing with them a treaty wherein their protectorate over all Abyssinia was formally acknowledged by the Negûs Nagasti himself.

This was the root of their continuous support of Antonelli and his Shoan alliance; the schemes of men like Baldissera and Orero would have brought a large area directly under their control, but not without making an enemy of Menelik, who would have declared himself independent of their protectorate. Now Antonelli's scheme was to hand over most of the border territories to Menelik, insisting in return that he should acknowledge the Italian protectorate over all Ethiopia; and the government, anxious at all costs to pose as suzerains of Abyssinia, to monopolize as far as possible its trade, and to prevent other nations from gaining a foothold within it, gave a consistent support to Antonelli. If treaties had been of any value his scheme would undoubtedly have offered a good and cheap solution of their difficulties.

When Antonelli reached Shoa he found the Protectorate Question in the following condition: in December 1889 Menelik, having been crowned Emperor at Entotto (near his capital), had himself written to inform the European Powers of his accession. This, of course, was a breach of the Protectorate established by Article 17, but, referring only to a fact of no great international importance, it might be taken as a mere diplomatic politeness. At the Conference of Brussels, (March 4, 1890), as already related, he had been represented by Italy. Hitherto, then, the question of the protectorate had not arisen; but when replies to the announcement of his coronation arrived from Great Britain and

Germany, in which both powers informed him that his communication ought to have been made through Italy, then Menelik's pride took fire. He at once wrote to King Humbert (September 27th, 1890,) denouncing Article 17 of the Treaty of Uccialli (establishing the Protectorate). His argument, as expressed in the letter or since ascertained, was that the word "consents" had been mistranslated; that in the Amharic version it was not stated that the Negûs Nagasti "consents" thenceforth to employ Italy in his foreign negotiations, but that he "has the power of" employing her; it appears that the Amharic equivalent is "icciallacciual,"—a word that might indeed appear formidable to translate,—and that it signifies "may employ."[1] But Menelik goes further than merely to assert a mistranslation; the following is the account he gives of the matter in his letter to King Humbert.

"While talking to Count Antonelli at the time when the treaty was being brought to a conclusion, I questioned him with great seriousness, and he answered me in the following manner: 'If it suits your convenience, you can employ us as your intermediaries; if not, you are free not to do so.' I said to him: 'If it is merely a question of friendship why should I employ anyone but you in my external negotiations?' I accepted at that time no obligatory agreement, and I am not the man to accept it, nor could you advise me to do so."

Is this true? Nobody can say for certain. If it was

[1] It seems to be agreed that the word has the signification that Menelik gives to it, but Count Antonelli asserts that it was the Amharic interpreter of the Negûs who is responsible for the mistranslation, and not the Italian interpreter.

true, Menelik would probably have had no scruples left in his subsequent negotiations; he would think himself justified in almost any kind of fraudulent dealing; but he had already shown a somewhat unfettered conscience in his secret negotiations with Mangasha.

When Count Antonelli arrived in Shoa it was only about three months before the final treaty by which the British and Italian spheres of influence were to be defined. He had orders, therefore, to give way on the question of the frontiers, provided that he could secure the maintenance of the protectorate; for the present it was Article 17 about which the Government were chiefly concerned. Menelik, however, refused point-blank to admit the protectorate or any equivalent to it, or even to undertake not to place himself under the protection of another nation. For a month, fruitless negotiations continued, when suddenly Menelik proposed that the frontiers should be regulated on the basis approved of by him, in return for which he agreed to acknowledge the protectorate as it stood according to Article 17, but for five years only. Antonelli at once closed with the offer. On February 6th, 1891, two treaties were signed; the first in two separate versions, Italian and Amharic, arranging the frontier question; the second in Amharic only, maintaining the protectorate according to Article 17: both were at once signed by Menelik and Count Antonelli.

Having quitted the presence of the Negûs, Antonelli proceeded, together with Count Salimbeni (now resident at Shoa), to read through and translate the Amharic version; to his horror he discovered that so far from having signed a treaty maintaining Article 17, he had signed one entirely abrogating it! It was obviously an attempt at fraud on the part of the Negûs.

He hurried back to Menelik and, after a stormy interview, tore up his own copy of the treaty and demanded the duplicate. But Menelik merely attributed the mistake to his interpreter and refused to hear any more of the matter, so Antonelli was obliged to content himself with declaring his signature void. Three days later (February 11th, 1891,) he and Salimbeni left Addis Abeba and returned to Italy.

Thus, for the time being, diplomatic relations were broken off between Italy and Shoa. But Menelik having taken one bold step followed it up by another; he wrote a letter to King Humbert complaining of the mistakes that had occurred with the Italian ambassador, and on April 10th sent a circular to each of the Powers of Europe, in which he gave them a short description of the true boundaries of his empire as he desired them to be understood. Starting from Arafali (south of Massowah on the Red Sea), he said, his frontier ran westward through Halai, Digsa, Gura, to Adibaro; from thence it extended north-westward to where the River Mareb joins the Atbara,—but it is needless to go through the complicated list of frontier towns that he gives. It is sufficient to say that he included two provinces (Okule-Kusai and Serae) occupied by the Italians, and that on every side he named the territories of outlying tribes as being within his empire; he was, in fact, quite European in his method of dividing up the native lands of the less civilized inhabitants.

There is also a note of defiance in his letter: "I have no intention of being an indifferent spectator if far-distant

Powers make their appearance with the idea of dividing Africa,—Ethiopia having been for fourteen centuries an island of Christians amongst a sea of Pagans. As the Almighty has protected Ethiopia to this day, I am confident that He will protect and increase her in the future."

This breach with Menelik is the beginning of the final downfall of Antonelli's policy; after such a rebuff as the last, Italy could no longer remain the ally of Shoa. Negotiations were at length opened with Mangasha, who received them with undisguised pleasure; at the meeting with the Italian officers he showered such titles as Ras, Dejatch, Cagnasmatch upon them, until a touch of comedy was added to the scene by the triumphal procession of General Gandolfi and his Colonels in all the flowing insignia of their new Abyssinian titles, their "shammas" supplementing with graceful irregularity the rigid correctness of the Italian uniforms.

Matters were soon brought to a successful issue. It was agreed that on December 6th, 1891, a great meeting should take place between the adherents of both parties near the River Mareb. At this—the celebrated Convention of the Mareb—a solemn oath of alliance was to be exchanged between the Italian officers and the Tigréan chiefs. It was arranged so that the two armies should be encamped one on each side of the river, the Italians on the North, and the Tigréans on the South. At the meeting-place each chief advanced in turn and spoke aloud the formal words of the oath that he was to swear, of which the culminating phrase was couched in the impressive terms: "my enemies shall be thy enemies, and my friends thy friends."

Amongst all the warriors who had come to tender their adhesion to the treaty, none were watched with so keen an interest as Ras Alula. Since the battle of Metemmeh the political weight of the old chief had become greatly diminished; he possessed no hereditary estates from which to draw men and supplies; those who followed him were for the most part poor adventurers and outcasts, often in the front of the battle, but usually ill rewarded, for he now had little to give them; the Italians had taken all he possessed, and to swear allegiance to Italy meant to resign his mountain stronghold of Asmara for ever. It was a struggle between his own interests and his loyalty to Mangasha,—or, more accurately speaking, to the memory of the Emperor John.

While the other leaders were proceeding with the necessary formalities, he sat apart until it should come to his turn to swear the oath of friendship; then, when the moment arrived, he arose, and all waited anxiously to hear him speak. With perfect dignity and self-restraint he went through the formalities, but when the crucial words were reached, instead of repeating them, he substituted a phrase that openly expressed his true feelings. "I am the faithful slave of Mangasha," he said, with a touch of pride, "and therefore I swear to be the friend of his friends." With this double-edged acknowledgment the Italians were obliged to content themselves. From a man like Alula it was tantamount to an open declaration of personal enmity; it meant that while they remained the friends of Mangasha he would abstain from any act of hostility, but that he still regarded them with an irreconcilable hatred.

CHAPTER III

BARATIERI'S REFORMS[1]

GENERAL Baratieri—His life—Civil reforms—Military reforms—Italian tactics—How far successful—The Ascaro as a fighting man—Instances of devotion.

As regards the new governor, General Baratieri, it is singularly unfortunate that to most people his name should recall only the battle of Adowa, for had he died six months before that disaster he would have left the reputation of being one of the greatest Italians of the century.

He was a man well-known in Italy. At the age of 17 he had already seen service, having been one of the famous "thousand" with whom Garibaldi freed Sicily from foreign rulers; since then he had led an active and successful life. As the result of some of his travels and writings he had become vice-president of the Geographical Society, as well as Secretary of the Italian Committee of the International African Association, so that he had been in touch with African affairs at a time before they were yet a matter of public interest. He had advocated colonial expansion even before the occupation of Massowah. He had been elected

[1] I must here acknowledge indebtedness to two able works on this subject: *La Colonia Eritrea* by Lieutenant B. Melli who lived in the colony for some time, and *I nostri errori in Africa* by an anonymous writer who appears to have held some civil post there.

deputy for Breno, and though he spoke but rarely, was always listened to with attention and interest; it had indeed been rumoured that he would become Minister for Foreign Affairs under Zanardelli, but the attempt at forming a Ministry was unsuccessful. It will be evident, therefore, that he was a man of unusual versatility, successful as a soldier, as a speaker, and as a writer, and, moreover, the friend of many of the best known politicians of the day. He had also shown signs of those powers of organization and grasp of a situation which are so very widely different from culture, and, for a man in his position, so much more valuable. Having arrived in Africa in 1887, he had served under Di San Marzano against the Abyssinians. Under General Gandolfi he had come into prominence as Governor of the Zone of Keren,—it was said, indeed, that he had constituted himself the rival of the General, an accusation which has since been repeated against Baratieri in the case of several other men.

Although a soldier by profession he had seen so much of civil life that his first care was to reorganize the administration of the colony. As his period of Governorship,—extending over four years,—was almost entirely occupied by wars and rumours of wars, it will be most simple to begin by a slight sketch of his internal government and reforms, so that they may not intermingle with the tangled skein of foreign policy.

His guiding principle appears to have been centralization; everything was to be done under his own directing eye,—a precaution perhaps necessary during a period when the colony was invaded first from the North West, and then from the South by the overwhelming masses of Dervishes and Abyssinians. He raised as far as possible the dignity of his own office by taking the title of "Excellency," and by increasing the ceremonies that surrounded it. Colonel Arimondi, as second in order of seniority, was named Commander of the Troops; but by a royal decree of March 10th, 1892, the Governor retained the power of conducting military operations in case of need. There were thus two commanding officers,—a bad arrangement that led to disagreements, and verified in a singularly convincing manner the dictum of the Great Napoleon, that it is better for an army to be led by one moderate general than by two of even first-class ability.

In order to delegate the supreme power and to distribute it amongst the various departments of the state, the Governor instituted six different offices, through which the work of the colony was to be done.

First. The Cabinet of the Civil Governor; a body of officers who formed a small council of a consultative nature.

Secondly. The Political-Military Office, under Major Salsa. This was the most important of all the offices; it dealt with the native questions and the secret information service, but its functions appear to have become considerably extended; it became a kind of little cabinet for external affairs and for war.

Thirdly. A Central Administrative Office,—to deal with the Balance and with financial matters.

Fourthly. A Technical Office, presided over first by a Civil Engineer, and then by a Royal Engineer; its duties were to superintend the construction and repairing of public works, bridges, etc.

Fifthly. The Office of Civil Affairs to direct the customs, the port, postal, and telegraphic arrangements, etc., etc.

Sixthly. A Colonization Office: chiefly concerned with those lands that the state had taken for purposes of agricultural experiment etc., etc. Composed to a great extent of officers.

There appears to have been also an office of legal counsel for purposes of advice, but this does not of course deal directly with the colony.

It will be seen that by means of these offices the Governor had little difficulty in making his supreme will reach every branch of the administration. It is said by Italian writers that they did little more than carry out his expressed wishes, which is probable enough, for he was the chief in both civil and military matters, and most of the employés were officers, or military men, on whom the habit of discipline would be strong. There seems, in fact, every reason to believe that the whole machinery of government revolved round, and worked at the word of the Governor himself.

The system has been criticised with great bitterness; the chief points at which exception is taken being, that although there were many officials and offices, there was very little actual work done; and secondly, that the duties of the various offices overlapped one another, so that the same piece of work would occasionally fall within the province of more than one department, thereby causing confusion. These criticisms appear to be well-founded; but as regards the first, the governor argues in his memoirs that it was very difficult to produce any great practical results with the small balance that was allowed to the colony; the aim was that Erythrea should pay for her own civil government, which was not to cost more than two million lire, or £40,000 per annum,—a sum intended (according to General Baratieri's memoirs) to cover the expenses of justice, public safety, civil staff expenses, pensions to natives, public works, roads, expenses of ports, light-houses, residents, schools, hospitals, telegraphs etc. The colony, within the Mareb-Belesa-Muna boundaries, included about 85,000 square kilometres and 250,000 people, and it was afterwards extended further south; it was obvious, therefore, that more than £40,000 was necessary to maintain efficient civil government.

To secure a more effective administration, the outlying districts had been divided into zones, to each of which a Royal Commissioner was appointed; and amongst the subject tribes Official Residents were stationed. Both Residents and Commissioners were under the orders of the Political-Military Office, and therefore indirectly under the eye of Governor himself.

As regards the administration of Justice: there was at Massowah (endowed with civil and penal jurisdiction over the Europeans and natives of that zone or district) a Justice of the Peace, a Civil and Criminal Court, and a military tribunal, as well as a special criminal court functioning as Court of Assize for the whole colony, including the territory of Assab.

In the zones of Asmara and Keren the civil and religious cases were decided by assemblies of notables,[1] or of Cadi, (Chiefs of tribes) according to the customs in

[1] Presumably corresponding to the assemblies of "old men" which are one of the fundamental institutions of Abyssinia.

existence, but with the intervention of the Official Residents.[1] Certain civil suits were entrusted to special Arbitration Tribunals, and criminal offences of a certain importance devolved on the military tribunals of each respective zone.

Such is a very brief sketch of the administrative and judicial organization of the colony under General Baratieri. What it might have developed into, it is hard to say; but from the first it had no chance of success. The civil government was inaugurated, so Baratieri himself tells us, by a declaration that the country was in a state of war, and during his four years of office the energies of both rulers and subjects were continually directed towards military preparations or actual campaigns.

As regards his military reforms: by a royal decree of December 11th, 1892, the following numbers were established for the defence of the colony.

Italian troops.—1 battalion of Cacciatori (chasseurs), one section of mechanics (for repairing artillery), one medical section, one section of engineering specialists.

Natives.—4 battalions, 2 squadrons of cavalry, 2 mountain batteries.

Mixed.—One company of gunners, one company of engineers, one commissariat company.

In all, 6,561 men of whom 2,115 were Italians, the remainder natives.

This establishment, however, was very soon increased; before the end of Baratieri's governorship 3 other white regiments had been sent out as a permanent addition, and 4 more native battalions had been raised, thus making 4

[1] Presiding as chairmen.

white and 8 native battalions in all, while a force of 1,500 men were enrolled in the Native Mobile Militia. It was the Governor's unceasing aim to substitute the regular for the irregular element; thus the Militia was instituted in order to bring under Italian officers men who would otherwise have served in the irregular bands of the native chiefs,—but, like most Militia forces, it was in turn considered primarily as a sponge from which the best men should be squeezed for the benefit of line regiments, every encouragement being given to Militiamen to enlist in the regular battalions, of which opportunity many availed themselves. Owing, however, to the presence of a large number of old soldiers the standard of efficiency among the Militiamen remained wonderfully high; 8 companies of them were formed on the territorial system.

A similar increase was made in the Artillery, though only by the addition of one black battery. No white batteries ever formed part of the colonial army, but many were brought from Italy in time of need; at Adowa there were 10 Italian batteries,—making 56 guns in all.

The Cavalry, on the other hand, was decreased; a squadron was employed against the Mahdiists, but against the Abyssinians no cavalry was ever used, owing to the unfavourable nature of the ground. The only mounted men were the officers, all of whom rode on either mules or horses.

Besides the above mentioned troops many irregulars were employed, whose numbers varied according to the wavering fidelity of the native chiefs; at Amba Alagi about 1,000 of them fought on the Italian side; at Adowa only about half that number.

As regards the formation of this native army, it differs very widely from the English infantry organization. Up to the middle of 1895 each native battalion consisted of 5 Companies of 250 men each, but before the Abyssinian war these were reorganized on the basis of 4 Companies of 300 men each; this at all events was their nominal establishment, and we may count that few if any battalions were less than 1,000 men strong. The Companies were divided into Centurias of 100 men each, and the Centurias into Buluks, or squads of 25 men each. The battalion was under the command of a Major, the Companies each, of course, under a Captain, who had at first only 2 Italian lieutenants and one Italian non-commissioned officer with him; there were thus only 4 Italians to each Company, but when their numbers were increased to 300, another lieutenant was added, giving a proportion of one white lieutenant for every hundred men. In addition to the Italian there were 2 native subalterns per Company, called Jus-bashi, while the native serjeant who commands the Buluk or squad of 25, is called the Buluk-bashi; below him is the native corporal or muntaz. The employment of Italian sergeants was abandoned, as it was found to create an unsatisfactory situation between them and the native officers.

A mountain battery was composed of 4 Italian officers, 11 Italian non-commissioned officers or gunners, and 163 natives.[1] For this branch of the service the Sudanese were usually selected, being found superior to all other races. It is noticeable that the artillery was almost entirely worked

[1] General Luzeux: *Etudes critiques sur la guerre entre l'Italie et l'Abissinie.*

by natives,—by other nations it has been found safer to preserve a larger proportion of white men.

As regards the tactics employed by the Italian generals, they may be termed transitional. The old and approved of method by which the British were accustomed to defeat the Mahdiists was the square; whereas nowadays (1901) our firing line advances with an interval varying from 6 to about 30 paces between man and man. The reason is obvious: the Zulus and Mahdiists were for the most part armed with spears, but the Boer uses a magazine rifle. The Italian wars against Dervishes and Abyssinians took place between these two epochs, and the formation adopted by them belongs plainly to a period of transition; it is described as follows by the French General Luzeux.

"We have said that the Italians preserved their close formation, but reducing it in many cases to a single rank. The troops, marching shoulder to shoulder, advance by successive rushes, but always resume at once their close order. This method is one that exposed the Italians to great losses from the Abyssinian fire, which was usually well regulated.

"General Arimondi, who died at Adowa, had evolved a corrective for the disadvantages of this order of battle; it was the employment of reserves echeloned in rear of the line.

"Already the Mahdiists, whose tactics are more or less the same as those of the Abyssinians, had succeeded in breaking the Egyptian squares and had pressed hard on the English squares; the tactics of both Mahdiists and Ethiopians is to envelope their adversary.

"Reserves in echelon are therefore necessary in order to

oppose it, and to take the offensive on the flanks that are being threatened by the turning movement.

"The thin line of men, elbow to elbow, supplies a fire, which, when carefully watched and directed by officers, can give a maximum of effect for a minimum of ammunition,—an important point in a country where transport is difficult.

"Moreover, the echelon formation permits the disposal of intact forces, with which to fall on those of the enemy, when the latter have been decimated by fire, or when they are extended so as to attain the desired enveloping movement.

"The tactics of Arimondi were good; but far too many of the Italian officers, who were transferred suddenly to the Abyssinian plateau from the manœuvring grounds of Italy,—where they practised methods that were entirely different,—did not apply these tactics with the readiness that is indispensable. Hence the dash of the Abyssinians was able, and certain to carry all before it."

We may remark that Arimondi's tactics were perfectly successful against the Dervishes, many of whom were only armed with spears or inferior firearms; but against the Abyssinians, who nearly all possessed magazine rifles, the case was entirely different.

As regards the native soldiers, the Ascari (as they are called), every Italian officer agrees in describing them as magnificent fighting men,—whether Christians or Mohammedans; at first it was feared that the religious antagonism might lead to want of unity in the battalions, but no such difficulty ever arose, and the men have proved themselves to be brave, faithful, and naturally apt for war. The Ascaro can march and fight on a ration of flour, out of which he makes himself a few small cakes; his eyes are said to he better than those of Europeans; his marching is phenomenal, —the ordinary day's march for a native regiment is equal to about 26 British miles,—and this is a quality common to all the Ethiopian race; for Italian prisoners have left on record how they were unable to keep up with the Abyssinian army, there being no halts during even the longest march until it reached its camping-ground for the night. But the point on which Italian writers are never tired of dilating, is the *esprit de corps* and fidelity to their officers shown by the Ascari. Amongst our own native regiments many instances might be found, but not so many, I think, as amongst those of Italy. There are numberless cases of men facing, not death, but mutilation for the sake of their officer, or their duty. Amongst hundreds of anecdotes I select three, as being typical instances of loyalty, courage, and self-sacrifice.

Amtsa-Hassin, a muntaz of the 2nd Native battalion, received a bullet wound in the neck at the battle of Agordat, but remained at his post until he received another wound during the attack, and even then continued to fight until he fell senseless to the ground. As the doctor, after the battle, was bandaging the wound in his throat, he remarked in jest: "Amtsa, now you have two mouths," whereupon the wounded man, though hardly able to speak, replied promptly: "Then the Captain will have to give me two rations to eat." This same man afterwards won the Gold Medal for valour at Adowa; he had been severely wounded while making a shield of his body for his officer, Lieutenant Pini.

Burru Aga Sechiel, a Jus-bashi (sergeant), being left (during the invasion of Tigré) with ten men to defend an inaccessible rock near Adowa, was, of necessity, abandoned by Major Ameglio, his commanding officer. His orders were "to hold it to the last and not to give it up to anyone unless he received a special message to do so," and he held it through a period of the greatest and most unexpected difficulty, even when he had heard the news of our disaster of Amba Alagi and of the consequent evacuation of Tembien by our troops, —when he could no longer expect any relief from the Italians.

Some chiefs of that region, amongst whom was the leader who had already been ejected from that hill by Colonel Pianavia, came several times to the foot of the rock to confer with Burru, trying by every inducement to make him surrender the impregnable natural fortress, but each time without success; nothing could shake the sworn faith to Italy of that brave soldier.

"Devices being of no avail, these chiefs had recourse to more terrible trials, and one day showed Burru his father closely bound, and threatened with immediate death; but the strength of mind and iron will of Burru did not fail him, so that this brave buluk-bashi, worthy of the heroic days of Sparta, declared, in order to cut short all discussion, that he would never surrender the Amba (hill) as long as a single Italian remained in the colony."[1]

Eventually he was compelled by famine to surrender; but not before arranging with his men to escape at the first opportunity, which they shortly afterwards succeeded in doing, and after a long march that lasted through many nights, rejoined their battalion. Burru Aga Sechiel was rewarded by being promoted Jus-bashi (native lieutenant).

[1] Major Gamerra: *Fra Gli Ascari.*

The most pathetic story of all is that of the orderly of Lieutenant Pennazzi who during the last moments of the native brigade at Adowa was wounded in both legs by a shell. His orderly not being able to raise him on to his shoulders and carry him to a place less exposed to the enemy's fire, dragged him as far as he could from the melée, to try and place him in safety. But not being able to do so, "he hid the wounded man in the hole of a hyena and gave him all the care that he could. Meanwhile the last survivors of the brigade had retired, and the orderly found himself alone, abandoned with a dying man, amidst implacable and fierce enemies.

"The slow agony of poor Pennazzi lasted over two days, and when it ended the Ascaro closed, with a stone and some earth, the mouth of the hole that had now become a tomb, and sadly took the way which led to Asmara.

"But, unfortunately, he was seen by a group of Amhara, who attacked him, made him prisoner, and carried him to the camp of the Negûs, where even an act of pity such as his, found no mercy and did not prevent his being mutilated by one foot and one hand being cut off."

These three instances are not culled from sensational pamphlets nor even from newspapers; they come from the book of Major Gamerra, who had spent years amongst the Ascari, who commanded the 8th Native Battalion at the battle of Adowa, and was afterwards a prisoner for ten months in Abyssinia: it would be easy to find many similar anecdotes.

CHAPTER IV

RUPTURE OF ALL NEGOTIATIONS WITH MENELIK

Italy still negotiating with Menelik—Traversi mission—Mangasha tired of his fruitless alliance with Italy—The two million cartridges are given to Menelik—He denounces the Treaty of Uccialli—Disastrous results of the gift—All further negotiations interrupted by the Dervish invasion—Victory of Agordat and capture of Kassala—Menelik profits by the respite.

When, on February 28th, 1892, General Baratieri became governor, he found that, as far as Ethiopian affairs were concerned, it was indeed a tangled skein in which he was involved. Only two and a half months had passed since the Convention of the Mareb, so that Ras Mangasha was still a genuine ally of Italy. But as regards Ras Alula, matters were more doubtful; the old chief was evidently dissatisfied with his position. He had been compelled to swear allegiance to his mortal enemies, he saw no prospect of recovering his province, and he found himself in the service of a man who then, at all events, and as late as the year 1896, had the reputation of possessing less ability than vanity. As for Menelik, he was, of course, no longer on such friendly terms with the Italians as when he needed their assistance to win his throne.

But the Governor had also another factor to consider—

namely, the ministers at Rome. The Cabinet held their own views on all these matters and it did not always coincide with his; they expressed their intention as follows: "To act in such manner that (as far as concerns European Powers) the Emperor shall remain within the orbit of Italian influence; further, to act so that the Emperor may be induced to adopt, and maintain towards us, an attitude such that the Tigréan chiefs will be prevented from assuming towards the colony of Massowah a demeanour, either less correct, or less deferential." In other words they had two aims:

To get some acknowledgment of their protectorate with which to satisfy Europe.

To keep the Tigréan chiefs in due subjection.

The question of the Tigréans may be for the moment neglected; the true problem that the government still aimed at solving was how to persuade Menelik—an able and independent monarch—to acknowledge himself under their protectorate. This was the difficulty in the settlement of which there was no time to be lost, for they feared he might at any moment enter into alliance with some other nation.

Now the Italian cabinet wished to gain a definite admission from Menelik, and there are, roughly speaking, only two ways of obtaining a concession from an unwilling man—namely, either to frighten him into giving it, or else to allow him some corresponding advantage in exchange. As any idea of terrorizing Menelik was out of the question, his country being too far off, it remained for them to buy him. The remnants of the loan that he had negotiated in

Italy naturally occurred to them; they could make use of these two million cartridges that had been promised him on the condition of his agreeing to the Treaty of Uccialli and the additional convention; neither of these stipulations had he observed, therefore they had an undoubted right to insist on fresh terms before delivering them. They started a mission under Dr. Traversi, armed with the two million cartridges, but it took seven months on the way, and did not reach its destination until February 1893.

In the meanwhile matters were not going well between them and Mangasha; Ras Sebath and Alula were plotting against the Italians, and were said to be on the verge of renouncing all allegiance to Mangasha himself;[1] the smallest sign of friendship between Italy and Menelik at once became a grievance to these Tigréans. And here it must be admitted that the Italians were not treating their allies with entire fairness; at this time they had laid a plan for buying the acknowledgment of their protectorate from Menelik, by obtaining for him the submission of his rival Mangasha,—a process that they termed mediating between Shoa and Tigré. Now it was hardly to be supposed that if Mangasha, the Tigréan chief, the son and chosen successor of the Emperor John, resigned his claim to the imperial throne, he would do so through the Italians or permit them to reap the benefit of his renunciation. He could obtain better terms by making his own submission to the Negûs in person.

[1] They both rebelled shortly afterwards, but Mangasha had still enough hereditary influence left to overcome them; Alula was pardoned, but Sebath was imprisoned on the height of Amba Alagi.

In February 1893 the Traversi mission with the cartridges reached Addis Abeba, where it was received with all due formality, but with great coldness. The cartridges were then presented with the result that might have been anticipated. Once he obtained this supply Menelik threw off the mask; on February 27th[1] he openly denounced the Treaty of Uccialli to all the Powers.

It was evident that Italy had wasted her trump card; and Baratieri insists that it was entirely contrary to his will that these two million cartridges were ever given to Menelik; he quotes passage after passage from his letters of that time to prove that this was so. But however important he may have considered the Negûs's denunciation, in Italy it appears to have excited little comment; the importance of Menelik was not yet realised. Baratieri complains, and not, I think, without reason, that the Government acted at one moment through their own agents (such as Traversi), and at another moment through him; there were two heads.

The results were undoubtedly disastrous. For some time past, the Somalis and inhabitants of Ogaden, allies of Italy in the south of Ethiopia, had been suffering terribly from the marauding expeditions sent out by the Negûs; they had with perfect justice appealed for help to the Italians, under whose protection they were living; but now it was evident that, not only were the white men unable to keep order in their own protectorate, but they were even arming the

[1] Signor Vico Mantegazza gives the date as May 11th. The only reason that appears to exist for the haste with which the cartridges were presented, is the fear of the Italians lest Menelik should conclude an alliance with some other Power.

oppressors. There was a general outcry of horror: "The cartridges will be used against us," was the message sent to the Governor by his ally the Sultan of Aussa.

It was from this date also that Mangasha began to give up the Italian alliance; he had agreed that they should keep two of his finest provinces, but found that he gained no corresponding benefit from them. "My enemies are thy enemies and my friends thy friends," had been the words of the Mareb Convention, but he now saw his allies sending a peaceful mission to the usurper, and he felt that with the new supplies Menelik might invade Tigré at any moment. His repeated demands for an interview were refused, as the Governor was unwilling, for diplomatic reasons, to meet him at that moment; henceforth he is but a nominal friend of Italy. The Roman government had lost both allies.

What was the true course of action that the Italians should have followed during these negotiations? It is almost impossible to decide. Captain De la Jonquière is of opinion that when Menelik proved treacherous they should have supported Mangasha with all their power, and this policy would certainly have had the advantage of keeping alive the internal dissensions of Ethiopia; it would of course have meant resigning for the time being their claims to the protectorate.

The course they pursued was undoubtedly the least advisable of all; they kept up two streams of negotiation, one from the Cabinet at Rome to Menelik, the other between the Governor and the Tigréan chiefs. The question was naturally asked from one end of Abyssinia to the other: "How can they be allies of both sides at the same moment?" It was not, in this case, a mere treaty of neutrality; at the Convention of the Mareb they had said to Mangasha: "Your enemies are my enemies, and your friends my friends;" yet within fourteen months they were arming his bitterest foe.

This, then, was the end of the alliance with Shoa. Menelik had borrowed money, had denounced the Treaty of Uccialli, and had been supplied with cartridges; he was not as yet the declared enemy of Italy, but after all that had passed, it was scarcely possible to attempt any further negotiations with him. And to the list of failures was soon added a fresh mishap—namely, that during the next ten or eleven months, the Governor was unavoidably prevented from giving his attention to Abyssinian affairs.

Here we come to an almost complete blank in their history,—for the space of nearly a year,—and this at the most critical period of all. No blame can attach to the Governor on this account; it was simply unavoidable, being due to a sudden invasion of the north-western frontier by the Dervishes, to repel which the colony was obliged to strain every nerve. On December 21st, 1893, (while the Governor was in Italy) General Arimondi attacked and brilliantly defeated the invaders at Agordat. On hearing the news of this battle the Governor hastened back to the colony and quickly decided that it would be wisest to strike a decisive blow at the Dervish base of operations, for he argued that their attacks might become dangerous "if they coincided, for instance, in December (1894) or in January (1895) with a raising of shields in Ethiopia." He foresaw, in fact, the risk of being simultaneously attacked by both enemies, and intended to strike them singly. As regards the "raising of shields in Ethiopia," we way note that his prophecy was fulfilled almost to a day.

With these ends in view he planned an expedition against the Dervish stronghold of Kassala; it was brilliantly successful, and ended in the complete surprise and capture of that town.

This campaign has, of course, no direct bearing on our subject, but it illustrates very strongly the dangerous position of the Italian colony throughout the whole struggle with Abyssinia. Erythrea was liable to be attacked at a moment's notice, either from the South or from the extreme North West, and, for the purpose of repelling her enemies, she possessed only one small force, which was continually being called on to cover enormous distances. On the other hand, the victories of Agordat and Kassala spread a feeling of confidence throughout Italy that accorded ill enough with the true state of the case. On the southern frontier matters were far from satisfactory. Baratieri had been compelled to turn his mind to the North West during all these months, but Menelik had made the very best use of his time, as will presently appear.[1]

[1] For the benefit of those who care to study the wars of the Italian colony I give a short account in the Appendix, of these Dervish campaigns. It was in them that the native battalions of Baratieri were first under fire; they also afford proof of the energy and ability of a man who is remembered chiefly by his failures.

CHAPTER V

WAR AGAINST MANGASHA. BATTLE OF COATIT

AFTER eleven months the Governor again turns to Abyssinian affairs—Finds Menelik and Mangasha reconciled—Colonel Piano's mission to Addis Abeba—Mangasha arming—Crisis impending—Batha Agos' rebellion—Suppressed by Toselli—Governor's ultimatum to Mangasha—Governor advances and occupies Adowa—Retires again—Mangasha advances towards Okule Kusai—Baratieri surprises him at Coatit—Two days' fighting at Coatit—Senafe—Official figures of the campaign.

I

WHEN General Baratieri, after the elapse of nearly eleven months during which he had been busied with Italian and Dervish affairs, was able to turn his undivided attention once again (in August 1894) to the Abyssinian question, he found matters in an altered condition. It was by this time nearly a year and a half since Menelik's repudiation of the Treaty of Uccialli, and during that period the Italian cause had advanced little, but that of the Negûs had been steadily and quietly progressing. In June 1894 Mangasha, tired of his profitless alliance with Italy, had proceeded to Addis Abeba, to tender his submission to the Negûs in person, and receive from him the crown of Tigré. Menelik, as usual, made the most of the situation; when Mangasha went through the formal prostration, with a stone hanging about his neck according to Abyssinian custom, the Negûs overwhelmed him with reproaches for having concluded an alliance with Italy, and told him that before claiming the crown of Tigré he must first think of re-conquering the ceded provinces. Amongst the courtiers Mangasha found himself regarded as a traitor to his race, and greeted with sarcastic observations,—especially by the faction of the Empress Taitu who had promised the crown of Tigré to her brother Ras Olie. Menelik, however, took care that he should not be driven to desperation.[1]

On the other hand, Ras Alula, who was known to hate all Italians, found a warm welcome at court; he and the other Tigréans were quickly won over to the Emperor's side, and (according to the common report) as many as 2,000 of them remained with him when Mangasha returned to Tigré. It was evident that the work was proceeding apace, —the great work of welding all the scattered fragments into one powerful, united Ethiopia.

At Rome the new Cabinet had started with a strictly economical policy. They intended to withdraw the boundaries of the colony to a triangular line between Massowah, Asmara and Keren, to give up the land south of Skitet (Schitet) to Abyssinia, and the land west of Keren to the Dervishes. The armed force was to be reduced to a third of its effective strength and the whole colony was only to cost Italy three million lire (about £115,000) a year, which,

[1] Menelik did not confer on him the title of Negûs, but it was understood that he might earn it by service against Erythrea. —*Memorie d'Africa.* Baratieri.

to make a rough comparison, is less than a quarter of what Great Britain spends in time of peace on her Militia.

It was, of course, impossible to carry out a program of this description, so after a commission had been appointed to enquire into it the idea was abandoned; but Colonel Piano, a member of the commission, was despatched to Addis Abeba, to endeavour once again to extract some semblance of an agreement to the Italian protectorate. He found Menelik busily engaged in constructing railways and telegraphs, coining money, talking of entering the Postal Union, ordering machines of all kinds, and affecting indifference for the Italian resident and the Italian Government.[1] "It would be a grave illusion," remarked Piano sadly, "to think that we enjoy in Shoa either the esteem or the friendship to which our past benefits should entitle us."

The Piano mission had therefore no better fate than its predecessors, and the continual despatch of these unfruitful embassies did not tend to raise the prestige of Italy in the eyes of the natives; it showed, or appeared to show a singular lack of dignity on the part of so great and civilized a power, that a member of her royal commission should be sent to ask for concessions of the Shoan chief, and be treated by him with open contempt. Neither would any great point have been gained by inveigling the Negûs into signing a shadowy reproduction of the Treaty of Uccialli,—some phantom agreement which he would have repudiated with the same cynical directness that he had already shewn in the case of the reality.

Memorie d'Africa: Baratieri.

Under these conditions it is perhaps not surprising to find, as the Governor tells us in his memoirs, that at "this time there was growing up throughout the length and breadth of Ethiopia a kind of negative patriotism" such as he had never before seen; founded on a general hatred of the white men. He relates that a song had spread amongst the people from Shoa as far north as Okule Kusai, of which the principal refrain was: "Of a black snake's bite you may be cured, but from the bite of a white snake you will never recover."

The alliance with Mangasha, which was the only remaining counterpoise to the power of Menelik, was now little better than a cloak under which the younger chief matured his hostile preparations. He had succeeded in surrounding himself in a nebulous mist of intrigue, the tone of his letters was still that of the most exalted friendship; he warmly congratulated the Governor on the capture of Kassala; he even offered to attack the Dervishes in Ghedaref, but when this offer was accepted he merely sent Ras Agos into the western province of Shirè, from whence to threaten them, while one of Menelik's most able supporters was installed as chief of Agamè, to be a kind of Shoan resident with Mangasha. Many of the succeeding events are probably due to the influence and diplomacy of this individual, Shum Tesfai.

Matters were therefore in the following condition. Mangasha was collecting a large army to act against the Dervishes, for which purpose he had even beaten the Kitet (Chitet), but few people believed that he really intended to fight for the Italians; the truth probably being that he had not yet quite made up his mind as to which alliance would suit him best. Tesfai was working for his master. Mulazzani, the Italian resident at Adowa, was becoming more and more apprehensive, and the Governor felt himself between two fires,—the smouldering discontent in Tigré and a possible campaign of revenge from Khartum. It was only a short time since Mangasha had invited him to an interview, but he had refused it, fearing some act of treachery.

At this moment, December 15th, 1894, the bomb burst, and in a most unexpected quarter,—Batha Agos, chief of Okule Kusai, suddenly broke out into open rebellion. It was a curious denouement of events from more than one point of view.

Okule Kusai, though south of Hamacen, is one of the most northern provinces over which Abyssinia has ever extended her rule; it was surprising that the conspirators should have selected a comparatively detached district, easily accessible to the Italians, for the beginning of their operations.[1]

More peculiar still was it that Batha Agos should have turned traitor, for he was bound to Italy not only by ties of gratitude, but by those of interest. In former times he had been at constant warfare with the Emperor John and Alula; he had sacked Adowa, the capital of Tigré, and then Alula had driven him away to seek exile with the

[1] It will be noticed that this was an exact fulfilment of the Governor's prophecy on June 8th. He had said that "either in December or in January there would be a raising of shields in Ethiopia."

tribes of Habab. Here, amongst a less warlike people, he had quickly gained reputation as a leader, and it was from this condition of an outcast adventurer that General Baldissera had raised him to the chieftainship of Okule Kusai. It was the white men who had been his only friends, and Mangasha's father and Alula who had been his bitterest enemies; and his defection cannot with any great probability be attributed to bribery, for he was now a rich man.[1]

At Agordat no chief had shown himself more ready to fight for the Italians than Batha Agos; yet with all these arguments in his favour he had never inspired confidence; there was "something crooked" in his expression. Only a fortnight before his revolt, the Governor had sent to Lieutenant Sanguinetti, the Resident in Okule Kusai, warning him to be on his guard. "Batha," he wrote, "is a man of natural duplicity; one has only to look him in the face to know it;" and his letter continued by warning Sanguinetti of certain rumours of treachery that were afloat.

The alienation of Batha Agos is attributed by Italian writers to the influence of the Lazzarists, a sect of French priests (supposed to be bitterly antagonistic to Italy), who had converted him to Catholicism; and his final action had been accelerated by fear that the Governor would summon him for a fresh campaign against the Dervishes, and thereby cut short his whole intrigue. On December 15th, Baratieri,

[1] This sketch of his history is taken from Signor Vico Mantegazza's book.

at Keren, was informed from Asmara that the telegraph wires were cut from there to Saganeiti, the capital of Okule Kusai,—this was all he knew, but he acted without a moment's hesitation. He ordered a caravan to start at once for Kassala, to enable it to hold out if attacked during his absence, and telegraphed to Major Toselli at Asmara to proceed at once to Saganeiti, giving his advance the appearance of a route march in case of there being in reality no rebellion to be crushed. Reinforcements were sent to Toselli from the garrisons of Arkico and Ghinda, and the largest available number of troops were concentrated at Asmara under the Governor's own command.

On the 16th, Toselli arrived near Saganeiti, where he found that Sanguinetti had been treacherously seized and imprisoned,[1] and was therefore obliged to treat with Batha Agos for the Resident's release,—a negotiation that was prolonged as much as possible by the Abyssinian chief, who did not realize that every hour brought reinforcements to Toselli. He protested his continued fidelity to Italy, but on the market-place he had already posted a notice proclaiming himself independent chief of Okule Kusai, ally of Mangasha, and "avenger of their rights trampled on by the Italians."

By the evening of the 17th, Toselli had 1,500 men and 2 guns, so he decided to attack early on the following

[1] He had invited Batha Agos and his brother to partake of coffee, when they sprang upon him suddenly and pinned him to the ground: "God will punish you," said the lieutenant to Batha Agos, whose knee was on his chest: "Italy is great."—"Ethiopia is greater still" was the confident reply.

morning; but on the 18th his attack turned out to be unnecessary. By midday he had occupied Saganeiti without fighting, for Batha Agos was gone,—no one knew whither. This sudden disappearance surprised Toselli, but he quickly concluded that the Dejatch had marched against Halai, a small fort further north, garrisoned by one company (220 men) under Captain Castellazzi; so after only an hour's rest he started towards Halai.

This was merely a guess on the part of Toselli, but it saved the situation, for Batha Agos with 1,600 men had arrived that morning outside Halai and summoned the garrison to surrender. Captain Castellazzi's position was difficult, as his supplies of ammunition were very small, so he succeeded in prolonging the negotiations until 1.30, in the hope of being relieved. Then the firing began. By 4.45 matters were becoming extremely critical when suddenly the rebels found themselves attacked in rear by the advanced guard of Toselli's column. They fled on all sides, vanishing rapidly into the mists that hung about the surrounding mountains, and leaving their Dejatch, Batha Agos, dead on the ground. The Italians had lost 11 killed and 22 wounded, but the rebellion was crushed.

Never probably has there been a revolt in a large province so quickly suppressed; it had only lasted three days. This contemptible result was due partly to the character of the natives, amongst whom, according to Baratieri, the feudal devotion to a chief had never taken any deep root, owing to the naturally divided nature of their province. It is covered with small villages separated from each other by the mountains, and these units had been accustomed in former days to elect their own leaders by means of popular assemblies, in an almost republican manner, so they saw no reason to risk their lives for the benefit of the Dejatch.

Historically speaking, however, this rising has one importance—namely, that it proves that so shrewd and experienced a judge of political affairs as Batha Agos already considered the Italians to be sustaining a losing cause. He was a man without scruples and with few illusions, whose actions, therefore, offer a simple index to his thoughts. He was one of those characters,—and who is there that does not meet them in the ordinary affairs of life?—that may be treated as a barometer; their friendship points only towards those who are uppermost, their enmity only towards those who are down; if, therefore, they greet a man warmly, he may know that his prospects appear bright; if coldly, that they are but moderate; if they pass him by, or still worse attack him, he may rely on it that he has already been abandoned by the rest of their world.

This was what the Italians full soon discovered; but for the moment the work of their secret enemies was checked by the energy of Toselli, and by the rapid measures of the Governor. On the 17th, two days after the rising, he had already written to Mangasha requesting him to disband the forces collected at Entisho (Entiscio), to give up the rebels, of whom a large number had sought refuge with him after the defeat of Halai, and to send Ras Agos to attack the Dervishes in Ghedaref as he had agreed to do. To this letter, which amounted to an ultimatum, Mangasha only returned an indefinite answer, so the Governor prepared to take active steps.[1] A week later, on Christmas Day 1894, he had collected 3,500 regulars at the fort of Adi Ugri in Serae, and wrote a fresh letter to Mangasha who returned no reply. Baratieri's advance began. On the night of the 27th, he occupied the Pass of Gashaorki, (Gasciaorchi), the northern key to Adowa; on the 28th he was encamped close to the town; Mangasha had abandoned his capital.

Here the Governor published a proclamation stating that he had come, not to make war, but to bring the peace that Mangasha had already sworn on the Bible to maintain; and here he received the submission of many important men, the most notable being Theophilus the Itchegué, or religious chief who lives at the holy city of Axum, not far from Adowa.[2] The clergy of Tigré, who feared the advent of holy rivals from Shoa, were the most genuine allies that remained to the Italians; it is not the first instance of ecclesiastics favouring the foreigners in time of invasion: in the British Isles we have been perhaps unusually fortunate in the possession of a clergy who, even when belonging to the persecuted sects, have shewn by many glorious instances that their interests are secondary to their patriotism.

Baratieri had counted on the moral effect of a triumphant entry into the enemy's capital, and to some extent he had

[1] News had been brought to him that Mangasha's young son was being received with great honour by the Dervishes in Ghedaref. Entisho also, was within a day's march of the Erythrean frontier, so that matters had come to a crisis which Baratieri determined to break up.

[2] The Itchegué refused to come in person to Adowa, fearing treachery, but he sent messages of friendship.

been justified, but Mangasha was still at Entisho (Entiscio) to the north-east, threatening his line of communications; the Kitet (Chitet) was still beating in all the Tigréan provinces. After four days, therefore, he perceived that he must retrace his steps, as his force was not sufficiently numerous to follow up and attack Mangasha amongst the mountains of that district, where hundreds of strong defensive positions are easily to be found. He decided to make Adi Ugri his base of operations, and by January 3rd was again encamped near that fort. While his preparations were proceeding a battalion under Hidalgo was detached, to complete the subjection of Okule Kusai.

This dash on Adowa has been adversely criticised, and from a strictly military point of view it was a failure. He had hoped to prevent Ras Agos who was still in Shire (Scire) (the western province) with 2,000 men, from rejoining Mangasha, but the Ras had succeeded in doing so by making a wide southern detour; the advance had been, in the words of Captain De la Jonquière, "a sword-stroke in the water." Still, politically speaking, his bold action was not without good results. It now remained for him to march against the enemy, and dissipate by a tactical success any wavering amongst his allies to which his enforced retreat might have given rise.

The campaign against Mangasha is notable for the extreme simplicity of its movements; the Ras was encamped at Entisho, but his advanced guard had been pushed forward as far north as the Belesa. Baratieri was at Adi Ugri on his north-west.

Mangasha's aim was to advance due northwards into

Okule Kusai, and thence perhaps as far as Ghinda or even Massowah. To accomplish this movement he would have to leave the Governor on his left, and give up all idea of keeping his lines of communication open, but this apparently is a matter of little consequence to an Abyssinian general as his troops live on the country wherever they go.

There were three ways by which the Tigréans could invade Okule Kusai: via Gura; via Coatit,—a little more to the East; or by a still wider easterly detour. In all three cases they were liable to be stopped by an attack on their flank, for the Governor at Adi Ugri was near enough to intercept them by whatever road they advanced.

Baratieri saw this and understood that his wisest course was to move forward (to the East) from Adi Ugri, and take up a strong position from which he could fall, at a few hours' notice, on the enemy's flank. He selected the heights of Kenafena (Chenafena) as the most suitable for his purpose, being near to Adi Ugri his base, and easily defensible in case Mangasha were bold enough to attack him.

On January 9th, therefore, he moved to Kenafena where he spent several days, and was able to satisfy himself that the enemy did not mean to attack him or to advance by the Gura route; they intended evidently to keep farther away, and to evade his attack if possible by advancing on Coatit or by a still more easterly road. One thing was certain: that sooner or later the country around them would be exhausted and then they would be obliged to make a move; an Abyssinian army can never remain halted for long.

On the 12th, he crossed the Mareb and advanced to

Adis Adi, where he effected his junction with Hidalgo. In front of Adis Adi is Mount Toculé, that rises, like a tower on the edge of the rugged plain of Zama; from this height word was at once brought to him that a long low column of dust could be seen to the east, near Mount Dighim. A long low dust-cloud of course means infantry: it was evidently Mangasha's column advancing by the road to Coatit.

Two alternatives, Baratieri says, occurred to him: one was to attack them while still on the march, the other to occupy Coatit and await them. In most cases the first alternative would have afforded the best chances of success, but in this instance he saw that it would involve another three hours' march in the sun, through a rocky, thorn-covered country; that the enemy would be able to see them from the first, and would therefore have time to make every preparation for receiving them. He determined to march on Coatit.

Before finally coming to this decision, he took the advice of General Arimondi and of the other senior officers.

By 3 p.m. that afternoon the advanced guard under Toselli had occupied Coatit; soon the other battalions had each taken up its allotted position without the enemy's having the slightest suspicion of their arrival; it was generally supposed in Mangasha's camp that he had succeeded in evading the Italian force, whereas now Baratieri was only awaiting the cover of darkness to move against him.

The Governor's little army consisted of only 3,900 men, (66 officers, 105 white men in the ranks, the rest being natives). Mangasha's force was estimated at about 12,000 riflemen,

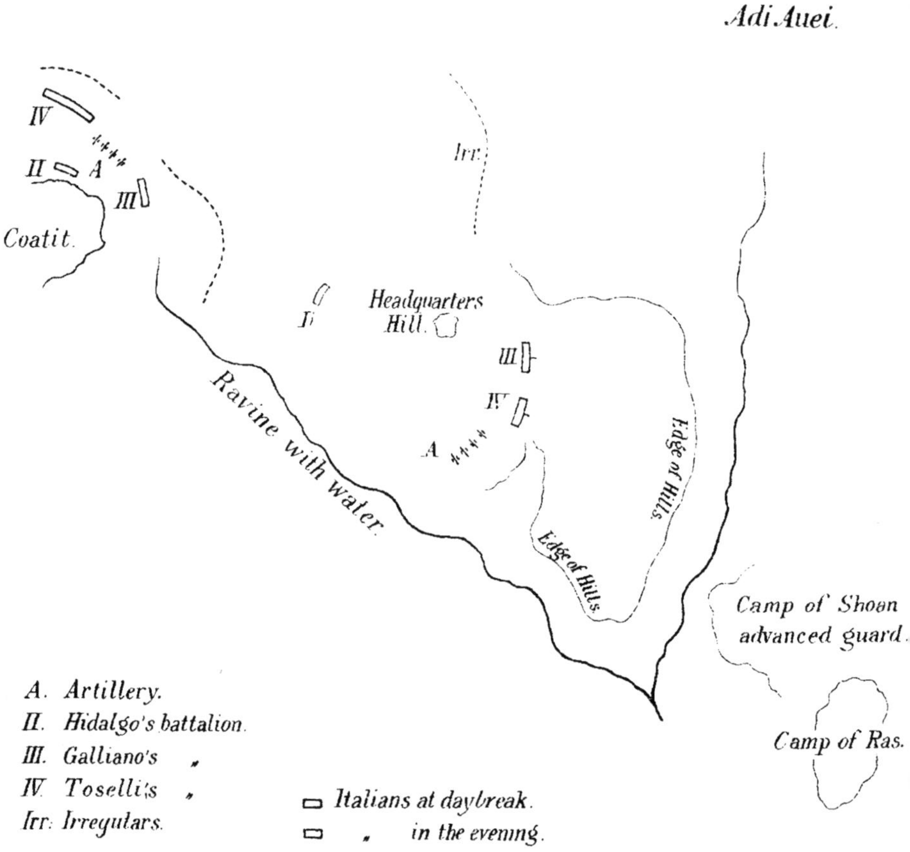
Adi Auei.
IV
II
A
III
Coatit.
Irr.
Headquarters Hill.
III
IV
A
Ravine with water.
Edge of Hills.
Edge of Hills.
Camp of Shoan advanced guard.
Camp of Ras.
A. Artillery.
II. Hidalgo's battalion.
III. Galliano's "
IV. Toselli's "
Irr. Irregulars.
Italians at daybreak.
" in the evening.

Face p. 71.

and about 7,000 soldiers armed with spears or not armed at all.

From the Italian outposts, it was easy to see the enemy's tents extending over a wide space in two roughly formed camps,—to the south that of the Ras himself, to the north that of his Fitaurari. In the darkness "we could count their fires scattered over a vast circle, while ours which had been reduced to the lowest number possible, were hidden by a considerable swell in the ground.... During the night there was perfect silence in our camp and in that of the enemy... there was no possibility of any hesitation about the attack, which I had already thought out... the folds of the ground favoured our initial manœuvring. Two hours before dawn I called the commanding officers and gave them their orders and instructions. Major Toselli (with the 4th native battalion) was to form the right wing, as far as a narrow gorge which would cover his right flank; in the centre Major Galliano (3rd native battalion) was to occupy a height; the paths and heights on the left were to be guarded by the irregulars (under Sanguinetti and Mulazzani); behind Galliano, Major Hidalgo (2nd native battalion) followed in reserve; the artillery was on the right with Toselli's battalion."[1]

"The moon shines over us, and the great extension of the Tigréan camps reveals their numbers and their carelessness.[2] In an hour and a quarter all our men are at their post and the movement of offence begins, with the first gleam of the morning (at 5.45), by a general advance

[1] *Memorie d'Africa.*—Baratieri.

[2] The official report on the battle.

wheeling slightly to the right, pivoting on the Artillery,—Toselli's battalion, Galliano's, and the irregulars of Sanguinetti and Mulazzani in succession: in the centre, in reserve and under cover, is Hidalgo's battalion, consisting of 4 companies, for it had been obliged to leave the 5th company in the position and with the task above mentioned (viz. of occupying a precipice on the right rear of the army in order to guard the water). The point to march on,—a conical hill on the summit of which rises a tukul, to the east, between us and the enemy, standing out darkly against the clear mirror of the dawn."

From the Governor's vivid picture one can see the little army creeping forward towards the pale light in the East, hiding behind the rugged crests like a wild animal stalking its prey.

"All goes well. A little after 6 a.m. the two battalions of the first line have some of their companies deployed, and the rest under good cover. With the first rays of the sun Captain Cicco di Cola's battery from its skilfully chosen position on a height, sends the first shrapnel at 1,900 metres (2,090 yards) into the rebel camp, while I betake myself with my staff and the banner of Italy, to the high conical hillock already indicated, at the centre of the line,—henceforward called Commando (Headquarters) Hill. The irregulars on the wing, attracted in the direction of the hills that rise off the plain, and owing to the great extension of their front, have unwittingly descended too far down towards the centre of our line, leaving almost unguarded on their left the height and village of Adi Auei which rises clear against the horizon, lit up by the light of the morning sun.

"A great commotion is visible in the hostile camp. Notwithstanding the sudden surprise, rapidly increasing groups of warriors swarm out with great promptitude and dash, advancing through the winding paths and small gorges, crossing them with wonderful agility, concealing their numbers, making a shield of the obstacles. They offer us only a small mark as they disappear from time to time, and gather in greater numbers under cover of the defences.

"The rifle fire runs along the whole line of the 3rd and 4th battalions, which keep well under control of their officers in spite of the *élan* of the attack; as is proved by the frequent volleys, and the bayonet charges of individual units, on that broken, furrowed, and thickly covered ground."

In this manner the battle was thoroughly engaged in front of the enemy's camp when suddenly the Governor perceived a cloud of dust, denoting a large hostile column, that was making a turning movement towards his left, and soon the irregulars sent word that they were hotly attacked; they had pressed forward too much towards the centre, so that there seemed to be a chance for the Tigréans to retrieve the day by turning their outer flank. This counter-attack soon became the true point of danger. Although the companies on the Italian right were rapidly gaining ground, the Governor was obliged to send word to the 3rd battalion (Galliano's) to incline to the north, and to despatch those companies that were not actually engaged to reinforce his left wing which would otherwise be surrounded; the enemy were making determined efforts to cut him off from Coatit.

Galliano at once moved northwards, as ordered, with three companies, but in accomplishing this movement his losses were very heavy, especially in one company, owing to its mistaking the advancing Tigréans for some of their own retiring irregulars, and being in consequence nearly surrounded.

On the original front this movement of Galliano's created a gap, so at about 9.30 two companies of Hidalgo were ordered into the firing line, under Captains Pavesi and Brabanti. On the arrival of these fresh troops the original advance was renewed, each company gaining ground by rushes or bayonet charges and then halting to fire, while the artillery was also pushed forward, even as near as 1,100 yards from the enemy. As for the Tigréans they pursued the usual tactics of the Abyssinian soldier—namely, those of concealing themselves for the purpose of making a sudden dash forward when it was possible to get to close quarters, but without success; in spite of their great preponderance in numbers, the superior discipline of the Italian troops had assured them victory on this front.

It was on their left that fell the real brunt of the day's fighting. Mangasha was here in person, as could be ascertained by the continual beating of the Negarit (War-drum), and under his eyes the Tigréans were pushing their way steadily onward amongst the euphorbias and olive trees. Matters were critical, as everything depended on the Governor's keeping his retreat open to Coatit. He was therefore compelled to call off Toselli and Hidalgo from their pursuit (on the right), and order them to retire towards the town, changing front left so as to keep the northern assailants at bay; so rapid had the Tigréans' turning movement been, that he had no choice but to retreat on Coatit and concentrate his whole energy on repulsing their northern attack.

No time was to be lost: the artillerymen were the first to move, then Hidalgo and Toselli succeeded, though with great difficulty, in performing this very dangerous manœuvre, but the Governor himself was barely able to make his escape from Commando Hill. Of his staff, consisting of eight men, no less than three were killed; and with such reckless courage did he expose himself in directing the retirement, that for a short space of time he seemed to those around him to have abandoned all hope of victory, and to be seeking death on the field of battle.

Once, however, that the change of front had been accomplished, he tells us that he had in reality no further anxiety. At every point the Tigréans were met by an impenetrable resistance; on the extreme north they had made their way through a hidden ravine to the church where the Italian wounded lay, but even here they were repulsed by Lieutenant Virdia, the doctor in charge, who armed his orderlies, mule-drivers, and slightly wounded men, and defended the cemetery wall. For some hours the firing continued, but the attacks gradually became less sustained until at length they died away altogether; the day's work was ended.

Which side had been victorious? It was hard to say. The small Italian force had surprised their enemy, but their attack had been repulsed; on the other hand, Mangasha's counter-attack had proved a failure. One thing is certain, namely, that the losses of the Tigréans had been far the heaviest and, as is nearly always the case, the drawn battle was virtually a victory for the regular troops, who have naturally the greater powers of endurance and recuperation.

All that night (the 13th to 14th) the Governor expected a fresh assault, but it never came. At dawn, however, the Tigréans opened fire. For a few moments the Governor thought of taking the offensive, but soon came to the conclusion that their position was too strong; he preferred to await the arrival of a caravan from Adis Adi, the more so as he knew that his enemies were ill supplied with water, and suspected that their ammunition would soon be expended; he determined therefore to stand entirely on the defensive. The orders he gave were, to induce the enemy to fire away as many cartridges as possible.

At noon his left was attacked, and an attempt was afterwards made to gain the water supply on the right, but, beyond a few ill-sustained efforts and a heavy fusilade, no very hard fighting took place; in fact so feeble did the enemy's efforts become that the Governor determined to drive him from his positions on the following morning,—a resolution that produced no results, for that very evening at 10 p.m., Mangasha retired, with a considerably weakened and disordered army, as far west as Senafè. The victory now rested decisively with the Italians.

On the 15th the troops were ready at dawn, according to orders, for the attack: instead of an attack they found only a pursuit, but it lasted from sunrise to sunset, and they covered 40 kilometres[1] over a really bad country during that day. Starting towards Adi Auei with Toselli, as usual, commanding the advanced guard, they passed

[1] According to De la Jonquière; this is equivalent to about 25 miles.

rapidly through that village to Mai Tzade, where at 11 a.m. they had an hour's halt, and on to Toconda, where they spent another hour. The Governor was making every conceivable effort to turn Mangasha's retreat into a rout, and although the Tigréans had had seven or eight hours' start, he had reached the hill of Toconda no very long time after they left it; he expected to catch them up at Senafè, for in the country immediately beyond this there was little water to be found, but it was necessary to take every precaution against ambushes, for the country abounded in good defensive positions; he was continually astonished at their not being occupied.

"I thought to find resistance at the difficult pass of Cascassè (he says in his memoirs), but it was clear, only the road had been widened by the current of fugitives,—branches broken from the trees, rags of clothing, utensils and tools thrown on the ground; here and there a wounded or exhausted man who, in spite of their most scrupulously observed custom, had been abandoned."

Thus the pursuit proceeded until, at 4.30 p.m., they reached the hill of Tarica, where the advanced guard signalled "enemy in sight." But no resistance was attempted, the white figures disappearing over the crest of the hill with loud shouts to warn their fellow-countrymen. When the Italians crossed the ridge, by the light of the setting sun, they saw at their feet the whole Tigréan camping ground in which the tents of the chiefs had already been pitched; the Negarit was beating the assembly.

Baratieri at once ordered forward his battery, telling them to open fire at the Ras' tent, which they did with wonderful rapidity, considering that they had been marching since early dawn. Meanwhile the advanced guard was preparing to attack.

"A crowd collected outside Mangasha's camp; shots, fired in the air in order to incite the warriors to battle, were distinctly to be heard amid the furious beating of the Negarit. A thick mist, as is usual in the evenings, was rising to the heights on which we stood (2,316 metres Senafè, 2,758 Amba Tarica, about 2,500 the hill), and was enveloping the whole scene, leaving only here and there an opening in its thick veil. Following rapidly on sunset came the darkness of the night, while two companies of the 3rd battalion, a small detachment of cavalry and the irregulars were descending the hill to reconnoitre."[1]

Under cover of the darkness Mangasha and his men slipped away, but although still three or four times as numerous as the Erythrean force, they abandoned everything:—"The tent of the Ras had been pierced by a cannon shot—perhaps by two; around it lay several corpses. Seventeen negarits (war-drums) were scattered about, and with them swords, small arms, bugles, lances and shields in a most varied supply." But the greatest find of all was a casket containing the correspondence of the Ras.[2]

On January 18th General Baratieri returned northwards, leaving garrisons in Senafè and Saganeiti, and ordering the

[1] *Memorie d'Africa.*—Baratieri.

[2] Signor Vico Mantegazza quotes passages from these letters proving that the rebellion of Batha Agos had been pre-arranged with Mangasha, only he had begun it too soon owing to his fear of being called on to repel the Dervishes.

occupation of the strong positions of Adis Adi, and Adi Caje. For the time being the war was over.

This small campaign against Tigré most undoubtedly gives proof, if any were required, of the great abilities of General Baratieri. The distances alone, which he was obliged to cover at so short a notice, offer no slight difficulty. In 32 days he had not only crushed the rebellion in Okule Kusai, but also invaded and temporarily conquered the great province of Tigré; with 3,900 natives and one battery he had discomfited and routed an army of 20,000 men,—of whom at least 12,000 bore rifles or guns. He had the advantages of being able to rely on many of the resources of civilized war, but, on the other hand, he was fighting in a difficult country amidst a hostile and treacherous population. These are achievements which I think compare very favourably with those of the most successful colonial expeditions in the world.

To turn to the official figures of the expedition. The campaign is counted to have lasted 45 days,—from December 15th, 1894, to January 20th, 1895. During that period there were some 8,000 soldiers in the colony, but only 3,883 were available for the corps of operations. These 3,883 are composed as follows:—66 Italian officers, 105 Italians in the ranks, 3,684 natives, 28 cavalry men armed only with lances, one mountain battery of 4 guns.

Their losses had been extraordinarily small, amounting to only 324 in all, 95 killed (3 officers) and 229 wounded (2 officers). Those of the Tigréans were estimated at 1,500 killed and about twice that number wounded, while their whole army had been dispersed. The disparity of the losses was chiefly due to the fact that the Italian force was always either on the defensive, or in a greatly superior position to their adversaries. Their fire-discipline had been splendid, especially when it is remembered that they included over 400 comparatively untrained native militiamen (who, however, according to the General, "displayed the same valour" as the regulars). The Governor quotes with pride the official return proving that, during those 45 days, his men had only fired 153,725 rounds, or about 40 per man. Assuming that the estimated losses of the Tigréans are right, this return gives a very remarkable average of hits: it would seem that for every 34 shots fired one man was hit, whereas in the Crimea it has been estimated that only one Russian was hit for every 570 French bullets and every 700 English.[1] But such statistics can have little real accuracy, and may be in reality misleading. In this campaign who can say how many Tigréans were killed by the artillery (the guns fired 228 rounds)? Or how many in the bayonet fighting of which there was a large share? All such calculations can be said to prove is that the shooting was good, and the fire-discipline excellent.

But the most astonishing feat of all, to those who are accustomed to the figures of European warfare, was the extraordinarily small cost of the campaign,—it cost only 500,000 lire, or about £19,000—a price often paid for a house in London. The Governor conquered,—temporarily it is true, a province about as large as Ireland, yet this insignificant sum is all that appears as war expenditure (*i.e.* expendi-

[1] Mullhall's statistics.

ture over and above the ordinary peace allowance) in the Italian returns for the campaign from December 15th, 1894, to January 31st, 1895. Its smallness is, of course, largely due to their being no mobilization expenses;—the battalions were all ready for war except 1,600 militiamen, who had to be called out for 38 days out of the 45; it is also largely due to the troops being natives, whose food, pay, transport, etc., is far less than that of Europeans, and whose widows would probably receive a lower rate of pension. The principal items are as follow:

5,500 rations[1] per day for 45 days	50,000	lire
Requirements of the Mobile Militia, 1,600 strong	110,000	„
Artillery and Engineers, sanitary materials, quadrupeds, repair of equipage etc.	100,000	„
Chief transport expenses—estimated	110,000	„
Intelligence, and other political expenses . . .	30,000	„
Gratuities to widows of dead Ascari	50,000	„
Payments and rewards to the wounded, medals etc.	30,000	„
150 fresh enrolments to fill up the vacancies left by death etc., expenses	4,000	„
General expenses, telegrams etc.	16,000	„
	500,000	lire.

The figures mean that General Baratieri waged war at an average expense of a little over 2 lire per man per day,—say 21 pence. The lowest expenditure in European campaigns during the last half century has been that of the German army in 1870, which cost about 5 shillings per man per day.

[1] These rations consisted of the flour served out as a marching ration to the natives. *Operazioni per la Difesa della Colonia Eritrea, dal 15 Decembre, 1894, al 20 Gennaio, 1895.*

No other nation has been able to do what the Germans did, so that even allowing for the mobilization expenses, for the higher rate of pay and better food required by white men, the more costly methods of warfare, and the greater determination of their opponents,—even allowing for all these differences, this little campaign of Baratieri's remains, to the best of my belief, unique from the economic point of view.

He was fortunate in his subordinates; Arimondi, Toselli, Galliano, Hidalgo, Pavesi, Sanguinetti, Mozetti (the doctor) are glorious names in the Italian army, not to mention others too numerous to record here.

So brilliant were these victories over the Dervishes and Abyssinians deemed in Italy, that it is beyond all doubt attributable to them that not only the General but some of his subordinates, and most of all the Italian Government and nation formed too low an estimate of the difficulties to be overcome during the campaign against Menelik.

CHAPTER VI

WAR WITH MENELIK BECOMES INEVITABLE

GOVERNOR'S triumphant return to Massowah—expels the French Lazzarist missionaries—Question arises, how to make use of the victories?—The Governor's opinion—Captain Perini's opinion—Dr. Nerazzini's opinion—Italian difficulties—Mangasha's overtures of peace—The Governor's schemes for forming a barrier of Mohammedan and friendly states between Italian and Shoan territory—Mangasha invades Agamè—Baratieri occupies Adigrat—Occupies Adowa—Prefers the advanced line of defence Adigrat-Adowa, to the established Mareb-Belesa-Muna frontier.

THE Governor's return to Asmara and Massowah was a long scene of triumph; the enthusiasm of the natives for the general who had led them to victory and who cared so well for their needs knew no bounds; triumphal arches were erected for him, native dances, beacon fires, festivities of every kind were universal; he was venerated almost as a god.

Nor were his triumphs received with less rejoicing in the mother country; the brilliant victories announced in the evening at theatres, cafés, and other places of public resort, called forth loud expressions of enthusiasm. Baratieri was hailed the worthy disciple of Garibaldi, from whom he had learnt to win battles with small forces. The Parliament and the nation vied with each other in making manifest to him their admiration. The Government and the King sent him telegrams of congratulation, and in reward for his work he was promoted to the rank of Lieutenant-General "per merito di guerra."[1]

He had indeed done well, but the final settlement of Tigréan affairs was still a long way off; he was victorious, in the same sense that Charles XII was victorious against Russia at the battle of Narva,—he found himself with a small army dictating peace to a large country. It was in the nature of things that in each engagement the Italians, like Montrose, must put it to the touch and win or lose their all; victory was a necessity of their existence, for they had only one force in the field, whereas their enemies were no sooner defeated on one side, than they reappeared from some other point of the compass.

One of the first cares of the Governor was to expel the French missionary association of the Lazzarists from the colony. They had been there 50 years and had made many converts, but according to Italian opinion they did not hesitate to intrigue against the government, acting in the interests of France; the French writers deny the accusation.

But the attention of all those in authority was soon diverted from matters of detail, to the (at that moment) more important questions of policy.

On January 21st Baron Blanc, Minister of Foreign Affairs, telegraphed to the Governor: "We are awaiting your proposals as to the best manner of profiting by our success." A short and very natural enquiry it seemed, but it inaugurates a new period,—an epoch of questioning, divided opinions,

[1] Melli: *La Colonia Eritrea,* p. 100.

endless discussions, heated telegrams and, finally, of disaster. It is here that we come to the parting of the ways, where every man has a different view; some say "forward," some say "back," and some say first one and then the other; some advise remaining half way; eventually each opinion in turn is condemned as having been the cause of failure.

The question to be decided was: "Having opened the gates of Tigré, what is to be done next?"

The Governor classified all possible methods of action under four headings. (I) Merely to secure the existing boundaries of the Colony. (II) To remain on the defensive as opposed to Abyssinia, but to invade the Sudan. (III) Vice versa,—to act on the defensive towards the Sudan and to extend their borders towards Abyssinia. (IV) To advance against both enemies. [1]

In reply to these alternatives the Cabinet said that they would not take any action against the Sudan; the only question, therefore, that remained, was whether to assume an offensive or a defensive policy as regards Tigré. On this point they called for advice from General Baratieri, from Dr. Nerazzini (the naval doctor who had accompanied the first missions to Abyssinia), and from Captain Perini, who had been at Adowa with General Orero in 1890. The opinions of all three are published in the Green Books, and it is interesting to note, not only the ideas they throw out as regards that period of Erythrean history, but also how difficult it becomes for a Government to stay its course

[1] Classified in his letter of Jan. 22nd, 1895, to the Minister for Foreign Affairs.

once it has been launched on a career of conquest amongst uncivilized populations.

The Governor's opinion was as follows: "The occupation of Agamè [1] and Tigré offers notable advantages both political and military; it will be my objective. But I do not consider it prudent to proceed to this occupation until our forces have been increased, and preparations have been made for the undertaking." In other words, he wished to pave the way by means of peaceful negotiation; to form in fact an Italian party in Tigré so as to undermine Mangasha's influence before taking the decisive plunge.

On the other hand, Captain Perini sent in a memorial to the Government urging the immediate occupation of Adigrat, (capital of Agamè), Adowa, and Axum (civil and religious capitals of Tigré). This was the opinion amongst (at all events) an appreciable number of the soldiers and military newspapers of Italy. They saw plainly that the barrier of mountains between Adigrat and Adowa was the strongest line of defence for the South of the Colony, as indeed has since been admitted by the Abyssinians themselves. Captain Perini urged that a fresh war with Mangasha was inevitable,—merely a question of months,—that it would be better to forestall it by occupying his strong places, and that there was already a large number of Tigréans who would welcome the Italians as deliverers from a condition of anarchy; that thousands of them would enlist in the victorious battalions of Erythrea.

These arguments in favour of an immediate advance are

[1] The Northern portion of Tigré.

unanswerable, as far as they go; but Dr. Nerazzini sent up a very able memorial, that, being more in accordance with Baratieri's views, carried the day. Nothing, he says, is more easy than to occupy Tigré, but it means the certainty of war against a united Ethiopia; Menelik, as Negûs Nagasti, would be obliged by his subjects to fight, even if he and his chiefs were willing to "stand by like sheep and watch an organized attack on Ethiopia, more especially on that city which is consecrated by religious tradition as holy, where almost all the Emperors are crowned. War would be inevitable, and from that moment all antagonism between Tigréans and Shoans would be blown away in order to show a firm front to the foreign conqueror." "A war against Ethiopia is a big war," he adds, with the emphasis of conviction.

Here, then, we get the two opposite opinions, both of them right. From a military point of view an immediate advance, coupled with a prompt despatch of reinforcements was the only course of action. But it meant war with Ethiopia; could Italy afford such a war? It was obvious that she could not; her treasury had already made great difficulties about the despatch of two white battalions that had been promised as reinforcements after the victory of Senafè.

Both these opinions have been fulfilled with such exactitude that now they each have the appearance of a prophecy. Captain Perini's is a correct technical view; but Nerazzini shows a wonderful insight into the situation, and he seems to have been the only man who at that time understood how quickly Ethiopia might unite against a stranger, or how formidable an antagonist she would then prove.

The position of Italian affairs both inside and outside

the colony was singularly unfortunate; it abounded in inevitably conflicting interests. After some years of struggling, Italy had just succeeded in balancing her accounts, and had returned a ministry whose watchwords were economy and retrenchment; yet her colonial field-force, only about 5,000 strong, was menaced on one side by Mangasha who might very easily succeed in raising eight or ten thousand followers for a fresh effort, while on the north-west frontier his allies the Dervishes were lining the banks of the Atbara with 20,000 men equally bent on revenge. How could such a crisis be solved without heavy expenditure? To invade Tigré meant war with Menelik; to evacuate Tigré meant war with Mangasha and the Dervishes. To set up another chief and turn Tigré into a "buffer" state was, in the opinion of the Governor, impossible, owing to the pride and independence of the Tigréans and the hereditary influence of Mangasha. There remained only one course, and that was boldly to face the war or rather constant wars, with Menelik; but this led towards a national deficit and would most probably have been very unpopular. On the other hand, a complete retirement from the situation, besides amounting to an almost criminal abandonment of her allies, would not have satisfied the aspirations, or befitted the dignity of the Italian people.

The only point on which Signor Crispi could congratulate himself was the almost equally precarious position of Menelik. The Negûs had just returned, it is true, from a successful raid on a Galla tribe of Wollamo, 150 kilometres S. of Addis Abeba, wherein his men had shown the true barbarian groundwork shining through the veneer of civilization, by massacring thousands of unresisting men, women and children. But in spite of this "victory" he knew that each of his Ras was working for his own hand; the King of Gojjam was his secret enemy, Mangasha was still his rival, Ras Mikael was in negotiation with Italy, and Maconnen was intriguing against him, even to the point of writing to Baratieri to say that in case of war, he would rebel against the Negûs. [1]

Amidst the divergency of opinions the Governor was enabled to pursue his own course unmolested, the more so as it coincided for the time being with that of Nerazzini. For the moment he intended to remain outside the Tigréan frontiers unless actually compelled to forestall an attack from within them: but the Italian resident, Lieutenant Mulazzani was sent back to Adowa with instructions to assist the smaller chiefs at the expense of the greater, to enrol Tigréans for service in the North, to develop the friendly relations with the clergy, and to discover and counteract, as far as possible, Mangasha's schemes. In this manner the Governor hoped to pave the way for an eventual occupation.

To secure the province of Agamè, he installed a friendly chief in Adigrat, its capital, although he might indeed have occupied that town himself without oppositiom from his government, for Dr. Nerazzini did not think that this step would lead to war with Menelik. The province had originally belonged to Ras Sebath, who had rebelled against Mangasha and was now imprisoned on the height of Amba Alagi. After the meeting of Entotto, [2] Shum Tesfai, Menelik's agent had ruled Agamè, but now, of course, Tesfai hav-

[1] Baratieri's letter to the Minister of Foreign Affairs, February 3rd, 1895.

[2] The reconciliation between Mangasha and Menelik.

ing fought at Coatit and Senafè, was obliged to fly. So the province remained without a chief until Baratieri gave it to Agos Tafari; all these personages play their part in the later history of the war.

By this time Mangasha understood that he had been made a catspaw of by Menelik, who, (there is very little doubt) had urged him to war against Italy not caring which side might prove victorious, as in either case one of his rivals would be humbled; the Negûs still preserved a secret agreement with him,—secret even from his own chiefs, so that it must have been an ill time for those who did not place a bridle on their tongue.

Mangasha spent his days in beating the kitet, arming his followers, and at the same time sending off peaceful overtures to the Governor; on March 2nd (1895) the following letter to the King of Italy was received by Baratieri and duly forwarded as a curiosity. [1]

"To the great, respected, supreme King Humbert I. Sent by Ras Mangasha, son of John, King of Sion, King of the Kings of Ethiopia.

"How are you? Thank God I am well.

"I grieve because they have done me a wrong, and General Baratieri complains that I have done him harm. At this time the Devil interfered in the matter, and Christian people exterminated one another.

"What has been done in the past was the work of the Devil. Now I seek for peace. I desire that you send a just man to decide between my wrong and that of the General.

[1] "I transmit a copy, as a curiosity"—Baratieri to the Minister of Foreign Affairs, March 14th, 1895.

I ask this in order to re-establish our friendship as it was at first.

"Written February 13th (Abyssinian date) in the camp of Addi-Omdai."

Had Mangasha's conduct always been sincere, such a letter might gain sympathy, for after all his lot had been a hard one and he was only 30 or 31 years old. It will be seen that he attributes his actions to the influence of the Devil, which, as General Baratieri remarks with unconscious humour, is an unmistakeable reference to Menelik.

In reply, the General refused to treat, unless Mangasha at once disbanded his forces: an impossible condition of course, but what is to be done with a man whom nobody trusts?

One of the most important projects of the Governor was his scheme for uniting the Mohammedan tribes on the South and East of Tigré, as a counterpoise to Menelik's Abyssinian coalition. It has a curious ring when one hears of a Roman government being the champion of Mohammedanism, but he had been working at this idea for some time with good results. Captain Persico had just returned from a most successful expedition amongst the Danakil tribes, and had in fact established friendly relations with no less a person than Sheik Thala, one of the most respected leaders amongst the Mohammedans of eastern Africa. Ras Mikael, chief of the Wolo Gallas, an enforced convert to Christianity, was also in negotiation with the Italians, although nominally the right hand of Menelik. These petty alliances may not seem of any great importance, but a glance at the map will show how large a tract of territory they included, and how well situated for a flank attack on Menelik, should he advance northwards. Had it not been for unpredictable mishaps, the Governor might have formed a barrier of his allies, cutting off Tigré from Shoa; it would have included the King of Gojjam, the Gallas, Aussa and the Danakil, in fact a broad line of country stretching from the shores of the Red Sea right into the centre of the African Continent as far as Nubia;—from the Red Sea I have said, but the line does not quite reach it, owing to the French sea-coast settlement on the Bay of Tadjoura, over which no Italian troops could pass and through which Menelik was constantly able to obtain European arms and munitions.

On March 10th (1895) Mangasha had collected about 4,000 men at Hausien for an attack on Adigrat, and Alula was said to be coming from Shoa to his assistance with 1,000 more. But the Governor on his part had not been idle; by March 14th he had 3,114 men near Senafè ready to assist Agos Tafari, who, though he possessed friends in Agamè, was not yet capable of resisting an invasion.

On March 25th the Governor entered Adigrat and, Mangasha having fled, came to the decision that he must make his stay in Agamè permanent. This occupation is a typical instance of a frontier difficulty. Baratieri had not been in haste to advance his borders, he only desired security; for this end he had set up a friendly chief in Agamè only to find that his ally was in danger of being ejected, and of involving in his flight the prestige of Italy; to avoid the inconvenience of marching in and out of Agamè whenever his help was required, he had no choice but to garrison a strong central position.

The occupation of Adigrat is a great event; it decides the character of all the future military operations. A few miles to the South of it the impregnable mountain position of Adagamus (or Edaga Amus) stretches right across the road to Abyssinia; it thus commands the natural route of invasion from Shoa, and, moreover, it is situated at the extreme point of an angle from which the mountains and roads run southwards towards Ethiopia and westwards to Adowa. Military writers appear to be of only one opinion as to its great importance both strategically and tactically; "it is," says Lieutenant Melli, "like an entrenched camp dominating all the ways that lead to Okule Kusai."

So far Baratieri had in no way overstepped the limits that Nerazzini's scheme of action prescribed; but on April 2nd he followed up his invasion of Agamè by occupying Adowa. This was indeed taking the bull by the horns; it was only two months since he had given his opinion in favour of making no immediate advance, yet he now considered the time ripe to seize the northern province of Ethiopia, about which there had been such diversity of opinion. The Government at once telegraphed to him to say that, for financial reasons, they could not approve of the permanent occupation of Adowa.

On April 3rd the Governor replied: "I am grateful for the consent to my occupation of Adigrat, an indispensable military position. It is impossible to hold Adowa in a merely nominal manner, for it is quite as important from a military point of view, and is, besides, a political and commercial centre. In the case of your Excellency not approving of the occupation of Adowa, our frontier will continually be threatened, and then it will be necessary to make a corresponding increase of the native troops indicated in my telegram. The economy would be insignificant, but the diminution of political and military prestige very great."

It is this step of the Governor's that has so often been considered an act of insensate Jingoism; yet he assures us in his memoirs that he never made a forward movement except for purposes of defence, and, as regards Tigré, at all events, a complete study of his governorship seems to prove that, although he had dreams of ultimate conquests, in the main his assertions are just. The occupation of Adowa was in reality merely the outcome, from a military point of view, of the seizure of Adigrat; if Adowa were left to the enemy, he could cut off an army at Adigrat from the rest of the colony; he could penetrate into the heart of Erythrea and compel the retirement of any Italian troops in Agamè. It was useless to close all the roads through Adigrat, if the remaining routes through Adowa were left open.

This, it is perhaps well to remark, is no mere theory; it is the course that was afterwards actually pursued by Menelik with successful results, and one of his chiefs admitted that had the passes round Adowa been efficiently occupied, "the campaign for us was over." [1]

[1] It is sad to see how the Governor argues in favour of his projected garrison and fort in Adowa, because he traces with a prophetic exactitude the various phases of the campaign that afterwards ruined him. He says in his letter of April 10th "the garrison of Adigrat .... its military action might be very efficacious in threatening an enemy who moves from the South towards the colony of Erythrea. But this military efficacy would be to a great extent paralyzed if the enemy's roving bands should spread themselves amidst the mountains as far as the line of the Mareb.

"I do not conceal the fact that but for your Excellency's

The Governor, therefore, in marching on the capital of Tigré was merely pursuing the military development of the situation to its logical conclusion; to this point the results had followed one another in direct sequence from the day when Batha Agos began his rebellion. Whether Italy would

intervention I had definitely intended to construct a fort at the splendid position of Fremona, within cannon shot of Adowa . . . in any case with a fort and permanent garrison we should have made secure for the Colony its finest province, and equalized our political and military forces with those of Shoa, and indeed of all Ethiopia,—perhaps preventing a war by removing from the Shoans a possible theatre of supplies and base of operations, and at the same time rendering vain his (the enemy's) hopes of finding there a valiant and tenacious ally to assist him against Erythrea."

In these few sentences written ten months before the war broke out, he sketches every single one of the most salient points of the Shoan Campaign; and as for his fort of Fremona, the French General Luzeux in "Etudes critique sur la guerre entre l'Italie et l'Abyssinie," severely blames the Italians for not having garrisoned it and placed guns there.

Menelik's movements in 1896 were as follow: Having spent some weeks about the fort of Macalle in the South, he was obliged to seek a fresh base of operation elsewhere in order to find provisions. He evaded the Italians at Adigrat and encamped at Adowa. The Italians, as Baratieri had said, "found their efficacy paralyzed by his roving bands amongst the mountains," and owing to lack of provisions were eventually compelled to move out of their fortified position.

Baratieri, then, was singularly correct in his plans, but he did not realize, and no one in Europe at that time, except possibly Nerazzini, did realize how many men Menelik could bring into the field or what heavy expenditure would be required to beat them. It was not yet known that though the Abyssinians were still semi-barbarous they carried wholly civilized weapons and had been taught how to use them.

have been wiser never to have occupied Adigrat, and to have bound herself down with iron determination to the less advanced Mareb-Belesa-Muna frontier that had been so strongly recommended by the Royal Commission in 1891, is another question. It would have meant enduring without retort the border raids of Mangasha, and being continually on the watch for rebellions fomented by him; it would have involved the maintenance of an efficient frontier force and would probably have entailed a constant drain of blood and money; nevertheless, in the light of subsequent events, one sees that it would have been the wiser policy.

The Mareb-Belesa-Muna line would have had the great advantage of not requiring such long communications,—their length was afterwards the chief cause of the Italian disaster. In fact, at the present moment there seems little doubt that it would have been the best line of defence, but it appears hardly possible to deny that, according to the knowledge then in his possession, the Governor was acting in a perfectly reasonable manner. He believed in occupying a strong advanced position; he thought that by doing so he would end the frontier difficulty. Considering the formidable nature of the position itself, considering his ignorance of the immense improvements in Menelik's army, and considering, finally, the strong influence that he appeared to exercise over many of the Abyssinian chiefs, there seemed to be every chance of success; as has already been shown, the military adviser of the Government, a man who knew the ground, was even more strongly in favour of an advance than he.

For good or evil the die was now cast, and as Nerazzini had prophesied, war against Ethiopia was inevitable.

CHAPTER VII

FOREWARNED BUT NOT FOREARMED

BARON Blanc writes to say that financial considerations do not permit of the occupation of Adowa—Memorial from the Treasury—Baratieri retires, leaving Major Ameglio in Adowa—Cabinet insists on expenses being reduced to nine million lire—Baratieri insists on thirteen millions—Baratieri asks to be recalled, April 23rd, 1895—Again asks to be recalled, June 10th—Asks for a third time, July 7th—Serious nature of the crisis—Colonel Sartorius' opinion—Baratieri summoned to Rome—Received in triumph.

"YOUR Excellency, with the customary ability that so greatly raises our military prestige, has accomplished at Adigrat the campaign of counter-offence that, by the occupation of Agamè, assures the colony against a return of the perils wherewith she was lately threatened by Mangasha." So writes Baron Blanc on April 6th, but he goes on to say that as regards Adowa, he considers it better that there should be no permanent occupation; that it should "remain under our hand but from a distance." The reasons for this opinion are financial, and are expressed in a memorial that he encloses from the Cabinet; he begs that in future the annual expenses of the Colony should be reduced to nine millions, and his letter ends as follows: "Dear General, Italy never had a commander more fitted, or circumstances more favourable for taking a decisive forward step in our

African enterprise. It goes to my heart to have to say that the country regards above all other things the question of expense, and the financial overbalance, from which abyss we have only just been delivered. Believe me, ever your admirer and friend, Blanc."

The memorial that he encloses is simply an outcry from the Treasury. It recites that, with General Baratieri's knowledge, the vote for 1895-6 amounted to 8,500,000 lire (about £326,000), an increase of 386,000 lire on the previous year; that after Batha Agos rebellion the Government had sent two white battalions, and had authorised the formation of two native battalions and of one mountain battery; that it had been understood that the white battalions were only to be considered as a temporary reinforcement, so that the permanent expenditure would not be raised by more than 2,000,000 lire (for the natives); but that now, instead of two millions the permanent increase would come to five millions (as the white battalions were not to be sent back); and that, finally, by a letter of March 31st General Baratieri says he is enrolling a new native battalion and occupying Adowa, which implies a probable increase of six or seven millions. "Hence arises the natural question, where is it to end?.... This point of the increased expenditure in Africa, will be the final stumbling-block of the Ministry."

After such an intimation it seemed evident that Adowa must be abandoned. Yet the Cabinet themselves were not entirely of that opinion: they had no wish to retire, all they desired was to avoid expense; two days later they telegraphed suggesting that a friendly chief should be left in power at Adowa; so when the Governor retired he felt justified in leaving behind him Major Ameglio with the 5th Native battalion, a section of Artillery, and some irregulars.

He was very reluctant to go; both in Adowa and at the holy city of Axum he had been well received; Tigré seemed to lie within the palm of his hand; and it is acknowledged to contain some of the most fertile provinces into which the Italians had as yet penetrated; indeed it was afterwards said that the acquisition of Tigré would have justified all the wars and expenditure incurred by Italy since she first entered on her colonial undertaking, but this is probably an exaggeration. Moreover, some twenty of the smaller chiefs, commanding about 1,200 men, had already made their submission, as well as the Itchegué Theophilus and his priests; there were signs in Tigré as in other provinces that the people were tired of the feudal system, and would welcome any government strong enough to ensure peace.

The retirement was followed by a sharp interchange of telegrams between him and the Cabinet. On April 9th he informed them that he could not reduce the normal expenses to nine millions,—that thirteen millions was the lowest sum for which the colony could be defended, as he did not consider it safe to send back the white battalions, or to stop the enrolment of the natives.

In reply to this, Signor Crispi telegraphed to him that it was "the absolute will" of the Cabinet that the expenses should not exceed nine millions. "In order to save Erythrea in Parliament, we must keep within these limits, and we do not wish to risk the fate of Italy for the sake of a financial error committed in Africa."

On April 10th Baratieri wrote a long letter explaining

the whole situation of the Colony, and followed it up by a telegram on the 12th to say again that the thirteen millions were a necessity; to which Signor Crispi replied on the following day intimating that if he could not return the three battalions he must find the means of keeping them himself. "Napoleon I. made war with the money of the conquered."

To this high-flown historical reminiscence, the Governor merely replied by two telegrams informing the minister in the first that the country was too much exhausted to supply any further contributions and insisting on the thirteen millions; and in the second reminding him that if Adowa were abandoned according to orders, Mangasha would return. This latter idea roused the ministers; they replied that "the government of the King certainly cannot desire that Ras Mangasha should take possession of Adowa, and your Excellency will not fail to find a method of preventing him."

On the following day (April 23, 1895) the Governor resigned his post. "In war," he wrote, "one is not sufficiently master of the situation to stop where one wishes,—least of all in Africa; but I understand how much public opinion is alarmed, and how the Government must take steps to calm it at the supreme moment of the elections, on which depend the supreme interests of the country.

"To meet this need, the most simple means of allaying the popular anxiety appears to me to be my recall. Some other man, not so deeply pledged as myself might try, in Africa, a compromise with Mangasha and with Menelik, that would permit of a notable reduction in expense..... what is most important is to appease public opinion; and I am ready for the expiatory sacrifice."

The Cabinet of course did not accept his resignation; he can hardly have expected them to do so; they said they could not deprive themselves of his services in Africa, where he had succeeded "with such profit and such honour to the Italian arms." The fact was they had not got money and did not want to lose the support of the victor of Coatit and Senafè;—they were in a difficult position. But they added an expression of policy which removes from the shoulders of the Governor much of the onus of having recklessly incurred the great war against Ethiopia. "We do not believe," said Baron Blanc, "in compromises with Mangasha or with Menelik. The designs of your Excellency, which, as you know, exceeded the possibilities of the moment, may serve as a basis of future action under improved financial conditions."

This is a very important declaration of the Cabinet, for it practically binds them to support the Governor in the future; they admit that they agree with him, but say that for the present they cannot afford his schemes; at the same time they ask him to wait until they can do so.

Notices concerning Menelik's preparations for invasion had long since been forwarded by the Governor to Rome, but as reiterated assurances that a great war was impending failed to produce any result, on June 10th Baratieri telegraphed to Baron Blanc, saying that he had not sufficient supplies to meet the emergency, and must insist on his resignation being accepted. It was again refused; then after some further correspondence, on July 7th (1895), he again asked to be recalled; this time the Government summoned him to Rome for a consultation. It was the third time that he had resigned in two and a half months, and it was beginning to produce the desired effect of showing the Ministry that matters were in an extremely critical condition.

The question may perhaps be asked, whether there was in reality any adequate cause for these continual resignations; only one reply is possible, namely, that they were entirely justified by the political situation. As early as April 9th Baratieri had telegraphed to Baron Blanc that Menelik was preparing for war in or about the following October,—and that in May he would already have begun hostilities against Aussa, where the Mohammedan population was friendly to Italy. On April 12th he had repeated this information. On the 25th he had written: "We must therefore be ready to meet a big war which has been hatching for years in Ethiopia. Menelik on March 20th sent many letters of protest against Italy, to Russia, France and Switzerland." On May 20th and 25th the Governor had forwarded similar tidings to those in his former telegrams; and on June 2nd a proposed plan of Menelik's campaign; while on June 7th he obtained a valuable piece of news from Colonel Sartorius, a British officer, who told him that at Aden a report ran that 160,000 Abyssinians were uniting against the Colony, but that he (Colonel Sartorius) had "formed the conviction that after the rains Menelik will advance against us, but that he will not be able to attack us with more than 30,000 men."

At this time the Italian colony, originally consisting of 86,000 square kilometres, peopled by only 250,000 inhabitants, had been increased to 150,000 square kilometres, and this great tract of country was defended by only 3,000 white troops, 8,000 native regulars, 1,500 militia and 1,700 irregulars; these would include the garrisons of all the towns and forts,—of those which, like Kassala, were intended for defence against the Dervishes, so that he could not rely on a field-force of more than about 7,000 men. The attack therefore of 30,000 well-armed Abyssinian warriors probably within six months, was very greatly to be feared; yet three months of invaluable time had passed away without his being allowed to make any extra preparations, although the whole dispute was caused by a sum of only £150,000; it was not surprising that the Governor insisted on being recalled.

It is plain, therefore, that he realized the impending danger far better than the Cabinet, but even he had no perception of the numbers, or the fighting power of Menelik's forces.

The opinion of Colonel Sartorius is in itself of exceptional value because it comes from an entirely external and disinterested source, and it tends perhaps to show that, amongst the English at Aden, the opinion prevailed that Menelik would not be able to advance so far north with more than 30,000 men. When, therefore, the Governor, and indeed the Italians generally, are accused of want of foresight and of under-estimating their enemy, it is very probable that they were merely sharing the errors of all the rest of the world. When Menelik did arrive in Tigré, it was with 100,000 men[1] and not 30,000 as here estimated; but it was impossible to foresee that a man of his calibre would suddenly arise to unite and lead the Ethiopian race. Baratieri says that the

[1] He left a large proportion of his army behind as garrisons; the actual numbers that he succeeded in raising are variously estimated at figures ranging between 160,000 and 200,000. According to some accounts be had 120,000 men at Adowa.

welding together of the various provinces was a miracle to all those that know Abyssinia: there was, in fact, an unknown quantity to be dealt with,—namely, the ability of the Negûs.

When, in August 1895, the Governor reached Rome, his stay in the mother country was one scene of triumph. It was not long before he succeeded in obtaining the extra four millions and an effective force of 10,000 men. Banquets, complimentary speeches, all the highest marks of popularity, awaited him wherever he went. But his triumph went deeper; ministers and generals came to see him; men like Nerazzini called on him with every sign of respect; when he presented himself at the Chamber to swear his oath as a duly elected deputy from the College of Breno he was received with the same honours formerly accorded to Garibaldi. As the victor of Coatit and Senafè entered, the whole assembly arose, and then amidst a scene of indescribable enthusiasm, he received the embrace of the president, as being the greatest living soldier and administrator of Italy.

PART II

THE WAR BETWEEN ITALY AND ABYSSINIA

CHAPTER I

THE BEGINNING

Short recapitulation of events up to July 1895—Twofold Italian policy—Alliance with native tribes—Secret negotiations with Menelik's chiefs—Ras Maconnen—Ras Oliè—Wagshum Burru—Ras Mikael and the Mohammedans—Importance to Italy of not suffering a defeat—Mangasha threatens Tigré—Engagement at Debra Aila.

On July 8th, 1895, General Baratieri, Governor of the Italian Colony of Erythrea, had been summoned to Rome for the purpose, firstly, of coming to a personal agreement with the ministry as regards the forces required to defend their African territory, and, secondly, with a view to convincing the Italian people that the sum annually voted for expenses must be raised from nine million lire to thirteen million. It was felt that his ability and the glorious memory of his victories would not only effect both these objects, but would also increase the general popularity of the Government.

To recapitulate very shortly the events that led immediately to the war: the Italians in 1889 had supported Menelik, King of Shoa, when he seized the imperial throne of all Abyssinia; but once safely seated on that throne, Menelik had thrown off his former allies, refusing to sign the Treaty of Uccialli which they presented to him, or to acknowledge the Italian protectorate over his dominions. The Government had therefore concluded the Convention of the Mareb with his rival, Ras Mangasha, ruler of Tigré (Dec. 8th, 1891). Owing then to various influences, Mangasha and Menelik had found it more to their interests to make common cause against Italy, than to continue their own feud. From the time when they concluded their secret alliance, at the Convention of Entotto (June 1894), war against Italy had been only a matter of time. In December 1894 Mangasha had begun the attack single-handed, by raising a rebellion against the Italians in their province of Okule-Kusai,—a territory that had formerly been part of his dominion of Tigré, and one that he was anxious to regain. This rising, known as the rebellion of Batha Agos (the chief who began it), had been suppressed in the most successful manner by General Baratieri, who then promptly pushed forward into Tigré, defeating Mangasha himself and expelling him from his dominions during the course of a short but brilliant campaign, wherein the native battalions and their Italian officers added the lustre of Coatit and Senafè to the glorious reputation that they had already won against the Dervishes at Agordat and Kassala. After a few months of uncertainty the Governor had decided, chiefly for purposes of self-defence, to occupy Adowa the capital of Tigré, but here he was treading on dangerous ground. Tigré is one of the historic Abyssinian provinces; to invade it, meant war against the whole empire,—for the native chiefs, though incessantly plotting against each other, have still a spark of national feeling that regards with bitter resentment the alienation to strangers of their ancient territories; and this sentiment is worthy of consideration, not because it exists amongst the chiefs, but because it is strong amongst the people themselves. Italy had therefore unwarily come face to face with the Negûs Nagasti himself, the King of the Kings of Ethiopia, who in a moment of national enthusiasm might perhaps find 200,000 warriors to answer his call to arms. Already the collision was within three or four months of taking place, but she had not the slightest realization of the danger to her colony; to oppose this horde of southern invaders she had reluctantly been persuaded by the Governor to allow him a field-force of 10,000 men, and a sum of thirteen million lire per annum (half a million sterling). The absurd insufficiency of this sum was due to the fact that three years previously she had been on the verge of bankruptcy, and since then no minister dared speak of extra expenses to Parliament, and no deputy in the Parliament dared suggest such an idea to his constituents. The nation was proud of its victories and anxious to retain its colony, but did not yet realize the expenses that such a policy involved; and, moreover, neither the Government, the Governor, nor the Governed had any real idea of the power and abilities of Menelik; he was regarded as a barbarian leader who, after deducting his garrisons, could dispose of perhaps 30,000 men.

It must be remembered that the Colony of Erythrea, extending, roughly speaking, from the line of Adigrat and Adowa on the South, along the Mareb, or Gash, (Gasc) westwards to Kassala, and thence northwards on both sides of the Barka as far as the Suakim territory, was really in no sense a colony; it was merely a strip of conquered territory, occupied by successive advances from the coast towns of the Red Sea; it was hardly as much a colony as Egypt or India; excluding soldiers and officials, the Italian population had scarcely any existence; in the future, however, it was hoped to turn the venture to a good account.

The Governor started from Rome on Sept. 15th, 1895, and reached Adigrat on October 3rd; the dates of the months are important, as the whole war lasted less than a year. There was obviously no time to be lost, for Menelik's attack had been expected during the month of October; indeed he had already made a start in June, but had been obliged to turn back owing to difficulties of climate and transport; the Governor at once proceeded to take up the thread of affairs that had during his absence lain in the hands of General Arimondi, the vice-governor.

The Italian policy was as usual based on the two-fold principle of arming their small force as far as expenses would permit, and of weakening the Negûs by detaching the more discontented chieftains from the coalition. As has already been stated, the Governor hoped to block the line of advance from Shoa by a system of alliances, viz., with the Danakil tribes, with Aussa, Lasta, and Gojjam, stretching along the southern frontier of Tigré, from the Red Sea to Nubia, in order to form a barrier of friendly states between himself and Menelik; but in addition to this he hoped to make friends of some of the most trusted advisers at the court of Addis Abeba. The Italians, and especially the Governor, believed to the very end in the possibility of Menelik's expedition falling through, and held that the true method of defending Erythrea, was by tampering with his followers, and by raising up enemies along his line of march northwards: it was part of their original policy of "surrounding Ethiopia with a band of iron" and cutting it off from outside influences.

Under different circumstances there is no doubt that this policy of dividing the enemy might have been the true solution of the difficulty, as indeed the British found it in 1868; but the Italians had so few advantages to confer on the men they were endeavouring to detach, that the Abyssinian chiefs never really thought it worth while to betray their race. Italy was so far off that even the Ras who were best disposed to her found their own Negûs a more dangerous foe than the white men. To attack Menelik would have assisted the Italian policy, but what benefit would they have received in return from Rome? Not even money. Before doing anything to incriminate themselves they wanted some armed support, and this they were never able to obtain from distant Italy.

Ras Maconnen of Harrar was the most important of the chieftains; he is first cousin of Menelik, and is noticeable as being more refined, and perhaps more thoughtful than the majority of his compatriots. It was he who had been sent to Rome to make all arrangements about the Treaty of Uccialli; and it was he who had negotiated the famous loan by which Menelik obtained two million cartridges. He considered himself more enlightened, and superior intellectually to the other Ras, and had fixed his eyes on the imperial crown. It was the idea that this could eventually be obtained by means of Italian support which had at first dazzled him, until he perceived that their support would be merely of a moral character; still he seems to have been more serious in his professions of friendship than the other Ras, for he knew the power of Italy; he became, in fact, unpopular amongst his fellow chiefs as being a friend of the Italians. His kingdom of Harrar, important from its situation near the sea coast, and its natural resources, was more open to civilization than the other provinces of Ethiopia; it was the passage through which the Negûs drew all his supplies of guns, ammunition, rifles etc., from the French settlement of Djibouti on the Bay of Tadjoura,—the English and Germans had forbidden the sale of arms to Abyssinia, but the French and Russians continued to do a fairly prosperous trade. Harrar was the ground where the agents of rival nations fought. The Swiss and French were the most numerous and successful; after them perhaps the Russians, then the Italians and Greeks; but it was an Italian man of business named Felter who seems to have become Maconnen's best friend. The Ras himself is possessed of a natural acuteness in business matters; cunning, patient, brave but cautious, Ras Maconnen is a man of whom, if he lives, the world will hear more. Menelik has no son, and Maconnen, to use General Baratieri's expression, is awaiting the fruit that is ripening on the tree.

During the period immediately before the war he tried hard to remain on friendly terms with both sides; it seemed as if, having once seen Italy, he wished to keep in touch with her because he could not believe that his compatriots would be victorious. On August 2nd, 1895, General Arimondi writes that Maconnen affects great indifference as to all that concerns Menelik, but is trying to obtain a free pass for 840 rifles that are detained by the British authorities at Aden. On September 11th Nerazzini[1] writes that the Shoan mission to St. Petersburg returned with ten large packages, which were consigned to the French resident at Djibouti, and forwarded by him in a caravan of seven or eight camels to Harrar. There is, Nerazzini says, a continuous trade in firearms conducted through Frenchmen and Greeks. Nevertheless, on September 28th Maconnen, according to another letter of Nerazzini, was making every endeavour to bring about a peaceful settlement of affairs;[2] he feared an Italian or even a British invasion from Zeilah on the Red Sea, during his absence at the war. And indeed, we may admit, he was right, for this was one of the Governor's most cherished schemes; but owing to England and France being bound by treaty not to invade Harrar, they remained neutral, and would not permit the Italian troops to cross their territory. Early in October Maconnen, by Menelik's order, expelled all the Italians from Harrar, but informed Felter before letting him go, that he was trying to induce the Negûs to make peace,—thus leaving himself a loophole of escape whichever side should prove victorious.

Of the other chiefs, Ras Olié, brother of Menelik's wife the Empress Taitu, and Wagshum Burru of Lasta were also in communication with the Governor, but Olié never got

[1] Agent of the Italian Government at Zeilah.

[2] It was a favourite pose of Maconnen to appear as the man who had experience of civilization, and was competent to arrange treaties with the white men; it had the effect of singling him out from the other Ras.

beyond fair words, and Wagshum Burru was imprisoned by Menelik who discovered his treachery.

Tecla Aimanot, King of Gojjam (formerly known as Ras Adal), had long been nibbling at the bait thrown out to him by the Governor. He undoubtedly nourished a hostile feeling against Menelik, but was not in a position to take any decided step: nevertheless, it was hoped that he would remain neutral.

Ras Mikael, chief of the Wolo Gallas, had in his youth been conquered by the Christians, and compelled to abandon his Mohammedan faith. He was not, therefore, a very warm supporter of Menelik, and was so deeply implicated in negotiations with Italy that when ordered by the Negûs in August 1895 to invade the Mohammedan state of Aussa (friendly to Italy), he first sent to warn it of his approach. To his warning the Sultan of Aussa scornfully replied that "he was ready to repel the attack, and that he advised Ras Mikael to remember the religion of his fathers, and to unite all Mohammedans for war against their common enemy."

It was this militant Moslem spirit, cleverly worked upon by the Italian emissary, Captain Persico, that brought Italy her best allies. The followers of Sheik Thala, the Mohammedans of Aussa, the Danakil tribes, the Azubo Gallas and others, had all suffered under the persecutions of the Christian Abyssinians and were ready for revenge.

About the negotiations there are several points to be noticed; the first is that almost every important chief except Alula was in secret communication with Italy;—possibly with the consent, or even by the advice of Menelik himself, who adopted this means of blinding the Italians. Secondly, that, even allowing for this consideration, there were a great many chiefs who were waiting to see what course events would take before committing themselves. For these reasons, therefore, it was a matter of the most supreme importance to the Italians to avoid anything resembling a defeat; once their prestige was gone they were lost; it only remained for their newly acquired subjects to rise in rebellion and the Italian cause became hopeless,—the first victories would go far towards deciding the result of the campaign.

Matters were in the position above described when Menelik gave his first formal signs of hostility at the end of September; but by the same telegram in which General Arimondi announced the refusal of Menelik to listen to Maconnen's peace proposals, and the expulsion of the Italians from Harrar, (September 20th) he also informed the Governor that Mangasha was threatening Tigré. Here was a splendid opportunity for striking his old enemy before the new one arrived on the scene of action. The Governor only landed at Massowah on September 26th, but as soon as he could get to Adigrat he began operations.

The militia was called out, and by October 6th, he had at Adigrat a well-appointed field-force of about 9,000 men in all,—116 officers, 672 white soldiers, 8,065 natives, 1,200 animals, 10 mountain guns; besides these a few hundreds of militiamen and irregulars.

Mangasha was at Debra Aila (also spelt Debrailat) about 130 kilometres, or 80 miles, from Adigrat, with a force of 4,000 to 5,000 men; he was expecting reinforcements from Ras Olié or from Wagshum Guangul of Lasta (son of Wagshum Burru), and was said to be greatly elated by the friendly encouragements of Menelik, who, doubtless, desired nothing better than to see his former rival and the Italians once more at each others' throats. Indeed it was said that Mangasha had sworn to end his life, like the Emperor Theodore when conquered by the British, rather than again fly from the field; the Tigréans, however, were tired of the war and unwilling to measure themselves against the trained battalions of Italy.

Baratieri, having the advantage of superior numbers, naturally decided to attack the enemy before they could be reinforced; his troops were disposed as follows:

At Hausien (Ausien, Hauzen) was Major Ameglio with one native battalion, one section of Artillery and the irregulars of Serae and Tigré.

At Mai Meghelta was Toselli with his famous 4th Native Battalion, 1 section of Artillery and the irregulars of Agamè.

At Adigrat was the Governor with 1 white battalion of Chasseurs, 3 native battalions, 1 battery, 1 section of Artillery, and 1 company of Engineers.

To each of these forces the Governor issued orders to advance by a different route. Ameglio was to proceed from Hausien to Agula and from thence to become the advanced guard of the main body; Toselli, on the Italian left, was to advance from Mai Meghelta by Asbi to Buia, to cut off Mangasha's retreat from Debra Aila. The centre was to march from Adigrat to Dolo.

Provisions were to be taken for eight days.

On October 6th the main body arrived at Mai Meghelta, Toselli having moved on to Asbi; it was ordered that each commander should reach his destination by mid-day on the 9th and be in position to attack the enemy.

During the 7th and 8th all three columns were marching rapidly along the mountain paths, and skirting the swamps with which the country abounded after the rains. In spite of those trying circumstances the white battalion of chasseurs and the engineer company marched as well as the natives, and by the evening of the 8th had reached Dolo.

At 3 a.m. on the 9th, the main body left Dolo and by mid-day had come (according to the plan of action) to Antolo, within striking distance of the enemy at Debra Aila.

On the left, however, Toselli, in spite of his well-known ability, had not been quite so successful as heretofore. His detour had not been wide enough, so that very early on the 9th he found his path barred by a detachment of the enemy's right flank. They retired, fighting, thereby drawing him on towards the main position. This was a singularly unfortunate event, for Mangasha being warned that his retreat was threatened, fled hastily before the break of day; by the time that the Italian attack began only the rear-guard of the Tigréans, some 1,300 strong, remained in position.

"The height of Debra Aila rises to the South West of Antolo, like a fortress,—the peaks dotted here and there giving the effect of towers and steeples, amidst the other projecting blocks; the whole bears the characteristic imprint of the Ethiopian Amba."[1]

It was against this position that the Governor sent out Major Ameglio to reconnoitre with the irregulars of Serae and Tigré and half a battery: "the Amba is still defended; and from its brow there breaks out a brisk fire. The formation

[1] Baratieri: *Memorie d'Africa.*

of the ground does not admit of the employment of a greater number of men; the Ascari are in good order and well in hand; the supports very near; hesitation would be fatal. And therefore Major Ameglio dashes forward to the attack while Major Toselli receives orders to make a detour towards the lower ground, (in view of, and near enough to bring assistance from Antolo,) in order to cut off their possible way of retreat towards Amba Alagi.

"But the enemy's resistance, though at first brisk owing to the tactical advantages of their commanding position, lasts a very short time. While the Italian battery continues to fire with calmness and accuracy, the firing line, in two rushes, arrives at the dead angle below the steep wall of the amba;—and taking breath under cover, scrambles up along the few accessible points. Meanwhile the enemy disperses and flies with the incredible agility of natives amidst big bushes, gorges, and along the ravines. The whole of the ground is furrowed and broken by boulders, encumbered with fragments of rocks from between which appear bushes and trees showing all the luxuriance of tropical vegetation.

"Under such circumstances, pursuit would have dissolved all tactical unity; therefore Major Ameglio had the 'assembly' sounded, and pitched his camp on the position where the Ras' tents had stood.

"The rear-guard of the enemy, that had fought, numbered from 1,200 to 1,300 rifles. We had 11 dead and 30 wounded; the enemy had about 30 killed and a hundred wounded."[1]

[1] The Governor does not mention that the Italians took about 200 prisoners in all, and 1,000 head of cattle.

Such is the description given by the Governor in his Memoirs, of the engagement of Debra Aila, which may be accounted either the first of the Abyssinian war, or the last of the Tigréan campaigns. As will have been noted, it was merely a rear-guard action, in which the Italians gained success, but without decisive results. The Governor hoped that the news would discourage his enemies, and assist in detaching the doubtful chiefs from Menelik's side; but it never, in reality, produced any of the effects on which he had counted. Both chiefs and subjects were now too much in earnest to be really influenced by a small victory against Mangasha who had already been so often defeated. It was felt that the Italians had yet to meet their real enemies,—a sentiment openly expressed in the half-scornful comment of one of the prisoners of Debra Aila: "For the present," he said, "you have been victorious, because God so willed it; but wait a month or two and you will see the soldiers of Menelik; they are as many in number as the locusts."

CHAPTER II

WAR AGAINST MENELIK. BATTLE OF AMBA ALAGI.

Tigré annexed to Italy—Arimondi in command south of Mareb—Toselli's force at Amba Alagi—Causes of Italy's disaster—Baratieri's over-confidence—His differences with Nerazzini and Arimondi—Menelik's skilful preparations—Final efforts at peace by Maconnen—Toselli at Belego—Telegraphic errors—Toselli retires to Amba Alagi—Abyssinian advance—Italian disaster at Amba Alagi—Its effect on her allies.

The victory of Debra Aila was quickly followed by a proclamation that Tigré was annexed to the Italian Colony, and the Governor promptly proceeded to consolidate and fortify his whole dominion. He entered Macalle, the former capital of the Emperor John, and decided that there he would establish his first line of defence; at Macalle as well as at Adowa he ordered a fort to be built, and expressed full confidence to the Italian Government that this triangle formed by the strong places of Adowa, Macalle and Adigrat would be sufficient to resist any invasion from the South. At the end of October he went northwards, leaving General Arimondi in authority over the newly conquered territory south of the Mareb.

Arimondi thus found himself in command of a force that never, until the war began, numbered much over 7,500 men, of whom 4,500 were regulars;[1] neither could he succeed in increasing them to any great extent by alliance with native chiefs. Ras Sebath, formerly chief of Agamè, who had rebelled against Mangasha and been imprisoned on Amba Alagi, was released by Arimondi after the victory of Debra Aila, and made ruler of the province of Enderta. He was the descendant of a famous warrior named Sagabadis, and had an undoubted right to rule over Agamè, but this territory had already been given to Agos Tafari, another descendant of the same chief, so Sebath had to content himself with the less important province. Both these men owed their position entirely to Italy, and Sagabadis must have turned in his grave at seeing the treachery with which they afterwards repaid their benefactors; but for the moment they were both faithful, and Sebath succeeded in raising 300 riflemen. Sheik Thala also joined the Erythrean force with 300 Mohammedans, but the Governor had expected him to bring 800.

On November 13th Captain Persico was sent with one company to Amba Alagi, which is a rocky position to the South of Macalle. On the 24th Major Toselli was ordered to follow him with three companies, two sections of Artillery and the irregulars of Ras Sebath: while he was halted there Sheik Thala's men joined him. Toselli was therefore in command of 1,800 men, thirty-six miles in advance of the most southern defensive position. This force was not intended to make any real attempt at defence, but rather to impress

[1] Baratieri's telegram to Minister for Foreign Affairs, Dec. 17th, 1895.

the surrounding chiefs and to gain information of the enemy's movements; the serious resistance was to begin at Macalle, where Arimondi had posted himself with the main body.

The causes that led to the future disasters of Italy may be comprehensively summed up under the following headings:

The lack of money.

Parliamentary government,—whereby the men in authority are led to spend more time in securing an immediate majority in the House than in studying the possibilities of mishap in a distant colony or dependency.

The universal failure to understand the power of Menelik or the immense strides that he had made during the previous years.

Too great reliance on the negotiations with the Ras, and with the Negûs himself (through Maconnen).

The over-confidence of the Governor, which was partly the result, one is inclined to think, of his being out-matched by Menelik in matters of secret information; it may also be said that he never, after the triumphs of his last visit to Italy, exercised quite the same watchful care as formerly.

It is the history of the negotiations during these two months (between the Governor's return from Italy and the first battle of the war) that shows how greatly General Baratieri under-rated his enemy, being deceived either by his own self-confidence, or by false messengers in the pay of Menelik.

Starting on the hypothesis that the Negûs could not bring more than 30,000 men as far north as Tigré, and that, even then, most of his chiefs would prove to be friends of the Italians, he assumes, even in his warnings to the Government, a confident tone. On October 15th he reminds the Minister for Foreign Affairs that due preparation must be made for the war, especially as the French and Russians continue to fan the flame; that Menelik can dispose of "immense forces" and that therefore the native regular battalions should be increased from 7,500 men to 9,600. An increase of just 1,900 men to meet the emergency! But it must be admitted that the Government would most likely have refused to give him more.

On October 27th he speaks of avoiding the conflict by making peace with Menelik; the basis of the terms is to be: (I) The boundaries to the south of Macalle—including in fact the disputed territory. (II) The protectorate of Italy over all Ethiopia. Such suggestions are absurd; and in the same letter he expresses himself as adverse to a campaign of conquest, but begs the Government to consider the question.

He never supposed that Menelik could place more than 30,000 men on the Tigréan border, although Nerazzini (whom the Italian Government had sent independently to Harrar) says in his letter of November 5th that Menelik's army "is very strong, and far superior in numbers to 30,000, which might be assigned as a minimum;" but Baratieri did not believe this. He stated, in at all events one letter, that the Negûs would act only on the defensive.

The action of the Government in sending an independent agent like Nerazzini to Harrar is open to criticism; it created a two-headed responsibility, and Baratieri evidently detested it. He complains that the native chiefs withdrew their confidence because they feared to entrust secret negotiations to more than one man, and that his own prestige was thereby lessened. The result was friction between him and Nerazzini, who wrote indignantly to the Minister for Foreign Affairs to say that when he sent a letter to Baratieri to be forwarded to the Government, it was read, but not despatched, and that he therefore appeared to be either idle or incompetent. As far as I have been able to discover, the truth of this accusation is not proved; but it is possible that the Governor may have been a difficult person with whom to work, for at the beginning of November General Arimondi resigned his post and demanded to be recalled. This was a renewal of his resignation in the previous April, which had been the first open sign of that rivalry between the two generals that lasted with disastrous results to the day of Arimondi's death; about this matter also the truth will never be proved, but such ill-feeling was the natural outcome of a system whereby Arimondi was named commander of the troops, but owing to the Governor being a soldier, never had an independent command.

Meanwhile Menelik was making his preparations with extraordinary deliberation and secrecy; never, probably, in the history of the world has there been so curious an instance of a commander successfully concealing the numbers of his army, and masking his advance behind a complete network of insinuation, false information and circumstantial deceptions. To take a few instances; on October 19th Nerazzini telegraphs the news that a French ship was in the port of Djibouti with a cargo of a million cartridges; that two Armenians were there at the same time with a draft in the name of Maconnen on the house of Menohem-Messa of Aden; Maconnen at this time was posing as the friend of Italy. It is said also that during this period there were Frenchmen and Russians instructing the Shoans in the use of arms. Presumably with a view to cloaking such preparations, the news was spread early in October that Menelik had been struck by lightening and had lost the power of speech; another report said that he had been killed. There does not seem to have been any foundation for the story, but it was so strongly attested that Nerazzini believed it; it must have been almost at that moment that Menelik's advance began.

The extent to which the Governor's self-confidence bore him may be seen in his letter of November 23rd (within a fortnight of the disaster of Amba Alagi), in which he sends to his government a detailed account of the situation, informing them amongst other statements that desertion is prevalent in the hostile camp; that Menelik will not come at all, but will halt at Borumieda and send on some of his Ras to attack Erythrea; that they will dispose at the outside of 30,000 men, who for reasons which he specifies will not prove very formidable; that he considers the occupation of Macalle as forming a connection with Aussa and thereby laying bare the Ethiopian empire; and that he was not in reality certain whether the Negûs intended after all to take the offensive or not etc., etc. This letter, be it observed, was written within a fortnight of the disaster of Amba Alagi.

While these optimistic messages were speeding across the telegraph wires, the great upheaval was proceeding from the Tigréan mountains of the North to the Gallas and Somalis in the South; every tucul and village in every far-off glen of Ethiopia was sending out its warrior in answer to the war-drum. According to ancient custom he joined his feudal lord at the place of assembly, armed with sword, shield and spear; but now the chiefs were serving out magazine rifles and copious supplies of cartridges. The churches were filled with women weeping for the departure of their husbands and brothers; so general was the commotion that Dr. Nerazzini at Zeila thought some great national misfortune had occurred, and therefore gave credence to the report of Menelik's death by lightening.

Not that all these warriors answered the summons without secret misgivings; many of them were civilized enough to know that the white man is the stronger, and departed, therefore, with full understanding of the gravity of their position. A shadow of the same sentiment is visible even in the opening sentences of the great war-proclamation issued by Menelik, in which he says:

"Hitherto God has graciously preserved our native land. He has permitted us to conquer our enemies and reconstitute our Ethiopia. It is by the grace of God that I have reigned hitherto, and if my death is near I have no anxiety on that account, for death is the fate of all men. But to this day God has never humiliated me. In the same manner He will sustain me through the future.

"An enemy is come across the sea. He has broken through our frontiers in order to destroy our fatherland and our faith. I allowed him to seize my possessions, and I entered upon lengthy negotiations with him in hopes of obtaining justice without bloodshed. But the enemy refuses to listen. He continues to advance: he undermines our territories and our peoples like a mole. Enough! With the help of God I will defend the inheritance of my forefathers and drive back the invader by force of arms. Let every man who has sufficient strength accompany me! And he who has not, let him pray for us." [1]

To the very last moment negotiations continued, for Maconnen had been authorised by the Negûs to come to terms with the Italians if possible. It has become the fashion since that time to consider these last endeavours as merely a part of the cloak wherewith Menelik covered his advance, but such extreme scepticism is hardly necessary; it is true that they did, in fact, lull both the Governor and the Italian nation into a false sense of security, for when the newspapers announced that Maconnen was demanding a meeting with General Baratieri to discuss peace proposals, many people concluded that after all there would be no outbreak of war. Yet the Shoans were perfectly sincere in offering to come to terms, but they saw plainly the great improbability of any result being arrived at, and therefore continued their military preparations; neither would the exchange of peaceful letters prevent them from fighting, if there arose a good opportunity of striking their enemy. The first blow, however, came almost accidentally, as it does on such occasions,—as it did in the Turco-

[1] Translated from "Menelik et nous" by M. Hugues le Roux.

Greek campaign and in the Spanish-American War; the two opposing forces are watching one another at a short distance, each side, so to speak, quivering with anticipation, until sooner or later the tension becomes so great that a sudden act of violence leads to the shedding of the first blood: the war has begun.

Arimondi, as has been related, was at Macalle. Toselli, with 2,150 men, had been advanced as far as Amba Alagi; but on November 24th he moved still further south, to Belego, his mission being restricted to collecting information and to preventing the natives from rising. He was not to make any attempt at serious resistance, but if attacked to retire on Amba Alagi, and thence to Macalle, in which strong position the Governor had ordered General Arimondi to establish his first line of defence; but definite orders had been given that in case of really serious attack, Arimondi and Toselli should withdraw to Adigrat, so that the whole colonial army might be concentrated against the invaders.

Toselli had already acquired such knowledge of the enemy's movements that he considered matters very serious and regarded Ras Maconnen as a doubtful friend. On the 29th, therefore, he wrote to Arimondi, asking for orders; on November 30th Arimondi replied by the following telegram:

"I leave you the choice of maintaining your position at Belego or of *retiring to the foot of Amba Alagi, or, according to circumstances, still further.*"

This was the telegram which, according to his narrative, he wrote at Adigrat, but the telegraph office there, and consequently Toselli, received a mutilated version that bore an entirely different signification, it ran as follows:—

"I leave you the choice of maintaining your position at Belego *or of retiring to the foot of Amba Alagi according to circumstances.*"

The alteration in meaning is obvious. General Arimondi believed that, having given Toselli full power to use his discretion according to the necessity of the moment, he need have no further anxiety about the matter. Toselli, on the other hand, believed that he was only authorised to retire as far as Amba Alagi, and no further; he considered himself bound when he reached that position to turn about and hold it at all costs.

Why these needless misunderstandings? Everybody knows how often small errors are to be found in telegrams, and they may be easily avoided,—especially in the case of a short message,—by repeating it word for word when acknowledging its receipt. We have lately seen the same error committed in Africa by one of our own generals, and it seems curious that within five years two such disasters should have occurred owing to the lack of a precaution so common that in every commercial house it is considered a mere matter of daily routine.

Fortune had evidently made up her mind to give Toselli no further chance of rectifying matters. Very soon after this event came his open breach with Maconnen; he had for some time perceived that the negotiations of that chief were being used as a means of getting secret information about the Italian forces, so that at length he informed the Ras openly, that if he meant in reality to negotiate he must make a definite proposition and meanwhile retire to Lake Ashanghi (Ascianghi). Maconnen, naturally indignant (for Belego is outside the boundaries of Tigré), retorted that Toselli himself had better go away; to which Toselli sent an angry reply and prepared at once for hostilities.

As matters now stood, Toselli, with 2,150 men, was opposed by a cabal of Abyssinian chiefs with 30,000, and he was still under the impression that Amba Alagi was to be defended at all costs, and that he would be reinforced on reaching that place. It was exactly the state of affairs that usually leads to a disaster.

To make matters worse, this erroneous belief was very shortly confirmed. On the 5th December,[1] Arimondi, who preferred the more advanced position, sent word to Toselli that he would join him at Amba Alagi. What could be more plain? thought Toselli, I am to wait there for a few more hours until the General reinforces me. As a matter of fact they never met again. Arimondi had sent this despatch without first obtaining permission from the Governor (although such a forward movement was contrary to orders), and at 7 p.m. on the evening of December 5th, Baratieri's reply reached him, forbidding his advance. He forwarded it to Toselli, but not until 7 o'clock on the following morning,—thereby showing that he did not realize how very close the danger had come, for the distance to Amba

[1] On this date Toselli wrote a letter to Arimondi that proves how deeply he realized the gravity of the situation. In it he says: "Though it may be possible by giving battle,—with your support, of course, and with your concurrence,—to gain a few more days for the colony, yet it is none the less true that, even if united, we could not solve the difficulties of the situation (unless by a miracle like that of Agordat: and who knows, Sir, that you might not repeat it!)."

Alagi is 35 miles, over a bad road. His letter never reached its destination; nothing therefore, short of a miracle, could now save the unfortunate advanced column from an entirely hopeless struggle against the overwhelming masses of the enemy.[1]

The position in itself is a fine one,—easily defensible by a force three or four times as numerous as that of Toselli. On the western side of the English road rises the Amba,—a bare mass of granite 3,013 metres above sea-level, tower-

[1] There are many letters extant from officers under Toselli's command which show that, although ready to sacrifice themselves to gain a few days for the colony, they perceived that their position was practically hopeless. Captain Canovetti, for instance, writing to his sister, said: "We expect to be attacked; we are 1,000 and have on our front 20,000 well-armed enemies. (This was some days before the battle.) If when you receive this I am no longer alive, you may remain assured that I have died for honour and duty and that an honourable death forms a good close to one's life."

A letter of Lieutenant Messina expresses similar feelings. He writes to a friend: "Though you have given no signs of life for some time, at a moment like this I want to make sure of sending you what are perhaps my last good wishes.

"It is no use deceiving oneself. At a few hours' distance are all the Ras, united and marching towards us.... As soon as some of our details come in we shall join our battalion which has orders to delay at all costs the advance of the Abyssinians.

"The results of this task you can easily imagine! We shall sacrifice our lives in order to give time for all the troops to assemble and advance. I feel perfectly cool and composed, but at the same time it is only true to say that my mind is full of thoughts about my dear old father and mother. I ask you, whatever may happen, to do your best to comfort them etc."

These letters are quoted in "La guerra in Africa" of Signor Vico Mantegazza.

ing upwards like a castle and completely commanding the main thoroughfare; but to the right and to the left are two small paths by which its flanks could be turned,—one over Togora Hill, the other over Falagà Hill. An enemy advancing from the South would be easily able to surround the central peak by following either of these smaller tracks which branch outwards from near Atzala; it was necessary therefore to hold both the hills across which they run.

Toselli of course perceived this,—and perceived also that he had not enough troops to do so; but he posted his men skilfully, having no doubt that in compliance with his repeated demands he would be reinforced in a few hours. At Atzala as a kind of advanced post covering the two paths, he placed the company of Canovetti and the half company of Lieutenant Mazzei.

On his left flank at Falagà Hill he posted Ras Sebath with 350 irregulars, next him (between Falagà Hill and the centre) the company of Captain Issel. In the centre, on Mount Alagi, itself, he placed a company under the celebrated Captain Persico, together with all his artillery, consisting of only four guns under Captain Anghera. On the immediate right, amidst the descending slopes of the mountain, were the irregulars from Okule Kusai under Lieutenant Volpicelli,—about 300 strong. On his right flank, Togora Hill, was the Mussulman contingent under Sheik Thala, some 350 rifles in all. The reserve, which consisted of only two companies and a centuria, was in rear of the centre, covered by the mountain.

Some 2,150 natives and 4 guns,—this constituted Toselli's whole force (it must be remembered that a company in the

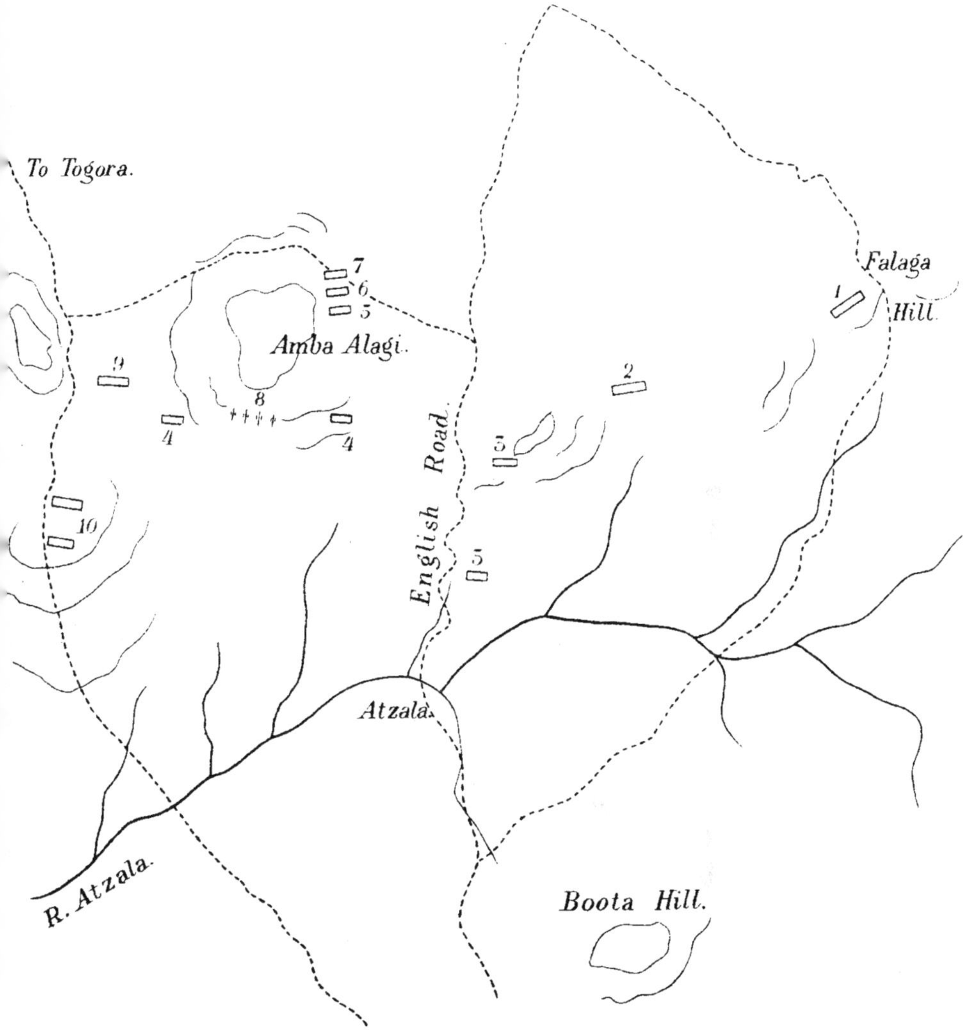

No. 1 Ras Sebat.
" 2 Issel's Company.
" 3 Canovetti's "
" 4 Persico's "
" 5 Ricci's "
" 6 Bruzzi's "
No. 7 Pagella's Centuria.
" 8 Anghera's Battery.
" 9 Sheik Thala.
" 10 Volpicelli.

Face p. 132.

Italian army consists of about 250 men); of these less than two-thirds were regulars, and almost 700 of the others were not even officered by Italians.

A collision was now inevitable, but Maconnen kept up negotiations to the end. On the 5th he had warned Toselli that although out of personal friendship for the Governor he had made every attempt to come to terms, yet when the Negûs arrived at his camping-ground, he, as advanced guard, would be obliged to move further forward. Toselli replied that "he was not to take a step further forward, but was to return to Lake Ashanghi; that if he advanced it was war." This message broke off all further negotiations.

At about 6.30 on the morning of December 7th, 1895, the outposts signalled "enemy in sight", and word was brought that some mounted men were to be seen moving on the plain to the South. Presently several distant volleys were heard,—fired by the centuria of Lieutenant Mazzei, which had been thrown out in front of Atzala, and the horsemen rapidly retired; but almost at the same moment a vast column, estimated to be about 7,000 strong, was seen descending from Boota Hill, and moving towards the Italian left, which was defended by only the 350 men of Ras Sebath and Dejatch Ali. These assailants were the force led by Ras Olié, who was soon hotly engaged with Sebath's 350 men, attacking them simultaneously in front and in flank, and compelling them to retire, though not until after an hour or more of fighting. This retreat of Ras Sebath on the extreme left naturally laid open the flank of Issel's company, and also that of Canovetti which had by now completed its retirement from Atzala,—disputing as it retreated every yard of ground and inflicting severe losses on the enemy. These two companies were compelled to change front left, and, in spite of a gallant resistance, were soon hard-pressed. "Although themselves diminished," says Baratieri in his report, "by brilliant counter-attacks they kept in check an enemy twenty times their number."

The position on the left was therefore somewhat critical; two of the Italian officers were dead and Lieutenant Mazzei was wounded. At nine o'clock, two and a half hours after the first shot had been fired, Toselli was obliged to advance the first company of the reserve under Captain Ricci, with a section of artillery under Lieutenant Manfredini, to the support of his left flank, or else the enemy would have seized the road to Macalle along which he was vainly expecting help to arrive. These young Italian officers led their men well; three times the enemy worked their way to close quarters, but each time Ricci advanced with such dash that they were compelled to retire before him, and Manfredini's two guns opened with shrapnel on their heavy masses, producing good results.

At 9.45, while the enemy were thus repulsed on the left, Toselli suddenly received word from Volpicelli that a great column of Shoans, led by the redoubtable Ras Alula and by Mangasha, was endeavouring to turn his right flank, and the firing was becoming as rapid on that side as on the left.

This was serious, but for the moment the Mohammedans seemed able to hold their own, supported as they were by Volpicelli's irregulars, so no immediate action was taken.

A quarter of an hour later, at ten o'clock, the centre,

consisting of Persico's company and Anghera's guns, was compelled to give ground before another huge column that had appeared from behind the hill of Boota. This mass of Abyssinian warriors, consisting of the followers of Ras Maconnen and Ras Mikael, was about 15,000 strong, and was moving rapidly along the English road[1] against the main Italian position on Amba Alagi. It was now three hours and a half from the moment when the first shot had been fired.

Another hour went by, and although the Italian officers were still holding their positions, the immense numbers of the enemy were gradually producing their inevitable result; the accounts given by survivors show how hopeless was the struggle. "The Abyssinians were many," says one Ascaro, "many of them died but the others came onward . . . the battery fired . . . but the Abyssinians kept on ascending. . . . Oh! how many there were." A better account was given to Lieut. Guido Moltedo by Ali-Aga, a non-commissioned officer, who, though wounded in the thigh by a projectile, succeeded in making his way to Fort Macalle. "It seemed almost useless, Sir, to fire battery volleys; four shots fell every time in the centre of the black mass which continued to advance . . . around the points where the projectiles burst one could see confusion . . . a gap was made . . . men were to be seen on the ground, dead or wounded . . . but the mass closed the ranks again and marched on towards us. They were many, many; the plain did not seem sufficient to contain them . . . the columns of the enemy could be seen circling from the right and from the left . . . it

[1] A road constructed by the British in 1868.

seemed as if they sprang up out of the earth. The infantry fired and killed some of them . . . useless . . . the enemy continued to increase."

At eleven o'clock Toselli saw that some decided action must be taken; yet what could he do? His orders did not allow him to retire. Not having been reinforced by Arimondi he concluded that the enemy, by some wide encircling movement from the East, had succeeded in engaging and delaying that general; he determined therefore to make a last stand on the position that he had been ordered to occupy.

The right was reinforced by the centuria of Lieutenant Pagella from the reserve, and the victorious companies on the left were drawn in towards the centre so as to render the whole line more compact, for it was becoming in many places, ominously thin. Having given these orders, there remained nothing for him to do; no precaution had been omitted that it was in the power of man to devise.

That hour, from eleven o'clock to midday, must have been terrible, for it was only then that he gave up all hope of the long expected support; towards the end of it he sent Lieutenant Bazzani for the last time to see whether Arimondi's column was not in sight, and then at 12.40 p.m., —some six hours after the attack had begun—he gave the order to retire. Already his centre, in spite of Captain Persico's desperate resistance, had been driven in, and his left flank had been turned by Ras Olié, who, on the retirement of the three companies, had been able to rally his men to a fresh advance.

The English road was occupied by the enemy, and only one line of retreat remained open—namely, a narrow path that winds at a considerable altitude along the side of a steep precipice 400 feet high, towards the hill of Togora on the Italian right. Manfredini's two guns were ordered to protect the line of retreat, but on reaching the ground they found Ras Alula victoriously occupying the crest of the hill, after having put to flight the Mohammedan riflemen of Sheik Thala. Volpicelli's irregulars were broken and in great disorder, but together with Pagella's centuria were lining a long spur, and still offering some resistance to the Abyssinians. In spite of the confusion, Manfredini succeeded in opening fire, and under cover of his two guns the lengthy train of mules with baggage, wounded etc., began to file slowly down the path, the only remaining company of the reserve,—namely, that of Captain Bruzzi,—being ordered up to form a rear-guard.

But all precautions were now useless. No sooner had the gunners ceased firing in order to begin their retirement, than the Abyssinians made a wild dash forward on every side, and the small rear-guard was quickly overpowered. Along their narrow path of retreat the thin line of mules, drivers, wounded men, and baggage became a living target, at a distance of only fifty paces, for the triumphant warriors of Ras Alula; some of the mules fell kicking on the track, others sprang over the precipice, taking more than one unfortunate Ascaro with them, while a hurricane of bullets was whirling all around from flank, from front, and in a very short time from the rear. The brave Sudanese gunners of Lieutenant Scala, who had defended the centre until they had hardly a round left, rather than allow their beloved pieces to fall into the hands of the enemy, hurled them, mules and all, into the valley below. Amidst a confusion of which the survivors spoke afterwards with a shudder, some endeavoured to return the enemy's fire, others simply thought of their own lives. A Somali called Mahmud, who made his escape together with Ali-Aga,[1] gives a vivid account of the scene. "The fighting soon began.... I heard the shots, but saw nothing as I was preparing our breakfast. (He was the cook of the battery.) Towards half-past eleven Lieutenant Scala passed on his mule. 'What are you doing?' he said to me... 'I am getting the food ready.' 'Leave it; to-day we shall not eat. Put everything in order, load the mules and fall in with the others.' While I was retreating with the rest, we were welcomed on a very narrow path by a fusilade from the Abyssinians, who were posted behind all the rocks. They fired from above us, from our flank, from the rear,—we were pushed onward by the Ascari of the battalion in retreat... What confusion! Mules rolling over the precipices—on one's right and on one's left dead men, or wounded men calling for help, and everywhere Abyssinians who were following to fire at us. The battery had been taken and the Sodanese cut down. A few Ascari of the artillery joined me. I left the road and, making a circuit through the mountains, placed myself in safety. I met Ali-Aga the other day. When I

[1] The N.C.O. whose description of the earlier part of the fight we have already given on p. 135; it seems that Mahmud caught up Ali Aga, who was wounded, and came on with him to Fort Macalle; they were six days on the way (owing to the precautions necessary in accomplishing those 35 miles) and during that time neither of them was able to get a substantial meal.

began my retreat the battery was still in position, so I did not see the officers, but if they are not here they are all dead."[1]

It is evident that the unfortunate cook had not waited long enough to learn with any great accuracy what happened to his battery; but we have also an account from a bulukbashi of Lieutenant Manfredini's section of Artillery,—evidently a brave man, who with two others arrived at Fort Macalle five days after the battle. It was noticed that these three were the first fugitives who brought their rifles with them.

According to their story the Abyssinians had rushed on to their battery (Manfredini's section) while in retreat, surprising it between the spurs of the mountains; the Shoans, they said, fired on them at a few paces' distance and finally threw themselves on to them with sword and lance. "I was at the second piece when a mule belonging to one of the gun carriages fell, in a very narrow passage, struck by a bullet, dragging Lieutenant Manfredini[2] into the valley below. Other mules fell, and were dashed headlong in the

[1] Moltedo: *L'Assedio di Maccale.*

[2] His career was short, but unusually brilliant; he had won a bronze medal at Agordat and another at Debraila; and his conduct on the day of his death was rewarded by the silver medal. From the day when he was gazetted to his regiment from "the school of application", he had applied to serve in Africa, for having lost both father and mother he no longer cared to live in Italy.—He had been away on leave, and his friend Lieutenant Moltedo gives a somewhat pathetic picture of his anxiety lest he should not arrive in time for the battle, and "his guns should fire without his being there."

same manner. That is what I know about my own section; of the other, which was in rear, I saw nothing, but they must certainly have been all killed. It is now five days, Sir, that we have been marching without food; I met the two others on the first night when I was directing my way towards Macalle. We marched only by night; during the day we hid in the grass or in a tree. On the 8th, towards dawn, there came up behind us three Abyssinians on horseback, and told us to surrender. We fired and killed two, the other fled; we cut the heads off these two—look at the sword! They showed it to me, it was still bloodstained. I proposed these three brave soldiers for the silver medal for valour. The buluk-bashi died at Adowa, but I saw the other two afterwards in the colony."

Amidst all the surrounding tumult Toselli preserved his calm composure and clear-headed energy, and gave orders in the hope of lessening the disaster. But the strain of long waiting and anxiety, also, doubtless, of his bodily exertions, was beginning to tell on him; he was physically worn out. "I saw him," so the Buluk-bashi of Manfredini's battery afterwards related, "on a path, supporting himself with his hands, and descending slowly down to the road." As a matter of fact he was the last to leave the summit. A few officers were with him—Anghera, Persico, Bodrero, Pagella, and some of his most faithful native soldiers; all were exhausted. The small band went on, gradually becoming diminished during the descent owing to continual losses inflicted by shots, some of which were fired from only ten paces off. Anghera fell, and then Persico. Having arrived, after a descent of an hour, on the road to Antalo, Toselli ordered Bodrero to go on quickly to find Arimondi if possible, in order to lessen the disaster; he himself refused all assistance. [1]

They were now at Bet-Mariam (the house or church of Mary), several miles from the scene of the disaster, and Toselli was too much exhausted to go any further. Having seen Lieutenant Bodrero depart in obedience to his order, he said to those with him: "I am at an end of my strength; now I will turn about and let them do what they like"; and with these words he faced towards the enemy, offering himself as a mark for their shots. [2] Thus ended a short but wonderfully successful life.

Bodrero placed himself at the head of the column, and with the assistance of Sergeant Garibaldi,—a worthy representative of that great name,—succeeded in checking the fugitives and leading them to Arimondi, who was at Aderat, and who knew nothing of the disaster. Of the other officers only Pagella and Bazzani were saved.

* * *

Such was the battle of Amba Alagi, in which Italy lost about 1,300 native soldiers and 20 Italian officers; so many of the latter had fallen that Lieutenant Bodrero was in command of the whole force now only 300 strong. But

[1] Official report—Green Book, 23bis, p. 57.

[2] More than one Italian has written an eloquent description of the death of their hero Toselli; but the short official accounts are more vivid than any. The above is practically a translation pieced together from the official narratives of Lieutenant Bodrero and Pagella.

during the next fortnight not a day passed without some miserable fugitive arriving at Fort Macalle,—some of them with ghastly sword-cuts on the head and shoulders, some of them with hands or arms hanging by a thread of skin, others with mortifying bullet wounds. Yet, even counting these survivors, the losses remained enormous; of the whole battery only 35 arrived in safety, and some of these being wounded would come in the list of casualties. Of Toselli's own battalion, the 4th Native, only 579 succeeded in saving their lives, and of that number 120 were wounded,—the battalion having gone into action certainly over 1,000 strong; of the irregulars a larger proportion turned up again afterwards, except of the Mohammedans of Sheik Thala who had no desire for further fighting. The latter retired to their homes, spreading far and wide the report of the Italian disaster.

It was indeed this loss of prestige which was the most serious result of the defeat at Amba Alagi. The series of Italian victories was broken. In spite of the brave stand which their troops had made against overwhelming odds, they were now regarded as the weaker side, and all the doubtful chieftains who were ready to submit to whichever army came first within striking distance of their frontiers, at once joined the Negûs. As Baratieri himself says: "the whole political edifice, indispensable to our colonial defence, was shaken to its foundation, and to some extent fell to the ground, increasing the boldness, confidence, strength, and pretensions of the enemy."

We may have our doubts as to how far this system of colonial defence had any really firm foundation, but now, at all events, every chance of a barrier of friendly states was at an end. The Italian party in Lasta was overthrown, and almost without exception the feudal chieftains in the district joined Menelik; the king of Gojjam presently followed their example; while the Mohammedans of Aussa and the surrounding districts renounced all ideas of a rising on the flank of Menelik's invading hordes.

It has been estimated that the Abyssinians lost as many as 3,000 men in the battle, but these figures are gathered from Italian sources alone, and however carefully compiled, can only be considered as approximate.

CHAPTER III

ARIMONDI'S COLUMN

ARIMONDI'S march to Aderat—Skirmish at Aderat—Bodrero and the survivors from Amba Alagi join Arimondi—Retreat to Macalle—Macalle garrisoned—Reasons for leaving a garrison in Macalle—Forced march of Arimondi's column to Adagamus—Description of the arrival.

IT was fortunate for Lieutenant Bodrero that General Arimondi had, after all, obtained leave from the Governor to advance as far as Aderat,[1] in order to support Toselli in the retreat upon which he fully expected that commander would enter, as soon as the enemy showed signs of a serious attack. He had started at 11.30 p.m. on the 6th (the night before Amba Alagi), first sending on a note to Toselli, informing him of his advance. He does not tell us the exact hour at which this note was despatched, but if fortune had favoured the Italians it seems as if it might still have arrived in time to avert the disaster, for the distance which it had to cross is estimated by Baratieri as being 45 miles, and by Melli as only 35; so that a native messenger even on foot could probably have covered this space within 12 hours; Arimondi says in his despatch that he counted it only a 15 hours' march for his whole column.

[1] In consequence of a letter from Toselli, written on the 5th.

Fortune, however, had set her face against them. This note, like the others, failed to reach its destination; but Arimondi, after an all-night march, arrived safely at Afghol at ten o'clock on the morning of December 7th. There he found no news from Toselli, but vague rumours came to his ears of an attack having been made on Amba Alagi, and some of his men fancied they could hear the sound of distant guns, while unmistakable columns of smoke were seen in the distance floating upwards from the hill. After a short halt he continued his march to Aderat, where he meant to occupy a strong position only seven miles from the Amba, and by four o'clock in the afternoon his advanced guard had passed the main height that he intended to defend. He was, in fact, just issuing his orders for its occupation when a note from Toselli was handed to him, followed very shortly by another. These had been sent off at 8.30 and 9 a.m. respectively. They had been seven hours in finding him, and he was only seven miles off! Not, indeed, that the situation could have been saved had they found him at once. These notes were the last ever written by Toselli,—who had now been dead for some hours,—and in them he informed the General that the attack had begun, adding that he considered the position very serious. They have now only one importance, namely, that they form a conclusive answer—if any were needed, after his letter of the 5th,—to certain detractors of his who insinuated that he had remained at Amba Alagi because he wished to have the credit of winning a victory unsupported. These papers, of course, prove that he held his ground not from ambition, but from a sense of duty.

Arimondi was in the act of answering them, when he

heard his advanced guard (Galliano's battalion) opening fire from the further crest of the hill. Already it seemed he was in contact with some small groups of the enemy which were being rapidly reinforced and increased; by 6.30 p.m. the engagement had begun in real earnest.

Suddenly, from out of the valley of Alagi, a small column in close formation and clearly defined amidst the surrounding groups, began to come in sight, and Arimondi was soon able to recognize it for certain as a body of the Italian colonial infantry. In half an hour's time it was under cover of his men's fire, and he was learning from Lieutenant Bodrero the details of the disaster.

The receipt of this information left only one course open to the General, namely, that of retiring slowly on Macalle; for the 300 men who had just joined him were in no condition for fighting, while his own 1,500 had been marching now for almost twenty hours without a prolonged halt. To retire, however, was already a difficult matter, seeing that the enemy, with the usual rapidity of Abyssinians, were moving round his right and threatening his line of retreat. On the left, as he perceived, the position was stronger, and Galliano was withdrawing slowly in perfect order; but on the right the artillery, being badly posted, could not open fire, and Ras Alula was pressing forward to the attack. It was a great day of revenge for the old chief,—a day for which he had waited six and a half years; he had by this time been for twelve hours at the head of his men, now on horseback, now on foot, leading them on with all the energy of his prime and all the skill won from long years of experience.

At 7.30 a simultaneous rush on front and flank was made by the Abyssinians, and on the Italian right Alula won his way up to the brow of the plateau within a hundred yards of General Arimondi and his staff. But a rapid fire was at once opened on him, and a vigorous counter-attack by the company of Captain Oddone drove him and his followers back off the crest. Seizing the chance offered to him by this temporary success, Arimondi gave the order to retire, and the movement at once began.

By a quarter past eight the fire had entirely ceased on both sides, and the force was proceeding on its way to Chelikot (Celiquot) headed by the survivors of Toselli's column. The joy of these survivors at finding Arimondi when all hope of doing so had failed, must have been truly heartfelt, and a load of anxiety must have been removed from the mind of Lieutenant Bodrero; for otherwise they would inevitably have fallen a prey to an enemy whose ancient custom it is to mutilate their prisoners in the most brutal manner. Between Aderat and Macalle, a march of thirty miles at the lowest estimate still lay before them, and there can be little doubt that they would have been cut off by the Galla cavalry, and overwhelmed by numbers long before they could have accomplished the distance.

General Arimondi tells us that even for him there were many sources of disquietude. He feared that the enemy would send on their mounted men to occupy the crest of Chelikot, which would have compelled his tired soldiers to fight another battle in order to avoid being surrounded. The last skirmish, at Aderat, though lasting only an hour and a quarter, had been hotly contested, and had at one time looked serious; the Italian troops had lost, it is true, only one man killed and fifteen wounded, but they might well consider themselves fortunate in escaping with so few casualties. In dead silence the 1,800 men filed across the plain of Afgol, at a short distance from the bivouac fires of the enemy, and followed by scattered bodies of the enemy's cavalry, who, Arimondi says, carried small lanterns with reflectors that threw weak rays of light across their course,—a curious device which one would have thought more dangerous than useful. A brief halt was made at Chelikot, which was unoccupied, most fortunately, for his men were almost dead-beat. By the time he reached Macalle (4.30 a.m.) they had been marching for twenty nine and a half hours (including two nights) without any long halt! And in that time, besides fighting a sharp engagement, they had covered, at the smallest estimate, fifty-seven miles along the road! From this performance some idea can be formed of what the Ascaro can endure. But even they had had their fill; as each man entered the fort of Macalle he laid his rifle down, threw himself on the ground, and was asleep.

General Arimondi, though himself weary, and greatly distressed at the news of Toselli's disaster, was obliged to come to an important decision. There were three courses between which he had to make his choice.

To remain and defend the strong position on the heights of Macalle. But this was hardly possible now that he had only some 2,000 men left.

To retire with his whole force at once, and thus to concentrate the entire Italian army at Adagamus, where he would be met by the Governor. This would mean destroying a splendid store of provisions collected at Macalle and blowing up the fort which had taken some time to build.

He could leave a garrison in Macalle and retire with the remainder of his men to join Baratieri.

He chose the third course, and left Major Galliano with his battalion, the 3rd Native Infantry, to garrison the fort. Under Galliano's command there were to be 20 Italian officers, 13 non-commissioned officers, 150 Italian soldiers, and about 1,000 Ascari; and his battalion, we may add, was considered one of the best in the colonial service. The fort was supplied with 2 guns. Of civilians, 2 Italians and 3 Greeks remained with Galliano.

Arimondi justifies his decision by five arguments, which he enumerates in the following manner:—

That it would have had a demoralizing effect to abandon the fort, which was regarded amongst the natives as a great stronghold of the Italians.

That he could not take the provisions with him, and did not feel certain that he would have time to destroy them.

That the fort would have a great value as a base for fresh offensive operations against the enemy.

That with his restricted means of transport it would have been extremely difficult for him to carry sufficient food for the extra 1,200 men during their retreat; and that many of them being Italians,—Engineers and Artillerymen who were in no training for long marches,—they would have delayed his retreat besides necessitating so much extra transport.

That although the occupation of Macalle diminished the Italian forces at the point of concentration by 1,200 men, yet he hoped that the Abyssinians, finding this strong fort in their path, would be compelled to leave so numerous a contingent behind them in order to invest it, that the gain to Italy would be greater than the loss.

It is impossible, of course, to say exactly what the General's difficulties may have been at that moment; one can understand that a commander who is hotly pursued by an enemy about fourteen times as strong as his own force would naturally be very unwilling to risk an engagement. One can understand, also, it would have been extremely difficult to organize the transport required, in a day or two,—which was all the grace that he could hope for,—and at the same time to destroy what was not required and blow up a fort of some dimensions. It would also have needed some "hardening of the heart" to deliberately delay his retreat when he was certain to be pursued by cavalry, to destroy stores of which the Italians possessed such a small supply, and to blow up, perhaps unnecessarily, a fort that would most probably have to be rebuilt at the earliest opportunity. So great do these difficulties appear that it may perhaps be argued that the General in reality took the only course open to him at the time.

Nevertheless, one cannot help feeling that it was a pity to allow these 1,200 men to be cut off and surrounded, and the Governor certainly appears to have regarded it as a mistake. To leave a weakly fortified and garrisoned fort in the midst of a hostile country, means binding oneself to relieve it sooner or later. A case, similar in many respects, has lately occurred in Natal, where the British army held Ladysmith which had originally been a base for offensive operations against the enemy. The experiment can hardly be said to have resulted in entire success.

In the case of Macalle, General Arimondi probably counted that, having only a barbarian enemy to face, the Italians would be able to inflict on him a decisive defeat before their fortress stood in any danger of falling, that the enemy would thereupon beat a general retreat, and that the garrison would thus be automatically relieved. If this was in reality his idea, he lived long enough to see his mistake, for Macalle never was relieved,—the Governor, in fact, decided that it was hopeless even to make the attempt,—and it was only owing to an extraordinary stroke of good fortune that the garrison did not become prisoners of war.

By mid-day General Arimondi had decided on his course of action and given his orders; so he called together the officers, to whom he made a short speech, explaining to them that the disaster of Amba Alagi was after all but an unfortunate advanced-guard action, and expressing his confidence in Major Galliano, and in the proved courage and valour of his Ascari. He ended by saying that he was going to accompany the troops to the Governor, *and that in a few days he would be back in Macalle.*

At four o'clock his column started, but hardly had they crossed the brow of the nearest hill than one of the companies was attacked by armed rebels. The whole country appeared to be rising, and the telegraph wires to Macalle had been cut at nine o'clock that morning. During his long march he was continually harassed, until at length, by way of reprisal, he ordered several villages to be burnt, and publicly shot some of the rebels found with arms in their hands; but this was not until the column had lost one killed and three wounded, as well as several of the women, who were murdered. Their first halt was at Ghemat, after another long march of eighteen hours broken by only half an hour's halt at Agula;[1] at 7 a. m. on the 10th they reached Adagamus, having accomplished 115 miles in three days and ten and a half hours. Considering that during this short period General Arimondi had fought two engagements, and had been obliged to stop to burn hostile villages; considering also that after the first half-day he was constantly harassed by rebels, delayed by a long line consisting of wounded men and heavily laden baggage animals, and by the presence of a large number of women, it is beyond all doubt one of the most wonderful marches of the century.

An idea of the motley composition of his column may be gathered from the following description of his arrival at Adagamus, given by Major Gamerra of the 8th Native Battalion, who rode out to meet him. "I went forward," he says, "beyond the line of outposts, and after a little met the head of the column, which was composed of the survivors of Amba Alagi.

"General Arimondi, with the 5th and 6th Native Battalions and with the irregulars of the Dedjazmatch[2] Fanta, followed at a short distance.

"I tried, but without success, to open a way for myself in

[1] Arimondi's official despatch to the Governor of Erythrea.

[2] The highest military grade after that of Ras; for shortness it is often called Dejatch.

this mass of wounded Ascari, women, children, mules, horses and provisions, so I renounced the idea of pushing forward any further to meet General Arimondi, who honoured me with his friendship and whom I had not seen for a long time. I then witnessed the sad procession of the survivors of Toselli's battalion filing past me, then those of Persico's company, and of Pagella's centuria which belonged to the 6th Battalion, and of Anghera's battery. Many a time I had to make a great effort not to betray the inward emotion and the sentiment of profound sadness which that procession and the sorrowful thoughts that it called up, awoke within me. Before me passed wounded Ascari on mules or supported by their comrades, women weeping, and children with an almost stupefied expression in their faces and in their eyes. The Sudanese widows of our brave gunners were the most inconsolable of all, or at least their manifestations of grief were the most noisy. The Abyssinian women who had lost their husbands were distinguishable, as a rule, by the tarbush of the dead man, which they had put on their head, with ill-concealed coquetry. Some of them in this unaccustomed head-dress had a really original appearance, and from seeing it one would certainly not have said that they were widows of barely three days. At intervals, and especially when they passed opposite me, they uttered loud laments and burst out into tears, but they soon composed themselves, and never forgot to readjust the tarbush on their head. With the exception of this shrill note, the filing by was very painful for me, and when, by God's will, after a long hour's waiting it was finished, I felt really relieved, and galloped to meet General Arimondi!"

CHAPTER IV

ENDEAVOURS TO REPAIR THE POSITION

"Rivincita"—Baratieri's difficulties—Strength of his position—Disagreements with Arimondi—Negotiations with native states—Aussa—Gojjam—Negotiations with Raṣ Maconnen—News from Macalle.

The situation after the battle of Amba Alagi was in many respects peculiar. The Italian Colony was suddenly called upon to repel an invasion resembling those endured by ancient Italy in the days of Alaric's Visigoths or Genseric's Vandals; as yet, indeed, they had only seen the advanced guard, some 30,000 strong, but when the main body appeared the Negûs's army reached a strength of about 120,000 warriors, so many of whom brought their wives and dependents that almost 40,000 [1] non-combatants were to be found amongst the tents. To meet this horde no adequate means of defence had been prepared; Baratieri had, beyond all doubt, underestimated the danger arising from constant friction with Menelik, and Italy, as is usual with the mother country, had discounted largely even from the reports with which the Governor tried to arouse her, so that in the end

[1] It is said that Menelik left 60,000 behind him, doing garrison work etc.; according to the latest estimate that I have seen, that of Captain Welby in "Twixt the Sirdar and Menelik," some 200,000 warriors answered Menelik's call to arms.

this two-fold reduction naturally produced an insufficiency in the demand for men, money, and munitions and a still greater insufficiency in the supply.

On hearing of the massacre of the Ascari at Amba Alagi Italy awoke,—the disaster had at all events that one good result. But it was already too late to arrange "the revenge" on which she at once decided, in the manner in which it ought to have been arranged. For a nation like Italy, whose army is primarily intended for home defence, it takes several months to organize a powerful expedition over the sea, and requires an immense amount of care and labour. Already the Abyssinians were within three days' march of Adigrat, whereas the troops in Italy were about eight times as far from that town; and in any case they could not possibly be sent to the front until a supply of provisions had been obtained, for the colony was too much exhausted to feed them.

To summarise briefly from a military point of view General Baratieri's position in December 1895. He had abandoned the conquered provinces of Tigré and Agamè to the enemy, leaving in their midst Galliano's gallant little force of 1,190 men to hold Fort Macalle. Adigrat was his base of operations, and there he had 6,000 soldiers,—infantry,—hastily collected and almost all of them natives; some 3,000 more were in process of being raised.

One hundred and ten miles lay between him and the seaport of Massowah, which meant that he could get no reinforcements from Italy in less than about twenty-three days,—their march from the coast to Adigrat taking from seven to nine days. As matters stood it was obvious that he could take no steps towards relieving Macalle; it would have been madness to march with 6,000 or 7,000 men to attack 30,000 equally well armed, strongly posted, and flushed with recent victory. Even had he wished to do so, the lack of provisions and mules would have been an insuperable barrier; he was compelled, therefore, to abandon the fortress to its fate.

His plan of campaign was to concentrate at Adigrat as many troops as he could feed, and there to await the Shoan attack,—the advantages of which plan may be seen by a cursory glance at the map.[1]

The position at Adagamus,—about nine miles outside Adigrat,—is a splendid natural line of defence, in fact so strong as to be practically safe from any direct attack. It stretches "like an immense wall across the road coming from Macalle, its right flank leaning on the inaccessible Amba Guructo, and its left on the insurmountable spurs that descend in the direction of the coast." It commands all the roads leading from the South to Adigrat.

[1] His plan of campaign may best be described in his own words. "The situation seems clear to me. I unite the forces at Adigrat, a position of obvious importance from a strategic and tactical point of view, and also from one of general convenience,—the preparations have been proceeding . . . since April last. I cannot attack the enemy because he is still beyond my reach, and too numerous. If the enemy advances and attacks us with united forces, I am certain of repulsing him, and his retirement might easily become a disaster. If the enemy divides his forces, I count on attacking one of the columns and overthrowing it. If the enemy directs his course towards the Mareb, I intend to profit by the circumstance to attack him in flank. Meanwhile the reinforcements begin to-day to disembark at Massowah." He did not suppose that the enemy would treble their numbers while his own reinforcements were arriving.

As a defensive position, therefore, it has few superiors,—and for offensive operations too, it affords unusual advantages. The mountain ranges of Tigré form a right angle, in the inmost corner of which is Adigrat, and near it Adagamus. From this corner (Adigrat), one range runs southwards to Macalle alongside of the English road, and the other westward to Adowa (also parallel with a road), so that Adigrat commands the junction of the two roads and of the two ranges. Thus the enemy at Macalle, (i) if he advanced due northward, would have to make frontal attack on Baratieri's fortified position, or (ii), if he marched on Adowa, would have to expose his right flank to the Italians, which would be an extremely serious consideration for an army that swept along with it some 40,000 women, children and other non-combatants. Except the two roads through Adowa and Adigrat there was, practically speaking, no other feasible way of invading the colony, so that Baratieri's force occupied a splendid post of defence. [1] It will be noted, however, that any attempt to relieve Macalle would have sacrificed all the above mentioned advantages. [2]

[1] The danger, as has already been pointed out, was that the enemy might try and establish himself at Adowa, now that it was left undefended; he would then be nearer to Asmara (the chief town on the Italian communications) than Baratieri himself, and could advance fearlessly, not caring about his own communications. In this manner he could force the Governor to attack him on his own ground. (The fort of Fremona at Adowa had been evacuated as soon as the news of Amba Alagi became known, for it was not in a defensible condition.) This danger was foreseen and provided for by Baratieri as described in (ii).

[2] "After finishing with the fort (of Macalle),—will the enemy advance against Adagamus? We shall have there a prepared

Having selected this position, in which he felt himself to be absolutely secure, more especially as the ground in front of it, for over a day's march, had been reduced to a desert, the Governor turned his mind to the immense mass of work before him. He began by sending Arimondi to Massowah to organize the transport, and this arrangement, though in itself natural enough, was regarded as a mark of disagreement between the two men; it has even been attributed to jealousy on the part of Baratieri. The truth was that since Arimondi had won the title of General on the field of Agordat, he and the Governor had found it hard to work together. In a large, weakly defended country, continually repelling invaders and garrisoned by only a few thousands of men, it was necessary that there should be one head, and one only. Arimondi was now equal in rank with the Governor and was nominally military commander of the troops, the Governorship being a civil office; but Baratieri was, of

position, we shall have the best base for defensive action, from the point of view of our commanding situation; also for the support of our wings, and for employing our artillery. As regards counter-offensive measures, we shall have an equally good position, owing to the formation of the ground and the direction from which the enemy will advance. Will he move towards Hausen? Warned in time, we will attack him either on the march or before he can develop his movement,—energetically with two columns, one of our advanced posts being Mai Meghelta, the other Adagamus. Will he direct his march to the district of Tigré at the Mareb? In three days we shall be able to strike his flank at Adowa, or forestall him at the Mareb, a far more easy and still shorter manœuvre if he directs himself for Belesa, via Entisho. Will he remain in his positions? He will find it hard to maintain himself there, weakened by hunger or by discords."

Baratieri's telegram to Government, Jan. 23rd, 1896.

course, himself a soldier, senior to Arimondi, and by Article I. of the constitution he was allowed "the faculty of assuming supreme command over the forces of the colony by land and sea, in all cases that may seem necessary to him."

Such a two-headed system, especially amongst military men, was certain to give rise to discontent, and already, twice during the year, Arimondi had sent in his resignation. But the fact of these disagreements cannot be counted as discreditable to either of the generals; the Governor had several times, for political reasons, been compelled to forbid some of the plans that General Arimondi had formed,—one, for instance, prepared with Turitto in March 1895, for crossing the Atbara and destroying a Dervish camp; in October, one for invading Lasta. Arimondi might naturally say that nothing more was left to his discretion than before his promotion to the rank of General, that his titles of Commander of the Erythrean troops, and Commandant of Tigré brought him practically no chances of acting on his own initiative; but the fact remained that in time of war the Governor was responsible for the conduct of the military as well as civil affairs, and, being a soldier, he wished to act as his own General. [1]

[1] During the advance from Adigrat in February it was openly said by journalists that the Italian camp was divided into two parties, one following each general; this was probably an exaggeration, but two journalists were ordered away by the Governor for their outspoken observations during that critical period. Arimondi's supporters aver that Baratieri lost no opportunity of secretly slighting him and checking his career,—the Governor of course denies it. The truth will never be known, but Italian writers appear to favour Arimondi, who is chiefly remembered by his glorious victory of Agordat and his brave death at Adowa.

At the moment of which we are speaking, relations between him and Arimondi had become more strained, perhaps, than ever before, as the Governor laid on him the blame attaching to the failures in Tigré. He accused him of having disobeyed his order to make Adigrat the base of defence; secondly, for the mistakes in the telegram and letter that had caused the loss of Toselli's column; and thirdly, for leaving a garrison in Macalle.

Whether Arimondi ever understood that he was under orders to make Adigrat his headquarters is perhaps open to doubt. As regards the other two charges, it appears to be a matter of opinion how far he was to blame; but the Governor would naturally be inclined to take an unfavourable view of the matter, for he found himself weakened by the loss of Toselli's 2,000 men, to which would sooner or later be added the 1,190 in Macalle, a disaster about to take place before his eyes, and one that would inevitably be connected with his name, although he was powerless to avert it.

The defence of the colony fell naturally, as had always been the case, under two headings,—the alliances with native states and the actual armed force to be employed.

The barrier of native states had broken down after the defeat of Amba Alagi. Although the stubborn resistance of the Erythrean companies had excited everywhere amongst those hardy populations a sentiment of admiration, and although Toselli's brave death on the Amba was, and still is, a theme for their war-songs,[1] yet the faith in the Euro-

[1] The song of Toselli, sung by the natives to Ximenes and translated by him, may be translated as follows:

peans was broken. The Italian party amongst the chiefs was not yet dead, but it was terribly weakened. Ras Sebath and Ras Agos Tafari still remained faithful, in spite of the disappointment at seeing their promised estates overrun by the enemy; the Itchegué (High Priest) at the holy city of Axum was friendly, and Ras Agos in Amhara endeavoured (or said he endeavoured) to keep the King of Gojjam true to his engagements: these were the chief weapons left in the hands of Baratieri, who, hopeful to the last, despatched Lieutenant Giannini to Aussa, to arouse the Mohammedans to a fresh effort. Moreover, he continued his organized system of secret intelligence by means of native spies; in fact, amidst a hundred difficulties, he endeavoured in every possible manner to retrieve the situation.

Meanwhile the enemy were quite as active as he. Had the Shoans occupied themselves only with the siege of Macalle during the next five or six weeks, Baratieri might perhaps have succeeded in arousing some of the turbulent elements in their rear; but on the 26th Lieutenant Giannini telegraphed that the Shoans had made a raid into Aussa, killing 600 men and burning the capital, Hadele Gubo, so that the the Mohammedan population were more than ever indisposed to rebellion. As for the King of Gojjam, Menelik had long ago entered into communication with him, for as early as

"Thou, like the General on the sea (?), wast occupying a height which could not be taken except by God himself.

"Thou didst deserve to return safe to land.

"The hilt of thy sword was shining like the star of the morning.

"Save thyself, thou dost not merit such a death!

"But he draws his glittering sword, and says: I will never abandon my young men." Ximenes, *Sul Campo di Adua*, p. 28.

January 3rd it was reported that an alliance had been concluded between the two monarchs, and that already King Tecla Aimanot had sent a contingent under his sons to join the Negûs. Four days later Menelik was actually arriving with King Tecla Aimanot himself at Chelikot, where he was met by his faithful Ras, the victors of Amba Alagi.

What in reality constituted one of the worst signs of this episode was the manner in which the information, forwarded first of all by Felter, was strenuously denied by the native spies. Possibly this was due to Menelik's machinations; but even for those of the spies who remained faithful, the service was becoming rather too dangerous to be agreeable. On January 23rd three of them arrived from Macalle with their hands cut off by the enemy; a few days earlier Major Galliano was promoted to the rank of Colonel, as a reward for the gallant defence that he was making,[1] but one of the messengers carrying the news to him was killed.

To add to the anxieties of the Governor, Menelik had made an alliance with his old enemy the Khalifa, and 5,000 Dervishes had advanced as far as Ghedaref on the North West of the colony. They were, it is true, chiefly armed with lances, but nevertheless some skirmishes took place near the Atbara, and it was found necessary to keep a battalion and some detachments of artillery in Kassala in order to watch their movements. The command of this district was entrusted to Captain Hidalgo, and almost every day a message

[1] Macalle was by now surrounded by the whole Abyssinian army, but was holding out bravely against the most determined assaults of the Ras.

arrived for the Governor, who duly telegraphed the news to Rome.

One gleam of good fortune, that afterwards bore fruit in a most unexpected manner, came to shed a flickering light of encouragement over the almost unbroken failure that now attended Italian relations with their former allies,—not that the Governor appears to have felt deeply discouraged by these failures, for he knew that a single Italian victory would bring many of his volatile friends back to him.

On December 12th, only five days after Amba Alagi, he had received a peculiar letter from Ras Maconnen, in which that chief apologised for his share in the battle, saying that "he had been pressed forward by the troops of the Emperor; that his men had attacked without orders. It was bad; he begged that worse things might be avoided. He wrote in this manner because he knew Italy. He asked for a trustworthy man with whom he might treat."

Such a letter, absurd as were the excuses, proved, at all events, that one of the most important of Menelik's advisers was even now by no means confident of success. It is in fact one of the many small incidents by which we know that the Abyssinian chiefs (including the Negûs), especially the more enlightened among them, had a secret fear of the power of Italy. Probably the only man whom no diplomacy, and no change of fortune, could have brought to desert his side was Ras Alula,—and consequently for him alone of all their enemies have the Italians any real admiration.

The Governor answered this letter of Maconnen's in a general manner,—for it was his aim and his duty to gain time,—and then forwarded it to his Government, calling to their attention the fact that Signor Felter, a personal friend of Maconnen's, was in the camp. But the politicians at Rome, evidently had no belief in the sincerity or importance of the Ras' statements; they suggested meetings in Italian territory to which it was certain Maconnen would not agree. After some further exchange of messages, on December 28th an angry letter came from Maconnen, breaking off all communications, and adding: "where the Emperor bids me, there will I heroically shed my blood."

Nevertheless the negotiation was kept open. On December 29th Felter was permitted to visit the Ras. Being a trusted agent of the Governor and at the same time the very man with whom Maconnen wished to talk matters over, his mission was of considerable importance and became indirectly responsible for the only piece of good fortune during the campaign.

And meanwhile all Italy, and indeed many people all over the world were watching the fate of the little fort at Macalle. Messages travelled to and fro, almost every day bringing one from Galliano. At first they had been cheerful,—for a month after Amba Alagi the real siege did not begin; but then they began to arrive less often, and read less hopefully. When, on January 12th, it was known that the water-supply of the fort was in the hands of the Shoans, then both the Governor and the army began to feel that the end was near, for they were not sufficiently strong to march to Galliano's relief.

CHAPTER V

REINFORCEMENTS FROM ITALY

Twenty million lire voted—Insufficiency of the sum—Undefined policy of Italy—Chief difficulty want of time—Lines of communication—Transport difficulties—The British expedition of 1868—Description of the work at Massowah—The march to Adigrat—Commissariat arrangements.

On December 19th, 1895, the Italian Chamber voted a grant of twenty millions for the war with Abyssinia,—that is twenty million lire, which would be equivalent to about £750,000 sterling. Now when the British marched to Magdala and destroyed the power of the Negûs Theodore it cost them nine millions sterling,—that is about twelve times the amount voted by the Italians for their war. But, on the other hand, there are three considerations that tend to justify the smaller expenditure of Italy; firstly, that the British spent money lavishly:—"C'était du luxe pour une expédition qui ne dura que quatre mois," says the French general, Luzeux; secondly, that the Italian Government from the first strenuously maintained their intention of merely standing on the defensive,—they never meant to march on the enemy's capital; and thirdly, that they already had, at the end of 1895, some 11,000 men and 2,000 animals in their colony, whereas the English of course had to bring everything from India (the Suez Canal not being in existence at that time).

Nevertheless, the sum voted by the Chamber was insufficient, judged according to statistics; for Mr. Bloch, whose financial calculations, at all events, have opened up many new issues, has estimated that no European nation can keep an army in the field at a lower rate than eight shillings per man per day; and as the Italians counted on a field-force of 20,000 men, they would therefore not have been able to keep them in being for longer than three months. Moreover, this estimate of Mr. Bloch has been proved by our recent experiences to be extremely low; in the Boer war we have spent over half as much again on our soldiers as the sum that he allows. Finally, he did not include in this calculation the possibility of a sea journey that would occupy about a fortnight, and would naturally increase Italian expenses.

It seems, therefore, beyond doubt that the sum voted was too small; but what was still worse, it tended to perpetuate the confusion in the mind of the ministers. Had they said, boldly, that they merely meant to defend the original boundaries of Erythrea, abandoning the newly annexed districts, it has been held (by Captain De la Jonquière) that the amount was in reality rather more than sufficient for the purpose. With this opinion it is hard to agree. But the ministers themselves went further; they hoped to obtain decisive results and to defeat Menelik so that he would not be in a condition to attack them for years to come. They did not realise that this would entail his being pursued into his own territory which was almost as expensive as making fresh conquests,—a course that they loudly disclaimed. They were not in reality quite decided as to whether the campaign was to be offensive or defensive.

Of course there is always one great excuse,—that neither they, nor anyone else in Europe, at that time regarded the Shoans as a formidable enemy; they were merely one of the many wild Abyssinian tribes.

After Amba Alagi the great difficulty of the Italians was the lack of time. They could not count on having more than another month before the enemy might be closing on Adigrat, and reinforcements could not reach that town from the mother country in less than about twenty-three days. Every man under Arimondi's command was working all day and late into the night, for week after week, and even then, so few were the hands available that their task would have been impossible, but for the providential respite of nearly two months, before Baratieri's fresh advance entailed the really great strain on his line of supplies.

The communications ran from Massowah by two roads southward to Adigrat. The first and chief line was Massowah—Arkico—Majo—Adi Caje—Adigrat, over a space of 110 miles; the second, rather longer, from Massowah—Saati—Asmara—Saganeiti—Adi Caje—Adigrat. He has been adversely criticised for not adopting the old British line of advance from Zula—Toconda—Senafè, which was shorter, but he rejected it because it involved changing the base from the port of Massowah to that of Zula on the Red Sea, and for this he could not afford time. The English road, also, would have required some repairing, and did not touch at the fort of Adi Caje through which he was anxious to pass.

As regards Land Transports. Having thus a line of communications 110 miles long, the next difficulty was to collect, in three or four weeks, enough animals to carry his provisions to the front. It was estimated that for the whole of his communications 12,000 camels would be sufficient. At the end of December he had only 3,000, but in two months the agents of General Arimondi had succeeded in collecting, in all, some 8,200 camels and about 3,000 mules. The remainder of the work had to be done by donkeys, which were, however, found to be extremely serviceable, easy to lead, hardy, able to feed themselves, and in fact adaptable in many important respects. Most of the camels came from the Arab coast, Somaliland, or Mensa, and some few from the colony itself, costing altogether, over £65,000—a large hole in the £750,000 voted![1] Considering that all these animals were collected from different parts of the world within less than two months, (many of the mules came from Cyprus) it may be admitted that the work was rapidly done.

Twelve stages were then arranged along the road to Adigrat, as halting-places for the camel caravans.

In supplying the mules with saddles, harness, and drivers, we come to the true difficulties of the situation. The Italian mules were found to be too big, so that others had to be sought far and wide. It was then discovered that the Italian saddles did not fit the smaller mules, and alterations causing fresh delay became necessary. Moreover, drivers were exceedingly difficult to find; almost every man in the colony had been called to arms, so that the Italians were obliged to go even as far as India for drivers, where the English, we are told, "conceded animals but not men." Whether this means that the Indian authorities refused to allow their

[1] According to Signor Vico Mantegazza in *L'Assedio di Maccalé*.

own trained drivers to be taken,—a somewhat natural decision,—I do not know; but the lack of such men is merely one of the innumerable difficulties that invariably arise from an attempt to do the work of four or five months in six weeks.

By way of a rough comparison I give a short account of the English expedition of 1868, although the cases are not in reality parallel, for its objects were very different to those of the Italians. The British aimed at capturing Magdala, a place 379 miles from Zula, or over three times the distance from Massowah to the Italian front at Adigrat. On the other hand, they had only to fight against an ill-armed enemy, whose numbers eventually dwindled down to some 8,000 or 10,000 men, and they had unlimited time at their disposal. The task before them was therefore infinitely more easy than that of the Italians, except for the fact that the Suez Canal not being in existence, India became necessarily the base of all operations. Contrary to our almost invariable custom we appear to have overrated rather than overlooked the difficulties to be encountered (which is said to have been due to the lessons learnt in the Crimea). Some 62,220 persons of all classes and professions were landed at Zula,—but this total included sailors, camp followers, mule-drivers etc., of whom many deserted; between 40,000 and 50,000 were doing useful work, about 14,600 being in the fighting columns. These figures give some idea of the difficulty of the country. For purposes of transport 36,094 animals of all sorts were landed;[1]

[1] These were the animals *landed*; but the land transport also purchased native-bred beasts. Their total eventually reached the astounding figure of 41,723 animals, without including horses

2,538 horses, 44 elephants, 16,292 mules, 1,651 ponies, 5,735 camels, 1,759 donkeys, 8,075 bullocks,—in fact every known beast of burden was represented. Presently a difficulty arose owing to the various detachments arriving by different routes,—the animals had been picked up in India, along the Persian Gulf, at Aden, on the coasts of the Red Sea, of Egypt, of the Levant etc., and their drivers did not speak the same languages. The result was confusion. The scene, for a time, must have resembled Noah's ark. Many of the unfortunate mules were discovered looking for food along the sea shore, others were appropriated by the more agile speculators amongst the native population; in fact it took the British about two months to evolve a business-like organization out of the babel of men and animals at their improvised port of Zula.

Nevertheless they had shown that they intended to carry the matter through to a satisfactory conclusion. There was no lack of material, and, once that order was re-established, the attainment of success became a matter of time. The French General Luzeux, after detailing and emphasizing our mistakes, gives expression to the following opinion: "Les Italiens avaient donc là un exemple, sinon à imiter, au moins à étudier." For the purpose of receiving wounded and sick animals, depots were formed at 60 mile intervals (five or six day's march),—they must have been needed, for of the 36,094 transport animals landed, only 7,421 embarked at the end of the campaign; (many of

or elephants; 12,008 were camels. (It will be seen, by those who compare them that there are some irreconcilable discrepancies between the Land and Naval Transport returns.)

them, however, had been given to friendly chiefs and otherwise disposed of). A small railway was built to cover the first ten and a half miles and then, after only two months of actual warfare, the enemy's stronghold was in our hands. A steady advance, averaging barely five or six miles a day (the country being difficult), had been maintained until the British finally stormed the heights of Magdala, only to find the body of their unfortunate enemy Theodore. The homeward march was successfully performed in six weeks.

To return to the Italian preparations which, it must be remembered, were accomplished in only two months. Nothing perhaps reflects greater credit than the energy that they displayed in this almost heart-breaking task.

Between December 25th, 1895, and March 10th, 1896, there disembarked at Massowah 1,537 officers, 38,063 men (most of them did not arrive until after the battle of Adowa, March 1st), 8,584 mules (required for artillery, mounted officers, etc.,—besides those for the lines of communication), and 100,000 barrels of materials. The disembarkation service being extremely short-handed, every man was compelled to work many hours' over-time, and every officer to face an accumulation of difficulties, that by their very nature could not possibly bring him either personal glory or any of those rewards for which an officer naturally yearns; for this is one of the prosaic untheatrical branches of the fighting organization; yet it is this machinery that drives the giant hammer at the front.

The following picture given by an Italian writer[1] will

[1] *L'Assedio di Maccalé* by Signor Vico Mantegazza, p. 493.

best describe the struggles of these weary men on the quays and jetties of Port Massowah. "At night-time a fantastic appearance was presented around the quay by the movements of a few hundreds of black men who worked by the light of torches, of Wells lamps, and of electric reflectors belonging to the Royal Navy, to unload the chalands, barges, steamboats, and to load from the quays the Decauville waggons and railway. There, too, was felt the scarcity of light barges, to facilitate the unloading from the ships, and the shortness of hands for the work. This last difficulty was continually on the increase, partly owing to the extremely restricted means available (all able-bodied men having gone to the war or set out with the caravans), partly because, with the increased labour, weariness of the duty became more prevalent, and its suspension also more frequent owing to the enforced absence of the labourers. It is easy to understand how dreary was the work, how continuous and how heavy, by bearing in mind that at times it became necessary to disembark simultaneously 5 battalions, 300 camels, 1,600 mules and about 2,000 tons of provisions and materials, and that all the materials had been laden without any pre-arranged order, this having been impossible owing to the haste with which they were sent off from Naples; that in the case of each fresh arrival they had to disembark the men, extract the cases of rifles with a crane, embark them on the boats, land them on the beach or on the quay, open them, take out the rifles, rub off the grease, and distribute them, taking away the cases to the warehouse; that the soldiers had to re-equip themselves in a different manner, more suitable to the new land in which they were; that their reserve stores of provisions had to be issued as well as their ammunition, etc.; that each battalion had to complete its stock of supplies, collecting mules, bridles, harness, baggage etc., that the animals had to be numbered and shod, which last operation required time, men, forges and hard work,—the highest number of mules which could be shod at the five forges, being a hundred a day; that watering these animals was a lengthy difficult matter, not so much owing to their number as to the scarcity of men to lead them, and the small number of and wide distances between the springs or the drinking-troughs; that the various materials and provisions had to be separated and set in order, and arrangements made for carrying them to their respective storehouses; that the clearing of the quays was a long and laborious matter; and that, finally, so great a mass of unfinished work was accumulated, that while one operation was being carried out, another was necessarily abandoned for the time being, owing to the limited means at their disposal, (cranes, quays, barges, men, etc.)."

By degrees some appearance of order began to emerge from chaos. Barracks, new storehouses, sheds etc. were built; the hospitals, which had accommodation for only 300 men, were added to until almost 1,800 sick and wounded could be taken in,—they became in fact six times their ordinary size, and this was proved by subsequent experience to be but little more than sufficient. In this estimate was included the old hospital ship "Saati": and besides these hospitals two large and two small infirmaries were established. Yet all these buildings formed in reality a very small allowance;

even calculating that the campaign had ended in a few months, as apparently was expected, this arrangement, only making preparation for some 3,000 sick and wounded (say 1,800 in hospital and 1,200 in the infirmaries), was hardly sufficient when compared with the results obtained in other wars.

As a general rule the battalions were only detained two or three days at Massowah; the batteries perhaps a day longer in order to rest their mules thoroughly, and have them shod. As each detachment stepped on shore the officer in command was handed a ticket telling him where he was billeted.

A British soldier would be astonished if he were offered the pay and food that is given to his Italian brother-in-arms. The latter receives two pence a day; while at Massowah we are told he received his "ordinary ration," consisting of bread, meat (gr. 400),[1] macaroni (pasta) or rice (gr. 200), oil and cheese (gr. 15), coffee and sugar, wine (cl. 24), rum (cl. 3), vegetables and various other condiments. If, therefore, the rations are good he may be said to live remarkably well, but we can hardly consider his pay munificent. The officers, belonging to the more numerous detachments continued to have their meals on board the ship by which they had come, and their rate of messing would astonish most English regiments,—it amounted to 3 lire and 50 centimes, or about 2s. 8d., per day.

The march to the front. When the troops started on their march every endeavour was made to lighten the load they carried, only what is included in the Italian "personal equipment" being permitted. Boots, a blanket and a few

[1] Gr. 453 = 1 lb.

etceteras were taken, all of them being rolled up in a small tent which was worn like a shoulder-belt; but even these articles when united to the ordinary supply of cartridges, the rifle, bayonet, haversack [1] and water bottle were found too heavy for that hot climate. The men complained particularly of the tent's weighing upon their chest. A special kit, says Signor Mantegazza, ought to have been devised for marching in the Italian colony, where the climate differs so widely from that of the mother country. Is not this an idea that applies equally to our own army whose duty it is to fight in every known portion of the earth?

Every officer of the Italian force, except the subalterns, was mounted,—an arrangement that is open to criticism, especially in a mountainous country; but it must be remembered that the captains are each in command of a company of 250 men, so that the fact of being mounted would greatly assist them.

As regards provisions,—a short notice must be allotted to these, before we quit a somewhat monotonous, though all-important subject.

Most of the eatables already named, when describing the daily ration of the Italian soldier, from the allowance of meat down to the onions and the rum, were supplied by contract with civilians. The grain for the most part came from Italy, but the consumption of meat so far out-ran the supply that a cargo of oxen was bought in Bombay; 8,211 head sailed for Massowah and landed there on February 10th, these Indian cattle being found far cheaper than those brought from Italy.

[1] Tascapane (bread pocket).

Of ice, which is a matter so important in hospitals, there seems always to have been more than enough, owing to the efforts of the Neapolitan Society, who turned out a splendid supply as regards both quantity and quality, in fulfilment of a contract with the Government, by which, for 4,000 lire (about £150) per month, they were bound to meet the demand in all the public services (hospitals, infirmaries etc.). The private consumers, both military and civil, were able to buy it at the rate of 3d. a kilogram (kilogram being $2\frac{1}{10}$ lbs.).

At Massowah, although there is a good supply of water for ordinary purposes, the drinking water is artificially distilled. At Gherar there were three powerful distilling machines, the property of the Government, which were leased to a private firm and produced about 100 barrels of distilled water a day, sold at the rate of about 6 shillings a barrel to the military authorities and about 9 or 10 shillings to the townspeople. It was also kept in reservoirs, and by means of railways the neighbouring towns of Arkico, Monkullo and Saati were supplied with good drinking water. To this arrangement, probably, was due the fact that the Italian army reached Adigrat with only 250 cases [1] of sickness, from all causes, or $1\frac{1}{2}$ per cent, which, after a sea journey and a rapid march, is an extraordinarily good figure.

Many pages of description might be spent over the transport and commissariat difficulties encountered by the Italian army, but such details do not in reality concern the general narrative; they belong to the specialist who is studying a

[1] Baratieri: *Memorie d'Africa.*

particular branch of his profession. Having thus dwelt at some length on the more important divisions of the subject—namely, the eating, drinking, clothing and marching, we may end up by asking why it was that for some days before the great battle of Adowa the Italian army was ill provided with food and other necessaries? What was the cause of their breakdown?

The first and principal cause (excluding accidents) was undoubtedly the lack of time. There existed, of course, an insufficiency of money that would sooner or later have reduced their resources, but as the battle of Adowa was fought on March 1st, that is only two and a half months after the news of Amba Alagi reached Italy, the £750,000 voted would hardly have been completely expended. On this point one cannot do better than quote what has been said by Signor Vico Mantegazza in his book, "L'Assedio di Macallé."

"Every man worked, beyond all doubt, in a way that one can scarcely imagine; and to this fact alone it is due that the greater privations and hardships were avoided,—privations attributable to nothing but the lack of preparation, resulting from our not having foreseen, even approximately, the coming events." [1]

Leaving, therefore, these preparations and negotiations in full progress, we may turn once again to the actual scene of hostilities—namely, the beleaguered fortress of Macalle.

[1] Those who read Mr. Wylde's book "Modern Abyssinia" will see that he considered the Italians very "happy-go-lucky" in their work at Massowah. He did not, however, see them until some weeks after the battle of Adowa, by which time all danger from Menelik had vanished, and they were probably suffering from a reaction.

CHAPTER VI

THE SIEGE OF MACALLE

Position of Macalle—Fort on the height of Enda Jesus, built by Toselli—News of the disaster of Amba Alagi—Galliano takes command—Weakness of the fort—December 9th, enemy sighted—Defences constructed—Partini goes to the enemy's camp—December 20th, first shot fired from the battery—January 7th, 1896, siege begins—Successful day for the garrison—January 8th, the great attack on the fort that lasts till January 11th—January 8th, water supplies lost—The 9th, Shoans repulsed—10th, attempt to regain water fails—11th, Maconnen leads the supreme effort—12th to the 21st, blockade—15th, the Jus Bashi's dream—The end.

In the heart of Tigré, at the western corner of the province of Enderta, and a few miles only from the English road, is situated the ancient and important city of Macalle, the capital of Abyssinia in the days of the Emperor John. In Europe it would be called a dilapidated old village, for it consists only of a small collection of tucul and a few ruins about which hangs the atmosphere of former greatness; but, nevertheless, it is endowed with a very real importance as being the market town of a country sufficiently fertile to provide food for even a large Shoan army, and as forming a suitable base from which to attack either Abyssinia or Erythrea; it is the Ladysmith of the Adowa campaign (if such an anachronism is permissible). In former wars, too, the little town had already gained celebrity, for it was from Macalle that there started forth in 1876 the horde of Abyssinians who destroyed the Turco-Egyptian army of Prince Hassan at Gura; it was here that Ras Alula planned the campaign of destruction against Saati, which ended in the massacre of the Italians at Dogali, and from here, finally, that the Emperor John started to lose both prestige and power in the fruitless expedition against the fortified Italian camp at Saati.

It stands in a hollow, whose greatest diameter is about a mile and a half, surrounded by mountains, on one of which (to the South-East of Macalle) is the old church of Jesus (Enda Jesus). This church, together with its graveyard, was turned by the Italians into a fort, the tombstones being broken up and fitted together to form the outer walls, during the few weeks between October 18th and December 7th (the date of Amba Alagi), when speed and cheapness were the only hope of safety.[1]

This small fort, therefore, only some 700 metres or 770 yards in circumference, commands on the North-West the village of Macalle, and on its South dominates another village—namely, that of Enda Jesus (so called after the church). On the other hand, in spite of its high position (2,220 metres above sea-level), it is commanded from the ridge of Mount Gargambessa on the North (2,235 metres), a ridge that in parts is not more than 1,050 metres from the walls of the fort. It was therefore evident from the first, that

[1] Captain Moltedo relates that, returning one night to his quarters a stone gave way under his foot and he fell into a grave; so hastily was the work done.

if the enemy could establish themselves on these heights, they would have a very good chance of silencing the Italian artillery and then, at their leisure, reducing the fort to a ruin.

On October 18th, shortly after Debra Aila, the work began under the direction of Toselli, and proceeded with all the energy that usually characterised that officer. On November 24th he was ordered southward,—an advance which soon afterwards led to his death at Amba Alagi,—but in those five and a half weeks he had done wonders; he had made plans of the whole fort, completed the wall round it (it still required the parapet), begun the powder-magazine, had half finished a blockhouse on the northern ridges, and had obtained leave to keep all the ammunition belonging to the regiments that retired northward after Debra Aila, thereby securing a store of (in all) 600 rounds per gun and 250,000 rifle cartridges. On the highest point of the hill, where the church stood, at a level of 230 metres, or 10 metres above the centre of the fort, he had established four mountain guns[1] under command of Captain Moltedo; the little plateau being protected by the stout walls of the old church, which were not of native work, but built with large blocks of stone by the Portuguese adventurers who freed Abyssinia from the Mussulman yoke several centuries before. His difficulties had been great; he had few resources beyond those that he made for himself; he dared not quarrel with the priests, who nevertheless refused

[1] Franconi's section did not arrive until after the battle of Amba Alagi.

to give up their holy ground to be profaned by Mohammedans unless paid for it,—the occupation of the church cost him 1,000 Thaler, as well as the promise of building them a new place of worship. He was handicapped by the paucity of white men, and, last but not least, by orders to economise.

During the fortnight following his departure the work continued to progress steadily, each day bringing its usual round of toil, varied only by the arrival on December 3rd of General Arimondi, who took up his quarters in the Negûs's palace,[1] and of Lieutenants Bodrero and Manfredini, both of them in an agonized frame of mind lest they should reach Toselli's column too late for the fighting. These young officers came and departed, and, on the 6th, General Arimondi started on his march for Afghol without any interruption being made in the daily routine. On the 7th, the day of the battle, smoke was observed to be rising

[1] This Palace was built for the Emperor John by a Piedmontese carpenter named Giacomo Naretti, who is, I believe, still alive. In 1876 Naretti went to Abyssinia with his brother (a photographer) and some artisans, under the auspices of a Greek; the others soon came home, but he remained there, found favour with the Emperor John, became one of his advisers, and married the daughter of a German traveller by an Abyssinian woman. This palace was one of his chief works, and in it he placed a throne, which he informed the Emperor was an authentic copy of that belonging to the Negûs's ancestor King Solomon. Toselli sat on this throne on November 20th when he was receiving the native chiefs after the ceremony of hoisting the Italian flag over the newly completed walls of Macalle.

When the Italians occupied Massowah Naretti came home, curious to relate, a poor man. He had amassed little, for it was power he loved and not money.

above Amba Alagi, but beyond casual conjectures, no further interest was aroused during the day. At midnight, however, Captain Moltedo, was awakened by the far-off cries from the women's quarters, and, as his senses returned to him, he became aware that it was the long strident "keen" with which Abyssinian women bewail the dead.

"What is the matter there?" he asked the sentry nearest to his tucul.

"I don't know," he replied; "first they have been singing, then they were dancing, and now they are crying. Some one must be dead!"

A few minutes later Moltedo distinctly heard a man dashing down the path that led to the camp of the Ascari. The sentry challenged him as he ran; it was a Somali of the 4th Battalion (Toselli's).

"The noise in the camp continued to increase. While I was thinking of dressing to find out the reason of this unusual commotion, I heard some one come up panting, and fall down almost in front of the door of my tucul; then he said in Arabic to the sentry who ran up: 'All dead.'

"I put on my overcoat and boots, without anything else, and went out of the tucul; scarcely had I reached the threshold than I saw on the ground an Ascaro without his tarbush, disfigured by sweat and dust, in an artillery overcoat of which the right sleeve was missing, having been cut off to uncover a large wound on the arm, from which the blood was still running. Around him all the men belonging to the guard were standing, pouring out a flood of questions, to which he replied only by disjointed words.... 'Anghera.... Manfredini.... Toselli.... Scala'....

"'What is the matter?' I asked.

"'Salaam Lieutenant.... the Abyssinians are here.... they will arrive shortly.... the Ascari of the 4th.... all dead.... Major Toselli dead.... Anghera dead.... Manfredini dead.... Scala dead.... cullu, cullu (all, all).'

"I felt the blood beginning to run cold in my veins.

"'How? when? Tell us.'

"'This morning.... the Abyssinians were many,.... many of them died, but the others came on.... the battery fired.... but the Abyssinians kept coming up.... Uh! how many there were.'

"'What section do you belong to?'

"'Manfredini.'

"'Did you see him?'

"'Yes.... dead!'

"'And Scala?'

"'Dead!'[1]

"'And Major Toselli?'

"'Dead!'"

Such was the first announcement of the disaster of Amba Alagi, tidings of which very soon spread all over the garrison. For a few moments the officers were slightly dumfounded by being suddenly awakened to hear such news; some of the men were going about crying for their friends who had been killed, and the darkness added, of course, to the difficulty of the situation, but the Ascari, in the majority of cases, picked up their rifles quietly and stood by awaiting orders. The most alarming report was that which turned

[1] This was a mistake; Scala was not dead, merely wounded and a prisoner.

out afterwards to be untrue, namely, that General Arimondi's force had been overwhelmed with the rest.

Soon the Major's orders were carried all over the fort, and every officer was at his post, placing his men to the best advantage,—not that it seemed of any use; for what could two companies and two guns do in a fort intended for more than twice their number, and so incomplete as not yet to have even the beginning of a parapet? Captain Moltedo tells us that, as he stood between his two guns and reflected on the death of so many friends, on the annihilation, as he believed, of a force of 4,000 men, on the near approach of the enemy and their future devastations after they had disposed of the fort, "his head seemed to go round like a reel." He did not, however, forget to remind the Major that two more guns under Lieutenant Franconi were on their way from Adigrat, and would shortly be surrounded by the rebellious peasants. The Major sent a messenger off at once to hasten their march and they afterwards arrived in safety.

Very soon, fortunately, the greatest source of anxiety was removed by the arrival of Lieutenants Bodrero and Bazzani, who were able to give them every detail of the disaster and to reassure them as to the safety of General Arimondi's column: great as the disaster was, it was not quite so terrible as the first panic-stricken natives had supposed.

It is from this night that the siege of Macalle begins, and is dated in official documents. There was now, as far as the Italians knew, nothing to stay the victorious Shoans from advancing on Adigrat before any preparations had been made to repel them. The small unfinished fort lay in their path; it was determined to garrison it in the hope of delaying, or dividing the invading swarms. Surrounded by the thousands and thousands of half-savage tribesmen, it was to stand out as "the advanced sentinel" of the Italian colony, and by this name Galliano's men proudly called themselves during the next 45 days. [1]

At 4.30 a.m. General Arimondi's force arrived, almost at an end of its marching power, and the distress amongst the women became terrible at finding only 300 survivors out of Toselli's force of 2,150; "they all came down and all wept.... with glassy eyes they looked at their poor tucul.... they looked towards Amba Alagi and then.... began again to cry out and to call 'Guaitai, Guaitai,' [2] to tear their hair, and to beat their feet on the ground, accompanying the cadence with a monotonous crooning.....

"From the side of the fort there entered a group of Ascari who were accompanying the wounded.... their friends were supporting them.... and one wife and sister, a short distance away, recognised in that group the husband.... the brother.... whom they were already mourning as dead. They ran to meet him with open arms and embraced him, greeting with the 'elelta' (cry of rejoicing) their brave.... unfortunate. In several cases a brother found his brother.... a son his father.... a touching sight that drew tears to my eyes, and one that I shall never forget in all my life." [3]

* * *

[1] The advisability of defending Macalle has been discussed on pp. 149 to 151.

[2] Calling their husbands.

[3] Signor Vico Mantegazza: *L'Assedio di Maccalé.* At the time of the siege Captain Moltedo was only a Lieutenant.

When General Arimondi handed over the command of the fort to Major Galliano, the following were the chief works that remained to be constructed. A parapet; still some 70 metres of the wall (according to Lieutenant Partini's official account,—Captain Moltedo says it was completed before Toselli left); the banquettes, and the ramps, the covered paths to the water (that turned out to be useless), and the defensive traverses within the fort to prevent the Ascari from being taken in rear, or enfiladed by fire from the high ground. These were merely the chief requirements, so it is evident that when General Arimondi left the fort, there was still much to be done before it was in a condition to undergo a siege.

Two questions stand out above all others as showing the entire want of preparation on the part of the Italians: the first is their lack of ammunition, and the second is the question of their water supply. It might perhaps be urged that ammunition appeared to be sufficient, as General Arimondi did not anticipate a long siege; this of course is true, but according to the official figures the garrison had only 300,000 cartridges in all,—250,000 in the magazine and 50,000 distributed amongst the men; they began the siege with less than 300 rounds per man! It may be imagined how their power must have been crippled by fear of throwing away a shot.

The lack of water can scarcely by any possible argument be justified. The whole supply of liquid for drinking, washing, or for any other purpose was obtained from two streams, one of them on the South of the fort, only 80 metres from the wall, but out of reach of their fire owing to the

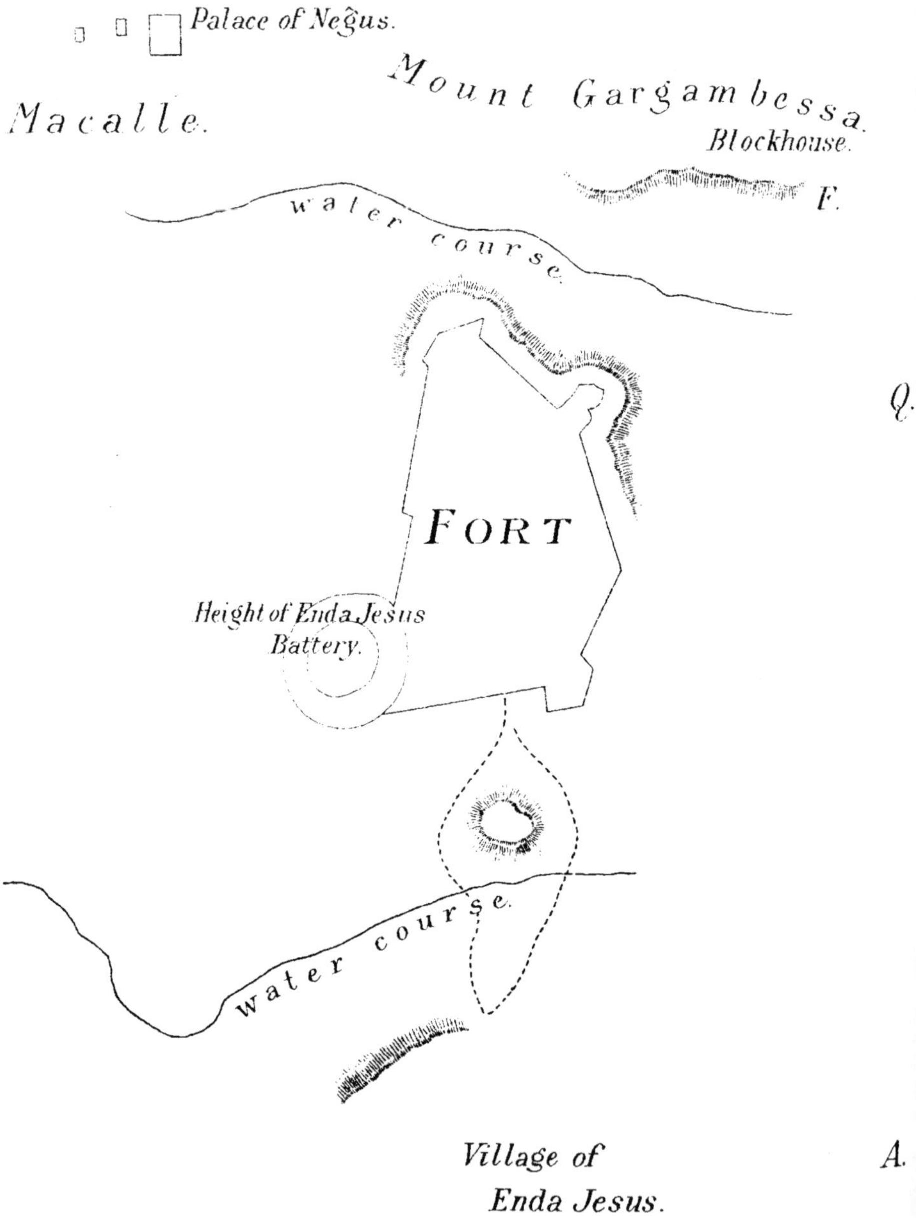
Palace of Negus.
Mount Gargambessa.
Macalle.
Blockhouse.
F.
water course.
Q.
FORT
Height of Enda Jesus
Battery.
water course.
Village of
Enda Jesus.
A.

Face p. 187.

precipice along which it ran; the defenders from their parapet could not prevent an enemy from seizing it, but the enemy, if they took the village of Enda Jesus, could prevent the garrison from reaching the water. The other rivulet, on the north, ran along the slopes of Mount Gargambessa, about 200 metres from the walls. This was the larger of the two, and it was chiefly with a view to its defence that the blockhouse had been built, for it could not be commanded from the walls of the fort. Toselli, of course, had perceived the vital importance of these two streams, but he had relied on occupying the blockhouse and thus having free access to the water on the North; about that on the South he did not care, for it had only a small and uncertain flow.

There was, therefore, absolutely no doubt that unless the blockhouse could be completed and defended, the water supply was at the mercy of the enemy, and the fort would become untenable; so that it would have seemed only natural for some kind of estimate to be made of the number of men required to hold both fort and blockhouse. This appears never to have been done. No sooner had General Arimondi left Macalle than Major Galliano began, so far from completing the blockhouse, to destroy it, because he had not enough men for its permanent occupation. In place of the supplies obtainable from the stream, he began to construct a reservoir within the fort itself. This reservoir, together with all the barrels and vessels of various kinds which he could collect, were in the end only sufficient to keep the garrison supplied for eleven days, and most of the animals died of thirst. So it may fairly be argued that when these

1,190 men[1] were left at Macalle, they were in reality relegated to an impossible position, the more so as according to all probabilities they might easily have been attacked on the 9th of December before the reservoir was even begun, whereas owing to the slowness of the Shoans they saw no serious fighting until the 7th of January ('96), a month later.

It is true that the decision to leave a garrison in Macalle was necessarily taken in very great haste by General Arimondi, and with the hope of returning to its relief at the earliest opportunity; but this is merely another way of saying that no forethought had been exercised as to his movements in case of a defeat.

Major Galliano did his best. He made a spirited little speech to his officers, reminding them of the honour which had been reserved for them in defending this extreme outskirt of the colony. He told off one company for each front, placed a guard in the blockhouse (ordering Paoletti to destroy one part, and to undermine the remainder as a death-trap for the enemy), and another in the village of Enda Jesus so as to protect temporarily both springs. Traverses were begun, and a parapet was built up of sacks filled with earth, or when these failed, as they soon did, of sacks filled with corn and oats. The tucul outside the fort were destroyed so as to give a free field to the rifle fire, and distances were measured. During the night small outposts were placed in the plain, at distances varying from 1,000 to 1,500 metres.

[1] 1,000 of these were natives; 155 fugitives from Amba Alagi turned up before the end of the siege, which brought the numbers up to over 1,300, including the wounded.

On the 9th, only two days after Amba Alagi, while all were busy, some of the enemy's cavalry were suddenly sighted in the plain to the South. Many of the garrison being outside the fort at their various duties, it was a moment of great anxiety for Major Galliano, who happened to be on the high ground of Enda Jesus where the artillery was posted. "Bugler, sound the fall in!" he shouted furiously; and very soon the garrison was ready with rifles and guns loaded. But it was a disagreeable incident, for had the enemy really intended an attack, the fort would not have been sufficiently advanced to resist.

Within the walls every officer fortified his post to the best of his ability, so that no detail should be overlooked; while in the centre of the fort Galliano had a strong traverse built from East to West, to protect the defenders of the northern parapet from being hit in the back by dropping bullets from the high ground about the village Enda Jesus, or the defenders of the southern parapet by those from Mount Gargambessa. Along the side walls there were small piles of sacks (three or four metres apart) between the men, so as to prevent their being enfiladed.

The accessory defences were due to the energy of Lieutenants Luccio and Paoletti; "the first that came into being were those on the southern side of the fort, with a width of about 3 metres, and extending 20 metres to the right and left of the path which leads from the southern entrance to the village of Enda Jesus; here at a distance of perhaps 30 metres from the fort, hundreds of little stakes were planted in the ground, jutting upwards perhaps 30 centimetres, (almost a foot) and divided by a space of little more than 20 centimetres (about 8 inches). They formed a very thick network, such that a man could not cross it except slowly and with difficulty under the fire of our front,—and not only this, but he would be in continual danger of stumbling and falling on the sharp points of the stakes. On the path itself, at the height of the network of stakes, was placed a 'chevaux de frise'[1] as a moveable door."

At either end of this band of pointed stake-work, began the ordinary entanglements, forming a thick hedge of wire (stretched from the top of one post to the foot of the next) all round the fort, at the distance of 20 or 30 yards from the walls. This was merely the regulation defence to be found in every drill book, but the Italian officers invented a fresh one, for the special benefit of the barefooted Abyssinians,—namely, that of planting sharp bottle-ends between the stakes on the south side, and all along the wire entanglements and the wall. This device, which they appeared to consider new in military matters, was probably a mistake; it entailed, they say, breaking up some hundreds of flasks and bottles. How very much better to have filled them with drinking water, and fastened them down until the siege was well on its way; the allowance per soldier during the last eleven days was only half a litre (less than a pint), so that each bottle might have held enough to supply a man for two days.[2]

[1] A horizontal axle traversed by pointed iron stakes at right angles to one another and to the axis, which may either be fixed or made to revolve, or the whole may rest on the ground on two series of points.

[2] There may of course have been some reason that prevented this being done, but it is not apparent.

On the evening of the 11th Major Galliano sent for Lieutenant Moltedo, who was in command of the Artillery, and ordered him secretly to lay a mine, connected with the powder-magazine so as to blow up the fort if necessary. If the garrison were reduced owing to want of food or water, he intended to march out and endeavour to cut his way through the besiegers; but if the enemy made their way into the fort he meant to blow up the whole place; "At the right instant," he said, "at the last moment, we will all fly into the air together."

* * *

From the 14th December to the 19th was a period during which a good deal of "sniping" occurred between the Italian outposts, the rebel peasants, and the Shoan raiders; but no serious fighting. On the 13th letters had come from Ras Maconnen which were forwarded to Adigrat, and on the 16th the order came from there to send a trustworthy officer to treat with the Ras. Many amongst the small group in Macalle (most of them young, and all of them ambitious) were the efforts made to obtain Major Galliano's nomination for this honourable employment, until it was pointed out to them that the post of danger was in the fort and not out of it. The chief duty of such an officer would of course be to renew the peace negotiations simply in order to gain time,—for Italy did not mean to make peace until Amba Alagi was revenged,—but it was unnecessary to publish this fact, as they did, before the cessation of hostilities, for the Italian newspapers are said to be assiduously studied at Addis-Abeba. On the 18th

Lieutenant Partini was sent to meet Ras Maconnen, who received him with every courtesy and allowed him to dine and sleep with Lieutenant Scala, the wounded artillery officer taken prisoner at Amba Alagi. On the 19th he returned to Macalle, where he was almost overpowered with questions as to Scala's experiences, the enemy's strength etc. He was able to give full particulars of Toselli's last fight, and estimated the force of Ras Maconnen at 25,000 riflemen, but—a characteristic Abyssinian touch—without artillery except the two pieces taken at Amba Alagi, for apparently the Negûs would not entrust his beloved guns even to the most faithful of his Ras. On the 20th Partini returned to the Abyssinians, taking a box of linen etc. for Scala.

While both sides were thus making half-hearted attempts at negotiation, the small garrison were surprised on the 19th to see an enormous column of infantry and cavalry filing past them amidst a cloud of dust, at a distance of only about three miles. These were Maconnen's men moving to their quarters at Gargambur about nine or ten miles north of Macalle. As his men formed the advanced guard of the Shoan army, their movement betokened a corresponding change of position on the part of the main body; Macalle was now surrounded by the army of the Negûs and cut off from Adigrat.

On the 20th the first cannon shot of the siege was fired by Lieutenant Moltedo; some scattered horsemen had been manœuvring about the plain, evidently aiming at inflicting loss on several small detachments of Ascari who were outside the fort, and, as their numbers were seen to be rapidly increasing, the alarm was at once sounded, and the Ascari retired at full speed; but the enemy continued to advance, endeavouring to cut off the guard in the village to the South, of whose strength they doubtless had accurate information. They did not, however, appear to know that death was hovering about the ground over which they were passing, for the four guns on the height of Jesus were loaded and the distances to the spot where the enemy rode had been measured out and marked down. Suddenly the whole group opened out, and with loose reins dashed towards the fort at full gallop.

"Second Section—Fire!" shouted Moltedo, and two shots crashed out, and two projectiles lit amongst the advancing horsemen.

"First Section—Fire!" Two more lit in the very centre of the group, and several men and horses rolled over on to the plain, whilst a loud "Hurrah!" arose from the Ascari lining the walls, who turned every man of them towards the batteries, waving their tarbushes and rifles. The enemy wheeled about, scattered right and left, and galloped away at full speed: in all thirteen shots were fired at them before they got out of range.

After this the fighting assumed a more serious character. On the 23rd there was a sharp engagement between a centuria under Lieutenant Giusto and some rebels supported by Shoans, in which Giusto had the best of the encounter. On the same day the outposts captured one of their own spies, a suspected man of a type probably common enough amongst those employed by the Italians on their secret service. He had been entrusted with a note (fortunately in cypher) to the Governor, which he at once took to the Shoan camp, at the same time giving the enemy full information as regards the strength of the fort etc., and when captured he was actually on his way back to gain fresh details for them. The Court Martial of course condemned him to be shot, but then, as he was being led out closely bound to the place of execution, they offered him his life if he would tell them certain points about the Shoans that were of special importance. Although within two paces of the newly-dug trench, he refused to say a word, even to ask for pardon, and died bravely like a faithful—spy.

* * *

The period of the siege between December 20th and January 7th may be shortly passed over; its chief events were the continued negotiations through Partini, and the visit of Mozzetti to the enemy's camp. He was the only doctor in Macalle, and being a very able man, the Abyssinians asked that he should be allowed to attend one of their Ras, Mangasha Atikim, who had been injured by a fall from his horse; so amidst friendly suggestions that he had better doctor as many of the enemy as possible, Mozzetti departed and performed the service with a success that seems to have earned their gratitude.[1] During this fortnight the Italians burnt the village of Macalle and the houses on Mount Gargambessa, having found supplies of arms concealed in some of

[1] Before he left, Mangasha Atikim told him that until he got to know Lieutenant Scala, he had had so bad an opinion of the Italians that he had given orders to shoot any that might be taken prisoners; but that now he regarded Scala as a friend; "and to you," he added, "who after Amba Alagi, so generously came to attend to me, I shall always remain grateful."

them by the peasants. The church was the only building in the village left standing, for they had every intention of respecting its sanctity, but before it could be prevented their Mohammedan Ascari seized this splendid opportunity of showing religious zeal by sacking a Christian place of worship. Amongst the arms discovered were 400 old Portuguese blunderbusses and guns, many of them having barrels inlaid with silver and some even with gold: what a splendid find for a collector would these old weapons have been! Unfortunately, a large number were of necessity condemned to be destroyed; the best of them, however, were saved, but it seems to be uncertain where they have since been taken.

It is on January 7th that there begins the period of serious fighting and close blockade which continued until the end—namely, the 20th of that month. The garrison were already aware of Menelik's arrival, both through their spies and by the altered tone of Ras Maconnen, who after asking in somewhat haughty terms for Lieutenant Partini's return to the Shoan camp, had sent to Major Galliano a second note that ran more or less as follows: "I have not come to make war on a little fort such as you command; we are many, and have no fear of your guns. Remember Amba Alagi and the end of Toselli; give over the fort to me and do not let us spill blood uselessly. I will consider the question of having you accompanied as far as Massowah, and of sending your baggage there. I know that you have been at some expense to send me a doctor and medicines, let me know how much the whole thing costs and I will send you the money." Pride goeth before a fall; it was an insolent letter,—but the Ras was irritated by Galliano's refusing to let Partini go to him.[1]

January 7th, at 9 o'clock, the enemy were observed to be moving on the plain to the South East, and by 10 a.m. several tents had made their appearance, amongst which was a red one,—the colour that belongs to the Negûs alone,—pitched at only 6,500 metres from the fort; for Menelik knew not only the number, but even the extreme range of the Italian guns. It being New Year's day according to the Abyssinian calendar, nobody supposed that they would attack until the following morning, but very soon some of their horsemen, followed by infantry, were seen moving forward from the South towards the village of Enda Jesus, in which the guard of about 30 men under Lieutenant Basile was stationed; by 10.15, according to the official narrative, a brisk fire had been opened all along the line. Very soon the guard and the small outposts (piccoli posti) began to retire in an entirely unaccountable manner, and Galliano in a rage shouted to his bugler, "Bugler, sound 'Guard halt.'" But the Ascari were, as a matter of fact, being outnumbered by the Shoans, some 600 of whom, invisible from the fort, were creeping forward, taking splendid cover. Nevertheless, the guard halted, and running into one of the houses

[1] Galliano had replied to his first letter, that he would not allow Partini to go unless he knew the reason for the request; that if the request seemed to him just, he would send him when a suitable guard of honour under a chief of importance arrived from the Shoans to escort him. This probably irritated Maconnen, who had wanted Partini to grace the arrival of the Negûs. The text of his reply is taken from Moltedo, *L'Assedio di Maccalé.*

of the village, opened fire from the windows. By this time the artillery would have been able to render them some assistance, but Galliano refused to allow a shot to be fired, owing to the smallness of their supply of ammunition. Very soon, therefore, the guard was again constrained to retire, and Galliano half-convulsed with fury, for he had not yet seen the main bulk of the enemy, covered as they were by the houses, again shouted "Bugler, sound 'Guard halt, and fire'"; it was a very unpleasant position for Lieutenant Basile.

The matter was soon settled by the enemy's dashing into the village, and at the same time opening with their artillery; the guard therefore continued its retreat, but it did so slowly, still firing. And now at last, from the fort the Ascari gunners, sighting at 1,050 metres (1,155 yards), sent some shots through the houses, driving the Abyssinians out of them like ants from an ant-heap, and at once silencing their guns. Had it not been for the shortness of ammunition the village might have been retaken, but as Basile was still holding the southern water supply it was thought better to rest content with this.

At 11.15, while this action was still in progress on the South, the enemy were also pressing forward on the northern front from the heights of Gargambessa, lines of almost invisible skirmishers creeping and running towards the block-house where Jus-bashi Selecca Agurgia (native Lieutenant) was stationed with orders to kill as many as he could, and then retire, setting light to the fuse of the mine. Although it was almost certain that the block-house could not be held, the Ascari fired coolly and steadily at the enemy as he came on, gradually working his way forward until he arrived within about 100 yards of them. The final combined rush was about to begin, when the artillery from the fort suddenly opened fire, and at the third shot got their distance. For a moment the Shoans hesitated, and before they could recover, Selecca Agurgia had escaped, and was in safety; the whole plan had been exceedingly well carried out.

Within the fort there was indescribable anxiety lest he should not have found time to fire the fuse, for if the block-house remained intact, it might become very valuable to the enemy. The Ascari were all watching with bated breath. "Lieutenant Paoletti, who had given the instructions to the Jus-bashi, was on thorns, because he did not see the block-house blow up; the Abyssinians were increasing.... A cloud of smoke and dust shot out from the redoubt, and the report was heard as far as the fort.... two or three Abyssinians were hurled upwards into the air.... I saw them as they were falling to the ground again.... the Jus-bashi had carried out his order.

"A 'hurrah' came from the whole fort.... the Ascari waved tarbush and rifle, continuous groans, clapping of hands, and hissing greeted the Abyssinians who were retiring behind the heights. I proceeded to follow the enemy with a few well-timed shots." [1]

The honours of the day rested, so far, entirely with the Italians; they had been fairly successful on both North and South, and the Jus-bashi was now able to re-occupy the remains of the block-house. But at one o'clock the attack was renewed from the South East (A.) and the Shoan

[1] Guido Moltedo, *ib.*

artillery opened fire at a range of 4,500 metres (4,950 yards), to which no reply could be made, as the Italian guns only carried 3,850 metres (4,235 yards). Moltedo buried the trail of his gun-carriage in the ground and fired some shots at the extreme range, but they were distinctly seen to strike about 800 metres short, so the attempt was given up. At the same time two more (quick-firing) Shoan guns opened from the heights north-east (Q.), inflicting some loss in the main body of the fort; it was obvious that the Italian pieces were both outnumbered and outranged,—and it was perhaps the more bitter that the guns on the North East were those taken from Toselli's force at Amba Alagi! The position in the fort, especially in the artillery redoubt of Enda Jesus, was becoming, if not critical, at all events far from pleasant, during this unequal artillery duel. But the black Sudanese gunners stood well to their work; dusty and perspiring they moved their guns from one place to another, regardless of the shrapnel bursting overhead, with a shout of "Allah" or "Mohammed" at each heave; as the smoke of their own fire blew round them they watched the effect of the shot, every hit being greeted with "Taib! Taib!" (Good! Good!).

Their activity began, after some time, to bear fruit. Regardless of the long-range fire on the South, which several times struck the old Portuguese wall of the church, they turned their guns on to the two northern pieces and soon drove them from the field, after which they did some good work amongst the enemy's infantry. Then the Shoans on the South East, finding they could get no good results from their long-range guns, withdrew, and at six in the evening the engagement ceased without further event. The Italian officers were in high feather that evening, and there was indeed every reason to rejoice; they had inflicted serious loss on the Abyssinians, while their own amounted to only 3 killed and 5 wounded, and above all things, they still held command of the water supply. The Artillery had fired away 174 shots from its very small store, and the outposts were drawn in far nearer to the fort than usual that night, but on the whole it had been a very successful day.

January 8th. On this day the enemy began a most obstinate attempt to take the fort,—an attempt that lasted intermittently by day and by night, until about one o'clock on the 11th January,—a period of over 74 hours' fighting, with few opportunities for rest. To the Abyssinians, who were probably 70,000 strong, this, of course, represented no very great hardship, but for the Italians and Ascari, attacked as they were on all sides at once, the strain on nerve power and general physique became terrible.

"On the morning of the 8th," says Lieutenant Partini in his official account, "the enemy who occupied the heights to the East dug a trench on them; at 8.15 his quick-firing guns began to play from there. At 8.45 the south front was attacked;—the guard on that side was obliged to retire, being commanded by the enemy's artillery occupying the higher ground, and being threatened by a turning movement of their infantry and cavalry. The water supplies were occupied by the enemy, who established himself in the angle of the two gorges, from whence it was found impossible to dislodge him. The fire of artillery and rifles on our front repulsed the attacking infantry.

"They then surrounded the fort with artillery—batteries being posted in five different positions—and continued all day to fire on us, inflicting serious losses, and playing on the powder-magazine, which had to be cleared because the projectiles penetrated into it and burst inside.

"It was not possible to reply to some of the hostile batteries, as our mountain guns did not carry so far as their quick firers."

From this very short account we can see that the Shoans had gained the water supplies on the South,—and in the evening it was found impossible to approach the water on the North, because, although it was not actually surrounded, the Italians dared not risk any losses in reaching it, owing to the smallness of their numbers; but when Partini says that it was impossible to reply to the enemy's guns he differs from Moltedo, who was in command of the artillery. The Shoans were firing from five points, viz., from two in the village (6 guns and 2 machine guns), from the South with 3 guns at 2,200 metres, from the North East (point F.) at 1,200 metres (number of guns uncertain), and from another position north-east at 4,000 metres with 4 guns. It was only the last-named position which outranged the Italian artillery; Lieutenant Moltedo claims to have silenced, at least temporarily, every other gun that came into action.

Nevertheless, the tiny redoubt of Enda Jesus was a dangerous place that day, being bombarded from five different points; one embrasure was hit three times running, and a shell burst between the wheels of a gun, wounding two Ascari and setting fire to some of the sacks.

One thing was certain—that the Shoans, after their successful seizure of the water supplies, had been repulsed in every attack. Nevertheless, the fall of the fort was now merely a matter of time, for the garrison could not fight without water, and they could not retake the streams, as their numbers were too small to admit of any serious losses. From the very first there had been no possibility of their standing a long siege, and henceforth they lived day by day on the vain hope of seeing Baratieri march to their relief,—Baratieri who had long ago decided that this was impossible.

That evening the outposts were placed only just outside the wire entanglements; at 11 p.m. the enemy suddenly attacked them and got as far as the wires, but were then driven back. At 1 a.m. they made another but less important effort; there was little sleep for the besieged that night.

On this day (8th) the enemy's artillery threw 500 projectiles into the fort, and the Italians fired 148; the losses were wonderfully small,—of the Italians, only 1 killed and 4 wounded; of the Ascari, 3 killed and 9 wounded; total of casualties, 17.

January 9th. The prolonged effort of the enemy was continued. From 1.30 a.m. to midday they advanced from various quarters, but were repulsed on each occasion, Galliano's guns making excellent practice. On Mount Gargambessa, about 1,200 yards distant, the Shoans had constructed a small entrenchment faced with stones, but in four shots the Italian gunners made so wide a breach in it, that it was hastily abandoned. Between the hours of two and three in the afternoon, the Shoan attack began to weaken and die away, but at midnight they opened fire vigorously on all sides. No less than five times during that night the garrison had to repel their attacks; at midnight, at 1.30, at 2.30, at 4.15 and at 5.30 a.m.,—this last engagement continuing until about 10 a.m. on *January 10th*, after which, by way of showing that they were in no way exhausted, the Italians sent out a patrol under a Muntaz (corporal) supported by a centuria, to try and retake the water on the South. But this effort was a failure, for the precipice was occupied by 500 Shoans; and Major Galliano decided to abandon all further attempts in that direction, owing to the losses they would entail amongst the already short-handed garrison.

On the evening of the 9th the first distribution of water was made from the reservoirs, at the rate of half a litre (less than a pint) per man; the officers resigning their share to the Ascari and placing themselves on an allowance of wine from their mess-stores. It was now that the real hardships began. After fighting in the heat and dust all day, and having been under fire all the previous night, an unfortunate Ascaro could only be given one glass of water with which to cool his parched throat; and as the days passed by, this small supply became muddy and yellow, hardly fit to drink; the sufferings of the women and the wounded must have been awful. On the evening of the 9th, the horses and mules which had not been watered for three days, broke their halters and made a dash for the gate that led to the streams; driven back from here with blows and stones they hung about the reservoir where they smelt water. Why these poor beasts were not put out of their agony it is hard to say, but probably Galliano expected to be relieved at any moment, and felt that they must have some animals left to carry the guns. Even allowing for this supposition, it seems an unnecessary piece of cruelty to have kept them alive; but he may have had some other reason of which one knows nothing.

During this day it was found that only 234 rounds of artillery ammunition remained, and the rifle cartridges were also beginning to run low. The two alternatives, imprisonment or death, were coming nearer and nearer; of which, imprisonment, for the Ascari at all events, meant mutilation by the loss of one hand and one foot. Amidst all these anxieties there was only one consolation—namely, that the moral of officers and men remained excellent; that they were still proud of being "the advanced sentinel," and still determined at any cost to keep the Tricolor of Italy flying over Macalle.

January 11th. With this day we come to the final and culminating effort of the Abyssinians to break their way into Macalle by force of arms. These 24 hours represent the 5th consecutive day of fighting, and the third sleepless night through which the little garrison had struggled, although the hopeless impossibility of their task must have been dawning on many of them. It was the most arduous day of all, for two reasons: first, because the Negûs Nagasti had ordered a final and supreme effort to be made; and secondly, because he entrusted it to Ras Maconnen, who was now in disfavour;—he had told Menelik that a few hours' fighting would place the fort in his hands, whereas it had held out victoriously for four days and nights. And so acutely did Maconnen feel the disgrace, that he led his followers time after time to the attack, and exposed himself recklessly throughout that morning wherever the shells were dropping with most deadly precision, in the hope of either restoring his lost prestige or dying a glorious death,—an end that would most undoubtedly have been his, had not old Alula and another Ras finally dragged him away by main force.[1]

The garrisons were, as usual, aroused between the hours of 2 and 3 a.m., but it was not until the time of sunrise—about 5.30 a.m.—that the attack began on their north front. Having succeeded in cutting the conducting wires of some of the fougasses,[2] Maconnen's men, of whom there were no less than 15,000, appear to have thought that they were taking the fort by surprise. Starting from the ditch on the north side, they were allowed by Galliano to reach the wire entanglements before their course was checked. Here a terrible duel took place; the men of Harrar, in some places only twenty yards from the parapet, were hacking at the wires with their heavy swords while a rain of bullets whistled round them from the fort, where "the Ascari had their cartridges between their teeth and between the fingers of the left hand in order to be more ready to load." (A doubtful expedient!) "The smoke of the enemy's rifle fire was being blown by the wind over the fort, and the flag was fluttering in the direction of Amba Alagi." (This was always taken as a good omen by

[1] The letter of Felter, which reached Galliano on the 13th, as quoted by Moltedo.

[2] Partini's official account says the wires of all the fougasses were cut; but this is evidently a general statement accounted for by the extreme brevity of his description.

the Ascari). "A long rumbling crash, deep like that of distant thunder, stopped the fusilade on both sides .... a column of smoke rose slowly above the little terrace (piazzuolo) on the North East, and in a few moments a rain of earth, debris, and small stones falls on the works; a fougasse had burst. The Abyssinians, startled and dumfounded, retired, followed by our fire, but only for a little while; presently they returned in greater numbers and still more furiously to the attack."[1]

The most dangerous element for the defender was undoubtedly the machine guns of the Shoans, which enfiladed the western front both from North and from South.

Near the village of Enda Jesus, a mass of Shoans was also to be seen crowning the various heights, and the Ascari along the southern wall were soon hard at work, supported by the artillery on the redoubt.

"At 7.15 the inside of the fort seemed like a hell; two fronts were attacked, those on the North and South; the machine guns kept up an incessant fire, and our guns thundered. The northern front was in danger, because the enemy was too numerous for us.

"At 7.30 the reserve was called up (about 80 rifles) under command of Lieutenant Partini; the arrival of this reinforcement certainly rendered the enemy less confident, but he continued his fire unabated.

"While from the Enda I was directing the fire against a mass of Abyssinians that was moving off towards the South, Partini arrived at the battery quite breathless.

[1] Moltedo, *ib.*

"'By order of the Major, send a section down below.... Do it quickly, as fast as you can—it's impossible to make head against them—they are too many—Quick! or they'll be in the fort.'

"Lieutenant Franconi, with his section, was sent to support the front in danger."

But hardly had the enemy at the village of Enda Jesus become aware of the movement than they poured forth a hurricane of lead from every available corner, and it was only with considerable difficulty that he got one gun on to the northern and the other on to the north-eastern redoubt.

There, a splendid but terrible sight awaited him. Hundreds and hundreds of Maconnen's men were dashing towards the fort, their dark faces and arms showing up against the bright-coloured silk shirt that an Abyssinian soldier wears on the day of battle. The leaders had already hacked their way through the wire to within a few paces of the wall, and were so close that it was almost impossible to lower the muzzles of his guns sufficiently to reach them without endangering the pieces themselves. At every shot the gun carriages were almost overturned, and seemed as if they would be precipitated on to the ground below. Soon it was found that one of them could no longer be raised or lowered; then a sight was broken off another, and the gun temporarily put out of action. Franconi was presently obliged to withdraw, but his few shots had been of use; the critical moment of the attack had been tided over, and the supreme impetus of the enemy's rush had been shaken; otherwise the Abyssinians would have pressed into the fort over each other's bodies, and on to the very muzzles of the Ascari's rifles.

And now the return of Franconi to Enda Jesus became a difficult matter under fire of the machine guns on the northern ridges. It was here that Carbineer Bianchi distinguished himself; at a time when the guns had been taken to pieces, and although even then it was doubtful whether they could be got into the Enda, owing to the good marksmanship of the enemy, to whom they offered a splendid target, Bianchi had one of them fastened on to his shoulders and amidst a shower of bullets carried it up into the battery. Now these guns weighed 98 kg.—14 stone 9 lbs. each,—so that this was a feat requiring some strength, as well as courage.

The other piece was soon afterwards successfully carried up, and the shelling of the crest of Enda Jesus village was resumed with three of them (one being out of action owing to the sight being broken). The enemy was making a last desperate effort, when one of Moltedo's gun carriages suddenly sprang backward,—its axle had been hit and crushed into atoms by a projectile. It was an ill moment for the gunners, but Furriere Patrono at the head of his squad, brought out a fresh carriage, and, although the manœuvre was both difficult and dangerous under fire, quickly succeeded in remounting the gun. By mid-day the Shoan attack died away, and after six and a half hours' fighting the garrison was able to get some food,—but nothing to drink.

Before they had finished their hurried meal the Abyssinians were on them again, and every officer had to rush away to his post. For half an hour the attack was once more pressed home with indomitable pluck by these semi-savages, who still believed that they could "rush" a scientifically fortified wall in the face of guns and magazine rifles. But this was in reality the last effort; at one o'clock they were retiring, and before 3 p.m. their last column was seen to leave its cover and wend its way up the heights. Now was the chance of the garrison! Unfortunately, they could not avail themselves of it; they could not risk a sortie owing to the losses that it would entail amongst their small numbers, and although their artillery was doing splendid execution amongst the disorganized masses of the enemy, Major Galliano was obliged to order it to cease fire and save its projectiles for a moment when the fort might be in danger.

As regards this day, which was undoubtedly the most trying of any, one can only admit that both sides fought well. The Italian officers were coolness itself, and the Ascari proved once more, if proof were necessary, that they knew how to face both hardship and danger. But what can one say of the Abyssinians? Surely no praise is too high for them. They were not, like the more uncivilized native races, ignorant of the effect of rifle and shell fire, for they had experienced both at Amba Alagi, and they themselves were trained to use both rifles and guns. Yet they rushed to the attack again and again, carrying scaling ladders, endeavouring to cut their way through the wire entanglements, facing the possibility of mines, treating life, in fact, as if it were of no account. The Italians themselves expressed enthusiastic admiration of the courage shown by Maconnen's men. On the northern front many Ethiopians were found dead between the wires and the wall; in one place five men together, with a scaling ladder about 13 or 14 feet long; in another place the body was found (with many wounds still bleeding) of a man who, having cut his way through the wire, had reached the wall and calmly begun to dig under it with a hoe, in order to bring it down. Even the greatest fanaticisms, such as that of Mohammed, have never produced anything finer than this.

The losses in the fort were comparatively light: 2 Italians killed and 1 wounded, 5 Ascari dead and 27 wounded, making a total of 35 casualties. The Abyssinian losses are not known, but a party of Ascari slipped out of the gates that evening and picked up 78 rifles and a great many swords,—although of course they dared not go far, and the chief slaughter among the assailants took place during their retreat.

From that day the Abyssinians gave up their attacks, which was fortunate for the garrison, as they had only enough artillery ammunition left for one more day's fighting. But the news of their success spread far and wide, and reached Baratieri together with a rumour that the water had been regained, and raised the drooping spirits of their friends and relatives, who, in the camp of Adigrat and Adagamus, or at their homes in Italy, were watching the struggles of the little fortress.

* * *

In an old-fashioned English book, the opinion was once actually expressed that Napoleon's defeat at Waterloo was easily accounted for by the fact that he began the battle on a Sunday. Without discussing this question, we may note the curious fact that the Abyssinians are of a similar way of thinking, and never fight on Sundays, or even on feast days, if they can avoid it. The 12th of January, 1896, was a Sunday, so the Ascari had time for complete rest, which was necessary, and for thinking over their position, which was inadvisable and was discouraged by their officers as being dangerous; at various times during the siege their semi-religious meetings had to be broken up and forbidden.

On the 13th there was an alarm and firing, but without result.

On the 14th the rations of water were reduced for the Christians, a little wine being added instead; but the Mohammedans continued on the same allowance. By this time the horses, mules and cows, who had drunk nothing and eaten little for seven days, began to die, and those that remained alive tottered about the fort at night, hanging round the reservoirs in search of water. This incident belongs to the class of horrors which, however disagreeable, should be carefully chronicled in every historical account, so that a fair picture may be presented of what war really means. Had this always been done, there would perhaps not be so many people in the world who, knowing battles only by their trophies, talk and think lightly of a struggle between civilized nations.

On this day while the officers were at mess, a shell came through the door and burst over their heads, fortunately, however, only wounding one of them, and that slightly. It was due probably to Abdallah, the servant of Lieutenant Scala, who had come with a message on the previous day, and, being regarded as a faithful follower, had been received in the mess-room; through him, doubtless, the situation of the officers' mess reached the Shoans, for several shots were deliberately aimed at it.

On that afternoon the sky was overcast, and great hopes were raised of getting water from the clouds; but no rain came. Nevertheless, the spirits of all in the fort remained good: "We will resist while we can," said Galliano, "and then go out to drink. What will happen God only knows!"

On the 15th, a Mohammedan Jus-bashi (Lieutenant) came to Major Galliano and said that Mohammed had appeared to him in a dream, telling him that water was to be found in the centre of the fort: "Let those dig who want to," replied Galliano, "and try for it." So, weary and underfed as they were, the Mohammedans divided themselves into squads, and dug feverishly for two days and two nights calling on Allah and his prophet to help them. They happened, by a piece of peculiar ill-fortune, to light on a rock, but this did not shake their faith; and some of them, had not the siege ended, would in all probability be digging still. Supposing they had chanced to light upon water,—which was by no means improbable,—what a miracle it would have been accounted! Far and wide the news would have travelled amongst the tribes of how Allah had revealed the hidden secrets of the earth to the true believers, by means of his chosen prophet. What a triumph for Mohammed! What a downfall for Christ! A miracle so genuine, and so honestly attested might have gathered hundreds of doubtful Christians back to the fold of Islam. When Captain Moltedo questioned some of them after the siege, he found that they regarded even their non-success as a triumph: "Signor tenente," they said, "you laugh; but your God makes no such revelations to you; if we had continued we should have found water."

On the 17th there was a false alarm that a relief column was in sight,—a fresh disappointment.

On the 19th another false alarm of relief. Captain Moltedo tells us how on that day he watched the distribution of water, which was now running very low. Furriere Patrono was the distributor,—"He had to call each man and woman by name as when 'paying out,'—and to be very careful that they didn't come a second time.

"The women, the Sudanese wives of our gunners, with babies on their arm, were there with their wooden bowls, which they always held over the barrel, in order to catch the drops that fell from the cup of the impartial Patrono.

"How many hands stretched out! how many thirsty people!

"And it was a sight to see with what care they drew back the cup or bowl through that barrier of arms and heads, so that not a drop should be lost! This tiny allowance of foul-smelling, dirty water, yellow in colour, was to them a delicacy. Some drank it in sips, others in one gulp, remarking, perhaps, 'To-morrow Allah will provide;' another, taking the smallest possible steps in order to avoid spilling any of the precious liquid, went off to enjoy it, to sip it beneath his little tucul, perhaps with his wife and children."[1]

It was on this day that a Sudanese gunner,—a man who had returned after Amba Alagi, with a sword cut on the head,—came to Lieutenant Moltedo and said that his wife had been confined; could he have a bottle of water to wash the baby? Even to this man, singled out by his honourable wounds, the favour had to be refused, for the liquid meant life to his fellows.

[1] Moltedo: *L'Assedio di Maccallé.*

Amongst the officers, although the water supply was a constant topic of conversation, they treated it lightly. That day Captain Benucci, who was in command of the distribution, gave out the following announcement: "Gentlemen, there is only water for to-morrow. I have been mistaken in my calculations; the barrels are surrounded with sentries, but the water inside is always diminishing." His speech was received with a chorus of laughter and various proposals. "To-morrow we won't drink anything, and the water of the day after to-morrow we'll drink in two turns." "We've got some Anesone which we'll give to the Abyssinians, and the water to the Mussulmans,—and then Baratieri will certainly arrive. Have you seen that smoke towards Hausien?"

A short time afterwards the rumour went round that a messenger had come into the fort from the Shoan camp, and then, while they were still discussing it, the interpreter came in, trembling with excitement, and summoned them all to the quarters of Major Galliano. They found their commander in his tent, leaning forward with both hands on a map that was spread on the table before him, apparently in a kind of lethargy. On its being announced to him that they were all present, he roused himself, and in a shaking voice addressed them. "Gentlemen, the Government of the King has decided on the surrender of the fort to the Negûs of Abyssinia! To-morrow at mid-day the white flag will be hoisted on the Enda, this being the signal agreed on for the cessation of hostilities, and for the freeing of the water supply. Every commanding officer will let me know how many mules he requires to transport everything,—wounded men, materials and ammunition. We shall march out with the honours of war,—it is the reward reserved to us for having arrested for 45 days[1] the conquering hordes of all Abyssinia!"

This, then, was the end. It was the result of Felter's mission to the Shoan camp,—perhaps the only good result that came of Baratieri's extensive negotiations during the entire course of the campaign: on the whole rather a curious finish to the brave but short life of the "advanced sentinel."

* * *

The following are the official figures relating to the siege of Macalle.

A. *Garrison.*

	20	Officers	Italian.
	13	N.C.O.	"
	150	Privates	"
	1,000	Natives.	
Total . . .	1,183		

There were also in the fort 2 Italian and 3 Greek civilians, and a few Shoan prisoners. The survivors of Amba Alagi amounted, according to Captain Moltedo (non-official figures), to 155, of whom 130 were wounded.

B. *Casualties.*

Italians	killed	7
"	wounded	8
Natives	killed	17
"	died of wounds	6
"	wounded	62
	Total . . .	100

[1] This was only 43 days from December 7th, but the garrison did not leave the fort for 2 more; the siege is always counted as having lasted 45 days, hence probably this slip on the part of Captain Moltedo, in his account of Galliano's speech.

In addition to these numbers, there were 130 wounded men from Amba Alagi, 2 of whom died; so that the garrison, when they marched out, had 200 wounded on their hands. Of the women there were about 100 according to Baratieri.

C. *Ammunition in the Magazine on December 7th* (first day of siege).

Balistite cartridges	200,000
Black powder „	20,000
Remington „	30,000
Rounds for Artillery	800
Extra cartridges	60

Expended during the siege.

Balistite cartridges distributed . . .	152,000
Black powder „ „ . . .	8,000
Remington „ „ . . .	3,000
Artillery—rounds fired	600

"The troops that were garrisoning the fort, or returned there after the battle of Mai Mesghi (Aderat), were not fully supplied with ammunition. It may be estimated that on December 7th there were in distribution 50,000 balistite cartridges. On marching out of the fort all those who carried arms were provided with 120 cartridges (total about 120 thousand). There would therefore have been consumed about 82,000 balistite cartridges (M. 1870/87), 9,000 black powder and 3,000 Remington." Lieutenant Partini's official report.

CHAPTER VII

AFTER MACALLE

MENELIK'S letter—Why he released the garrison—His march to Hausien—Takes cover behind his prisoners—Error of the Italians in not occupying Adowa—The Governor's schemes of defence—His ideas—Those of the Government—The proposed diversion from Zeila—Lord Salisbury's action—Abortive peace negotiations—Mangasha's letters to Queen Victoria, the Sirdar and the Governor of Suakim—Sir Francis Wingate's opinion on Italian affairs.

"FROM the camp of Dolo, 16 Teru, 1888. From the Conqueror of the Lion of the tribe of Judah, Menelik II, named by God King of the Kings of Ethiopia, this comes to his most respected and honoured Majesty Humbert I, King of Italy. The Peace of God be with your Majesty. You desire peace and friendship, and General Baratieri has informed me of this, and I am much pleased. In order to give proof of our Christian faith, as was our desire, we have sent out, with all their belongings, escorted by Ras Maconnen and in good health, those who were in the fort of Enda Jesus, though they were worn out by thirst, hard-pressed, surrounded, and almost trampled under our feet. It would be well to inform us what person your Majesty will name to treat of peace. As for me, it would also be to my interest to make an end of the matter by sending my ambassador."

Such was the announcement sent off by Menelik four days after the white flag had been hoisted over Macalle. It will be observed that the conqueror of the lion etc. writes in a slightly involved style, and employs a calendar that is not in general use. But the question at once arises, why was it that he let the garrison go free? It is a point that has exercised a large number of minds in various countries, and there have not been many who have felt inclined to accept the Negûs's own solution, that he did it "in order to give proof of his Christian faith."

General Luzeux, in his pamphlet, does not hesitate to say that he was paid to do so; the custom of ransoming prisoners still exists amongst the Abyssinians, and he considers it more than probable that the Negûs should have turned the situation to his own profit. It certainly does, at first sight, seem inexplicable that their conqueror should have not only freed Galliano's men, but even have provided them with mules to carry away their belongings, unless he obtained some compensating advantage,—not from the Italian army, but from the Government who knew that the fall of Macalle would raise a storm of anger throughout Italy. Nor could any sensible man blame a minister for such an action; if Menelik was willing to let the garrison go at a reasonable price, the best thing to do was to pay it to him. It was not perhaps a very honourable-sounding solution, but having placed a handful of brave men in an impossible position, it was a duty to save them from either a massacre, or from (perhaps) years of suffering in a semi-barbarous country. It was, in fact, better to pay for these mistakes in money than in lives.

Another suggestion is that the garrison was liberated on the promise of not taking any further part in the war. As the battalion was on the Italian left wing at the battle of Adowa, five and a half weeks later, this idea has a peculiarly venomous ring: to the best of my belief there is no foundation for it whatsoever. [1]

The truth, as regards this matter, will be known with absolute certainty only in the future, but General Baratieri in his Memoirs positively asserts that when the garrison marched out "no other agreement, no other restriction, either verbal or written was proposed, or much less accepted," [2] and one who carefully considers the insecurities that surrounded Menelik will, I think, be inclined to accept this statement of the Governor's. The Negûs most undoubtedly had a very sincere desire for peace. In spite of his recent successes he was in no enviable position; he was quite aware that his enemy was in reality stronger than himself; his food supplies were running short, and he perceived that any march to a flank in search of a new feeding ground would be dangerous for him. He had every reason to distrust more than one of his Ras; any reverse might attach some of his most influential followers to the Italians, who would again be considered the stronger side. He dared not, after his experiences at Macalle, attack the Italians, now over 16,000 strong, in their fortified position at Adagamus; while, on the other hand, he could not long maintain his own army in the field for want of supplies. Unless the Italians attacked him, which apparently they were determined not to do, it seemed as if his invasion might die a natural death: it would probably

[1] Since writing the above I see that Mr. Wylde supports this view. He was in Abyssinia shortly after the end of the Adowa campaign; he does not, however, give his authority.

[2] *Memorie d'Africa*, p. 292.

end in retirement, like that of the Emperor John before Saati. On the other hand, if a treaty were now signed, the victory of Amba Alagi and the fall of Macalle, would ensure him the reputation of having been the victor, whereas the Italians would seem to have sued for a cessation of hostilities after their two defeats; and to a man of peace as Menelik has always been, nothing could be more desirable than to retire from strife with an honourable record against so powerful an enemy. These four considerations,—the lack of provisions, distrust of his Ras, the peaceful temperament of Menelik, added to the risk involved by his being the attacking party, and, above all, the immediate necessity of a march to a flank, may seem vague and unpractical reasons; but the history of the next six weeks brings out irrefutable instances of each of them, proving how very real and present they must have been to his mind.

The release of the garrison, together with a letter stating how easily he could have destroyed it, seemed therefore the best way of placing the Italians under an obligation to him, and opening the way for peaceful negotiations. Moreover, why should he make prisoners of 1,300 men, whom he would then have to feed? How far preferable to make a favour of releasing them! Lastly, he perceived that they would form a splendid cover for his march towards new and unravaged territory, where he could pick up fresh supplies. This latter manœuvre he at once began to carry out with all possible rapidity and secrecy.[1]

[1] De la Jonquière says that it was Maconnen who was paid; that he alone would have raised objections to the release, because by Abyssinian custom, all the prisoners would have

It is about this march of Menelik that General Luzeux says: "It denotes in the mind of that sovereign a real understanding of the affairs of war." Now it has already been explained that for the Shoans to advance along the English road from Macalle, meant eventually running their head against the impregnable position of Adagamus where 16,000 Italians awaited them. It has also been explained that an advance on Adowa was the natural move for them to make, from a political and strategical point of view; as from there they could rouse the population all round Baratieri, and they were, in actual distance, nearer to his stores at Asmara, than he was himself at Adigrat. His communications were seriously threatened if Menelik succeeded in reaching Adowa.

The Negûs set about it in characteristic fashion. On January 24th Galliano's garrison marched out of Macalle, but it was found necessary, according to Menelik, (and in this opinion Felter concurred) to surround them with an escort, —so greatly were the Shoan warriors irritated against them.

belonged to him, as the commander to whom the siege had been entrusted. Also that Felter's influence over him was due to the Ras having negotiated loans with European banks through Felter, and that when the Italian government kindly lodged some hundreds of thousands of francs to his credit at these banks, Maconnen, thankful for being relieved of his debts, withdrew all opposition. Captain De la Jonquière quotes no authority for this information, and simply gives it as a matter of common report.

In this connection it is interesting to read in Major Gamerra's memoir that, while a prisoner in Shoa, he was told that Maconnen was hated by the other Ras because they believed him to have accepted huge sums from Italy.

Maconnen's men were therefore appointed to protect them from the others.

For the first two days both the garrison and its escort pursued its way due northwards towards Adagamus, and on the afternoon of the 27th reached Dongolo, which is almost half-way. There, to their great surprise, they were halted, and compelled to march north-westward towards Hausien, which they reached on the 30th. In this manner they had prolonged their march over several extra days, by making an entirely unnecessary tour to the left.

What was the object of this manœuvre? It was simply a device of Menelik to cover his own march westward; he himself was moving past Hausien on Adowa, and he wished to keep the garrison and its escort as a barrier between his right flank and the Italians. If the latter attempted to fall on him during the march they would first encounter a friendly escort of many thousands, surrounding their own ill-fated battalion; these they would naturally find it difficult to attack. Baratieri had relied on throwing his force against the Shoans, if they attempted this movement, and assailing them so suddenly that they would have no time to escape; but now, although his spies told him of the advance, he was shut out by a thick band of Maconnen's men marching under a flag of truce. He says, indeed, that most of the Italian troops, having only just arrived, were in no very fit condition for such enterprises, and that in any case his lines of communication were not sufficiently established to permit of such a prolongation.[1] But there is no doubt that

[1] It is 23 miles from Adagamus to Hausien, and 37 miles from Hausien to Adowa.

even had they been fully prepared, anything in the nature of a surprise would no longer have been possible.

Menelik was therefore able to establish himself safely at Hausien, where he liberated Galliano's battalion, but kept nine officers and a sergeant as hostages until he had arrived at Gundapta, his final halting-place near Adowa; the whole movement being, as the Italian writers admit, a complete success,—though, as they also say, perhaps not conspicuously redolent of good faith.

General Luzeux, however, undoubtedly lays his finger on a most important point when he says that the Italians ought to have occupied Adowa, and blames them for not having fortified it.[1] It is interesting to find that since he published his pamphlet, this opinion of his is confirmed by a conversation which Captain Moltedo relates, between himself and the Balambaras Uold Emanuel. "The object of the Negûs," said the Balambaras, "was to move into a region where his numerous army could live: towards Agame (the territory round Adigrat), that rich province, it was useless for us to attempt to go, it being too easy for a defender at Adagamus to stop us. Ras Sebath some short time before, at the head of only a few men, contested the pass with Menelik and prevented him from invading it. You can imagine how much more difficult it would have been for us to attack you in that position. No other resource remained open to us but the rich valleys of Faras-Mai (the country about Gundapta), and afterwards those of Adowa. The aim was concealed from the first, which permitted us to gain the

[1] *Vide* discussion of this question of the Adigrat—Adowa line of defence in Part I, Chapter VI, pp. 94—95.

crest of Hausien, from whence we could easily throw ourselves into Faras-Mai. It is many years now that you are in Tigré, but little have you learnt," (his own words) added the Balambaras. "If you had occupied the pass of Hahaile-Lallalai,[1] *the campaign, as far as we were concerned, would have been finished*, for, after exhausting Faras-Mai, we should not have been able to enter the hollow of Adowa, and then, for want of provisions, we should have been compelled to retire. You permitted us to enter and to live. Adowa is rich in water, rich in the abundance of grain, tief, barley etc., and in provisions previously collected there, unknown to you; it is near to Shirè and Tembien, also rich provinces. Adowa was our natural line of retreat through Socota, a road not yet pursued by our troops and therefore with its harvests intact."

As soon as Menelik had entirely accomplished his change of quarters he released the ten hostages,—to their intense relief: it is said that many of the Ras wished to have them shot, but that they were powerfully defended by Ras Alula. Taking advantage of the communications relating to them, the Negûs had, without loss of dignity, repeated his peace-

[1] "A very difficult pass on the watershed of the Tacazze and Mareb, with two tracts of country, Hahaile-Lallalai (high) and Hahaile-Tacbai (low), inhabited by mountaineers who have the reputation of being audacious and brave. After Macalle, while I was a hostage with Ras Maconnen, I was surprised on reaching this pass to hear a continuous fusilade. I enquired as to its cause and they replied it is the brigands of Hahaile who will not allow the soldiers of the Negûs to requisition supplies." Moltedo: *L'Assedio di Maccalé*. This pass is between Hausien and Adowa.

ful overtures; and they ought, one imagines, to have been well received, for General Baratieri found himself, on February 1st, in an unpleasant position. His commissariat and transport were of doubtful efficiency, his troops were unseasoned, and his communications were threatened.

Having traced the situation so far, we may return for a moment to the directing centres from which emanate all the various developments of the campaign—namely, the opinions of the Cabinet and the mind of the Governor. The condition of his mind at this moment is an interesting study, but, unfortunately, one cannot feel certain that the truth is yet obtainable, or that there are not unpublished letters which would supply missing clues.

His ideas of the defence are extremely wide. They include suggestions for expeditionary forces from different points along the coast of the Red Sea, the general purpose being that of shaking the confidence of the Shoans by attacking the country in their rear; of detaching powerful chiefs by invading their individual territories; of cutting off all communication with European nations, several of which were well known to be disembarking arms and ammunition;—in fact, "of surrounding Ethiopia with a circle of iron."

These ideas were developed with his usual brilliancy, but with curious limitations. He was by this time aware of the numbers of the Abyssinians, but he does not seem to have realized their power. As long as he is dealing with his own forces, or with problems such as distances, mountains, numbers of men in proportion to numbers of guns etc., he shows his old ability; but when he comes to estimating, not his own resources, but those of the enemy, there at once creeps in a curious note of confidence with a kind of substratum of uncertainty;[1] he gives the impression of a man who is continually saying to himself: "I have 20,000 European troops, well trained and well armed. What danger could there possibly be from any barbarian nation against so large a force?" But there are times when his bold assertions to his Government, seem intended to carry conviction to his own mind as much as to those whom he is addressing. What he apparently awaits with all certainty is the moment when the enemy will make some mistake,—a thing that they carefully abstain from doing. As this dawns on him, he gradually assumes the appearance of a man who, having started to chase a grass-snake, suddenly finds himself face to face with a viper; he still believes he can kill it, but he does not exhibit the same buoyant confidence as heretofore; nevertheless, with so many people urging him on, he cannot well draw back.[2]

[1] No doubt very largely due to his defective Intelligence Department.

[2] No amount of writing will better explain how Baratieri felt than his own letter of January 8th, 1896. "I would have asked for other battalions and other batteries, but I am limited to asking for as many as will suffice to cope with the present situation; taking count of the greatest number that it is possible to feed, in view of the paucity of the preparations. The difficulties of provisioning European troops far away from their base, amidst mountains, where steep paths take the place of roads, without enough transport-animals, and without advanced stores previously replenished, are so infinite, that the numbers, instead of being an assistance, might, after a certain point, become embarrassing. When the forces from Italy join us at

The fact was that had Baratieri been able to fight a purely defensive campaign, then he would perhaps have been able to tire out the Shoans and keep them at bay until their provisions were exhausted. But this was not what the Italian Government wanted; it was not what was expected of him in Italy or in the army. What was required of him was a victory. "Rivincita,"—revenge for Amba Alagi, was the note that had roused enthusiasm in the Chamber, and in the streets. The troops at Adigrat themselves were largely composed of volunteers who had come abroad to win glory. Now, as there existed amongst the Italians a party, composed of Anti-Africanists who considered that Italy was not yet in a condition for colonial expansion, Signor Crispi naturally felt that, having demand-

Adigrat, I feel perfectly confident of beating the Shoans either united or divided. After a success, our pursuit might disorganize their forces and perhaps enable me to follow them further, but (as I have already written) a campaign of conquest against Abyssinia requires a preparation of some months, and requires means that cannot be improvised in a country devastated by wars, and by the hordes that have lived there so long. It is not through overweening confidence, nor through regard for the country that I do not ask for more reinforcements, it is because I have no means of assuring their provisioning. Should the Government decide on a war of conquest, it will be necessary first to prepare everything, and then to send the troops as late as possible so as not prematurely to consume our resources."

In other words "I would ask for more if I could, but I believe I can manage to arrange matters with those I have got." But at the time when Baratieri wrote this, he cannot have supposed that the Abyssinian forces would ever amount to over 50,000 or 60,000 men; hence probably his hesitation when he found they reached about twice that number.

ed £750,000, he must have some success to show for it, or else his party would become discredited and his colonial schemes would be at an end. No document has as yet been published proving that Signor Crispi actually ordered Baratieri to fight, yet the General gives one a strong impression of having finally risked a battle against his better judgment.

To maintain himself in a hostile country and rout the enemy as was expected of him, he required not 20,000 men, but at least two or three times that number; and to provision so many troops was out of the question unless several extra months were spent on storing up food and munitions at the various towns of the colony,—not to mention the increased expense.

Another opinion expressed in Baratieri's memoirs shows plainly his hopes that the enemy would commit some fatal error: "Nobody then (*i.e.* about January 29th, '96) thought it probable (and to those who know Abyssinia even superficially it is still a miracle) that so great a mass of men, such a number of different contingents, and such a mixture of hot-blooded feudal spirits could maintain themselves together for so long, and in territories like those they occupied." (*Memorie*, p. 319.) He was not the only man to whom this combination came as a surprise. Captain Moltedo, for instance, relates how some of the natives, even, expressed to him the opinion that the Shoans would never be ready to undertake a serious war merely to expel the invaders from Tigré,—a nation that had been so long hostile to Shoa. The fact was that nobody had counted on meeting a man as able as Menelik; his power was an unknown factor. Had the Italians been dealing with the former Emperors, Theodore, or even John, the case would have been different; but Menelik has hitherto known how to attract and keep by him the most influential men of his race.

As regards the ministers at Rome, the following instance will give an idea of the opinions that prevailed amongst them, even when the campaign was already half over. On January 18th, Baron Blanc sent a draft copy of the conditions of peace to General Baratieri, to be used when the Italian arms had proved successful. The chief provisions were the following. That if a Negûs Nagasti continued to exist,—though the Government admitted that they would prefer his elimination, so that they might have an array of equally important chieftains under their authority,—he and his Ras were to acknowledge the Italian rule as far as Lake Ashangi, and the Tacazze River. All Ethiopia was to be an Italian protectorate, and was to maintain such troops only as might be agreed to by Italy. No concessions of land, commerce, industries, railways etc., etc., were to be granted to the subjects of any foreign nation except by permission of Italy, who was to keep a Resident at the capital, invested with full civil and criminal jurisdiction over all foreigners. The investitures of all the Ras were to be approved by Italy. The customs and duties would in future be regulated by her, the Abyssinian money coined at her mints, and no loans were to be contracted without her authorization,—but she would not be responsible for any previous debts of the Negûs. She undertook, however, to develop the commerce, agriculture, and education, etc. of

Abyssinia, and all that could contribute to the economic and civil welfare of that country. The Italians were to have the power of buying land. All internal disputes were to be referred to the Government at Rome, and in case of external danger the Governor would send troops,—at the expense of the chief who asked for them. The Negûs and his Ras would be under the obligation of joining in the defence of the colony of Erythrea, "with all their means and all their forces if called upon to do so by the Governor."

Such was the draft of the future peace. It was not intended, of course, to be heard of until after a great victory; but even so, what could be more absurd? Having now (1901) been in print for some years, it has doubtless afforded many a happy hour to the Negûs and his more intimate friends.

During this period also (on Jan. 15th) the scheme, long before suggested by Baratieri, of creating a diversion by invading Harrar from the Port of Zeila (opposite Aden) took a tangible form. The idea was undoubtedly a good one. It would have utilized the Italian men-of-war in the Red Sea, and also the various regiments that were ready to embark, but for whom no food could be found in Erythrea. It would probably have detached Maconnen from the Shoan army, for his capital is only about twenty days' march from the coast; and a general feeling of unrest would have been caused amongst the Abyssinian chiefs by this southern invasion of their homes. But the idea was abandoned owing to diplomatic difficulties. France and Great Britain had agreed not to annex or establish a protectorate over Harrar (by their treaty of 1888). The French would have regarded an Italian occupation as almost equivalent to one by Great

Britain; they protested against the force passing through British territory, and Lord Salisbury being unwilling to create a rupture, refused our allies leave to land at Zeila unless they could obtain the assent of France.

Another scheme for making a diversion by means of an expedition from Assab was also abandoned owing to the difficulties that it presented. These two failures can only be regarded as a great misfortune for the Italians. Whether they would have sent a sufficiently large force to act with decisive effect is perhaps doubtful, but such stabs in the back were certainly the best available method of detaching the more powerful chieftains from Menelik's army,—a policy still feasible, and one that represented to Italy almost the only remaining chance of success.

It was therefore not surprising that Baratieri was well disposed to consider the peace negotiations re-opened by Menelik after the release of Galliano's battalion, for which purpose he appointed Major Salsa his representative. He had been empowered to act in his own name, as the Italian Government was not in direct communication with Menelik; no answer had been returned to the Negûs's letter of January 24th quoted at the head of this chapter, for Baron Blanc considered it insolent.

On January 28th the Governor telegraphed to Rome for instructions as to the general lines to be followed during the negotiation, and received the following answer from Baron Blanc. "In the present condition of our military operations, and until Italy has won a victory over the enemy, the government of the king does not see that it can enter on serious negotiations, or obtain useful conditions which will assure our position in Ethiopia for the future. We feel that we must settle the question in such a manner that hostilities will not be annually reopened against us, and that those who interfere to our prejudice will no longer have the power of working to arouse them periodically." The letter ends by allowing the Governor full liberty to use his discretion while working on this basis, but it was, of course, obvious that negotiations begun in such a spirit would lead to nothing; the Government did not want peace, they wanted victory. On February 7th an interview was arranged with Ras Maconnen, but as Major Salsa was only authorised to accept terms that allowed the Italians all territories over which their flag had ever been hoisted, and was, moreover, obliged to renew the claim to a protectorate over Ethiopia, it was not surprising that the meeting produced no results. Maconnen on his part offered to return to the Treaty of Uccialli, omitting the clause establishing an Italian protectorate; but these abortive attempts were finally brought to an end four days later (February 11th).

One more event deserves to be chronicled before closing the history of the negotiations, and returning to trace the actual course of the campaign. On January 28th a messenger from Ras Mangasha arrived at Cairo bearing three letters from that chief, one for Queen Victoria, another for the Sirdar (Kitchener) and the third for the Governor of Suakim. The text of the letter is as follows (I quote the English translation printed in the Italian Green Books):

"To Queen Victoria, Queen of Kings, Empress of the Great Red Sea—From Ras Mangasha, son of King John, King of Kings of Zion and Ethiopia.

"With all due respect I beg to offer Your Majesty my greetings, and I hope you are well. Thank God I am well.

"My father all his life lived under the shadow of Your friendship, and it is said that such as the father does so should the son, following his footsteps.

"The former friendly relations between Your Kingdom and the Kingdom of Ethiopia have not been changed. But now the Italians have come and have occupied my country. I beg Your Majesty will not be unmindful of the old friendship which exists between Your government and my father which he advised me to maintain.

"I have delayed writing to Your Majesty because the roads are cut; otherwise nothing would have prevented me from writing. Neither mountains nor rivers will prevent me from writing or failing in my friendship to a friend.

"Seal of Ras Mangasha, son of King John, King of Kings."

Dated 23 Nekasi (corresponding to 28th August, 1895).[1]

The letter in itself is innocent enough,—merely a demand for assistance against his Italian invaders; Mangasha was sufficiently clever to avoid expressing his real thoughts in writing. But his messenger, who had left the Negûs's camp just after Amba Alagi, Dec. 7th, 1895, (in which action Mangasha took no part, being with the Negûs at Lake Ashangi) had much important information to convey. "He related that Mangasha was obliged to turn to Menelik, in

[1] This date must surely be a mistranslation; the letter did not start until after the battle of Amba Alagi, which took place December 7th, 1895. Baratieri in his memoirs, p. 324, says the letter "Gave no indication of its date," which seems to point at some uncertainty.

despite of himself, for assistance, as he could not raise an equal number of soldiers, arms or ammunition; but he assured us that Mangasha never has, and never will recognise him as King of Kings. He added that similar motives keep Ras Olié and Tecla Aimanot (King of Gojjam) in subjection, and that Menelik himself recognises Mangasha as a superior and remains standing before him. According to this Abyssinian, as soon as the Italians are conquered, Mangasha will have himself proclaimed King of Kings, and hopes for the assistance of England against Menelik, all the more that he will have with him Tecla Aimanot."

This mission has great importance for several reasons. In the first place it affords some interesting side views of the political situation within Menelik's camp. In the second place, taken in conjunction with other facts, it disproves the assertions of some critics who are apt to think that General Baratieri over-estimated the chances of detaching the more discontented of the Ras from Menelik;—certain people have thought that those chiefs were negotiating with the Governor merely for the purpose of deceiving him. Thirdly, through this letter we gain the opinion of Colonel Wingate, now the Sirdar, on the situation of Italian affairs.

From the Italian consulate-general in Egypt, Signor Raggi writes to Baron Blanc: "In the course of a long conversation with Wingate Bey, (a most able man, and one who knows these people well, owing to the long stay he has made in the Red Sea districts, and to his having now been head of the Intelligence Department for a considerable time) he said (giving it as his personal opinion and with all reservations due to the fact that he had not full knowledge of the matter, being ignorant of the actual course of the negotiations between General Baratieri and Menelik) that it was worth considering whether a treaty with Mangasha against Menelik would not be more profitable for us. He is inclined to think that the former, owing to the prestige that comes to him through his father, would have an ascendency over the populations,—an influence due to their natural conservatism, and their desire to maintain, at least nominally, their ancient constitution."

Colonel Wingate then went on to suggest that Menelik could be deposed, or relegated to the South of Ethiopia; that Mangasha would be bound down by treaty with Italy and then created Negûs; that the Italians should assist Mangasha to extend his dominion south of Tigré and should thus, through him as Negûs Nagasti, bring all the other Ras under their rule.

This was Wingate's opinion as to the best policy for the Italians to pursue. It hinges almost entirely on the amount of hereditary prestige possessed by Mangasha; but it proves that the head of the British Intelligence Department, like Baratieri, considered the true solution of their difficulties to lie in negotiations with the more powerful factions of the Abyssinian coalition.

As regards the actual answer to the letter, the British and Italian governments together concerted a suitable reply. Eventually Lord Salisbury wrote back a polite letter in which he assured the Ras of Her Majesty's friendly feelings, but expressed regret for the hostilities between Abyssinia and Italy, "which is the friend and ally of this country," and a hope for peace. He ended up: "I am to add that you cannot give a better proof of your friendship for Her Majesty than by endeavouring to contribute to such a settlement. I am, your sincere friend, Salisbury."—Thus making perfectly clear the position of the British Empire—namely, that it was the friend of both combatants. This letter was seen and approved by the Italian ministry before being despatched.

One other point of interest related by the messenger was that in the Shoan camp there were a great number of rifles and ammunition, with some artillery and machine guns, under the orders of a Russian, who was instructing the natives in the management of these arms; some Frenchmen also were there, but he did not know how many. On being informed that Menelik was treating for peace, he said he was not astonished, for the Negûs already distrusted the other chiefs, but that even if he made peace they would continue the war. Menelik, he added, was of a timid nature; it is a curious fact that from several sources this idea has been conveyed, that "the Conqueror of the Lion etc." is in reality a man of no great personal courage, or at all events of no liking for war.

The advice of Colonel Wingate was on the whole received with approval by the Italian ministers. They did not altogether favour the extensive powers that he proposed to give to Ras Mangasha, but Baron Blanc authorized the Governor to negotiate with him and Tecla Aimanot, and also with Ras Maconnen, employing if necessary the "secret financial means that are always so efficaceous in African warfare."

The idea was even mooted of creating a breach between

Menelik and Tecla Aimanot and Mangasha, by letting the Negûs hear of the letters and information sent to Cairo; but the suggestion was abandoned. In the first place, the letters themselves (the contents of all three were identical) contained nothing that might not have been written in the Negûs's interests, while the information given would be called merely the chance words of an ignorant messenger,—nothing more. Secondly, they did not possess the original documents, without which no Abyssinian would have doubted that the Italians had invented the whole story to suit their own interests.

CHAPTER VIII

SAURIA

BARATIERI finds his communications threatened—February 1st, 1896, leaves Adagamus—February 13th, reaches Sauria—12th, defection of Ras Sebath and Agos Tafari—13th, Sebath captures Seeta Hill—14th, Occupies Mt. Alequa—Two small Italian columns defeated—16th, Captain Moccagatta's defeat—Osman Digna attacks Kassala—17th, Hills of Seeta and Alequa recaptured—Condition of the army at Sauria—Volunteering system—Eagerness to fight—Faulty organization and equipment—Baratieri's instructions to officers—Transport breakdown—Intelligence department—Baratieri undecided—February 25th, Crispi's telegram—Stevani's small victory—28th, Baratieri orders retirement, but summons a council of war—29th, Makes up his mind to advance.

WHILE considering the course of military affairs, it was described how on February 1st Menelik was occupying the territory of Gundapta, north of Adowa, and the Italian army 20,000 strong was still at Adagamus, near Adigrat. Baratieri, as has already been said, had 110 miles of communications behind him (Massowah, Arkico, Adi-Caje, Adigrat, and a second line Massowah, Saati, Asmara, Sanganeiti, Adi-Caje, while at Asmara a large number of stores had been collected). It was doubtful whether either his commissariat or his transport could cope with any extension of the distance, nevertheless a movement was necessary, because the Shoans were threatening his lines of communication; already Menelik was nearer to Asmara than he.

Baratieri's movements began as soon as the ten hostages had returned to his camp. To detail them shortly and concisely:

On February the 1st he left Adagamus, changed front half right, and arrived on February 3rd at Mai Gabeta.

On 7th he advanced still further to Tucuz.

On the 13th he occupied the heights of Sauria from which the enemy had withdrawn about four miles to the South.

On the 14th Menelik retired to Adowa itself, and in these positions the two armies remained facing each other until March 1st, when the decisive battle of Adowa was fought.

These movements of Baratieri have been subjected to a great deal of criticism. The purpose of the advance was, of course, to cover Adigrat which he had made his base, but it is urged that his communications being already too long, he should have retired instead of advancing and formed a fresh base at Gura. This may be so from a military point of view, but even his critics admit that, considering the state of feeling in the Cabinet and in Italy, such a withdrawal was quite out of the question, for Gura is a town situated many miles to the North, half-way between Adigrat and Massowah; and in any case it would not have been just or politic to abandon the loyal natives to an Abyssinian revenge.

It was from Mai Gabeta, on the 6th, that Major Salsa's negotiations with Maconnen began, and they continued until the 12th, as already related.

On the night of the 12th the Italians suffered a serious loss in the defection of Ras Sebath and Ras Agos Tafari, who with 600 rifles deserted to the enemy. Sebath having formerly been a prisoner of Mangasha until released by Baratieri after the battle of Debra Aila, his conduct was regarded by the Italians, with justice, as an instance of the blackest treachery. There is, however, this much to be said for the Ras; he had fought bravely at Amba Alagi, where he lost 35 killed and many wounded out of his 350 followers; and he had apparently intended to stand by the Italians, but as matters progressed he was shrewd enough to see that their preparations were insufficient. After Amba Alagi he had said: "Six weeks ago I warned the Governor that his enemies were very numerous, and that it was time to make provision and send all the troops here, as otherwise we were running a serious risk."

It was now evident that he regarded the Italians as being already beaten, and did not mean to be crushed in the ruin.

On February 13th Baratieri had 21,000 men and 50 guns at Sauria; in the various garrisons throughout the colony he had about 10,000 more, (about 4,000 on his communications from Sauria to Adigrat alone); and 2 new divisions were being sent off from Italy, making in all a total of about 50,000 men. But as far as Tigré was concerned the campaign would be either won or lost before these last two divisions arrived.

The defection of Sebath was not long in producing serious results, for he had taken with him not only 600 men (whose numbers quickly swelled to 1,500 owing to his being joined by armed Tigréan peasants), but also an accurate knowledge of the Italian lines of communication. Between Adigrat and Sauria the country consists of a series of mountains, rocks, and hills. One of the latter, called the hill of Seeta, was occupied by only a few men of the Kitet; while Mount Alequa, a more extensive height, was defended from Mai Mergaz by a contingent under Captain Moccagatta, consisting of 232 white men and 138 natives,—370 in all. These were the two points selected by Ras Sebath as most suitable for a debut in his new service. On the 13th and 14th he captured Seeta Hill, and, unknown to the Italians, effected a lodgment on Mount Alequa. The Adigrat garrison replied by sending against Seeta a body of 70 men under Lieutenant Cisterni and 36 under Lieutenant De Conciliis; while, with a view to securing Mount Alequa, Captain Moccagatta had already despatched 100 natives under Lieutenant Cimino, and 70 white men under Lieutenant Negretti, accompanied by a caravan for Adigrat under command of Lieutenant Caputo. It seemed as if here there would be some splendid chances for the subalterns to distinguish themselves; but both the little columns were repulsed with loss, and of the young officers Cisterni alone came back; De Conciliis and Cimino were wounded and taken prisoner, the others were killed. On the 16th Captain Moccagatta, who knew nothing of these defeats, advanced in person to reinforce Mount Alequa with 140 men, but, falling into an ambush, left 97 dead and 20 prisoners in the hands of the enemy.[1] The

[1] Sebath, who then had about 1,000 men, dressed some of them in the uniforms taken from the dead, and allowed the Italians to get within 200 yards before firing. He is said to have written a greatly exaggerated account of his success to the Negûs.

result of this "méthode des petits paquets" as General Luzeux names it, was that the communications were temporarily cut, and that the army ran short of provisions; while on the same day news arrived that in the far-away North West of the colony, Osman Digna had arrived with 20 Emirs to attack Kassala,—for Menelik had not omitted to include the Dervishes in his great coalition. At this moment, it will be admitted, that Baratieri's position was not enviable. Though still in touch with an enemy at least 100,000 strong, he was obliged to weaken his front in order to protect his communications. Colonel Stevani was sent back with a whole regiment to occupy Mai Maret, and a new line of supplies was organised through Mai Maret itself to Debra Damo, a place slightly north of Adigrat. On the 17th Colonel Valli, also detached from the front, joined Captain Moccagatta with the 7th Native Battalion and two companies under Captain Oddone, and together they recaptured the two hills of Seeta and Alequa, restoring the communications; but Sebath and Agos Tafari with most of their men succeeded in escaping, and were soon raising rebellion far and wide amongst the peasantry. On the 23rd, however, better news arrived. The Dervishes had been repulsed before Kassala, so that no immediate danger was now hanging over the head of Baratieri; but many of his mules had been killed, or appropriated by their drivers, who vanished, and until the 25th his force at Sauria was reduced to little more than 13,000 men. On that day Valli's battalion returned to the front, while a relieving force from Adi Caje permitted Stevani's regiment also to rejoin.

These small defeats, and the consequent interruption of

supplies, did not tend to improve either the moral nor yet the physical welfare of the army at Sauria. The condition of that army is a subject on which much has been written, from many different points of view. Some writers have blamed the Government, others the General, others the constitution and even temper of the army itself; but upon one point nearly all are agreed—namely, that the seeds of failure had long ago been sown, and that the defeat of Adowa was merely the outcome of previous mismanagement. Where so many experienced judges, many of them eye-witnesses, have expressed their views, it is a delicate and difficult matter for any outsider to venture; he can only give voice as briefly as may be, to the convictions that have gradually become rooted in his mind during the study of many narratives, and during conversations with those in a position to have accurate information.

In the first place, the regiments for service in Africa had been constituted as far as possible of volunteers. Now this, in a nation where compulsory service is the rule, was undoubtedly the best system from a theoretical point of view; and we may add that the officers came forward splendidly, and the men, on the whole, very well. But every volunteer is not a hero; there are many different motives which send men to the front, and the rank and file may be roughly classified under the following heads.

The genuine volunteers—men who had sent in their names from patriotic motives and who arrived full of a real enthusiasm; these formed the majority.

Men who wanted for some reason or other to get away from Italy.

Men who had been persuaded to volunteer because they were considered useless at home.

The Non-volunteers,—those who had been ordered to come, so as to make up the necessary numbers; these as a rule turned out well enough. But it was naturally a tempting chance for officers commanding in Italy to shelve their "black sheep" on to the colonial battalions.

It will be seen that, side by side with the enthusiasts, there was a distinctly undesirable section of soldiers, and it was noticed that when the season of real hardships began, these latter did not hesitate to express their discontent,—a feeling that appears to have been more or less prevalent amongst even the keenest. The fact was that many of them were in reality too enthusiastic; they had come out, apparently, under the idea that they would at once be led to the attack, that after the excitement of a short but brilliant campaign they would be able to go home to enjoy their laurels. It seems, as far as may be judged from memoirs and narratives, that the more cautious their general became, the more impatient became his army. While he realized that these stray detachments, drawn from every regiment in the service, which as yet hardly knew each other or their officers by sight, were not fit to cope with an enemy four or five times as numerous as themselves, his men were chafing at his slow movements and his elaborate fortifications. Even Captain Menarini, who has written so brilliant and interesting a narrative about his brigade,[1] is an instance of this sentiment. In one passage (p. 19) he says, referring to a small advance:

[1] *Brigata Dabormida alla battaglia d'Adua.*

"The forward movement silenced those who were discontented at the inexplicable retreat of a few days before, and brought a gleam of hope amongst all, that our General had now at last made up his mind to attack;—but unfortunately it was merely another illusion."

This is only one of the many instances that prove how confident, and how eager for battle were, not only the men, but the officers from General Arimondi downwards;—though in the light of subsequent events it seems hard to believe that such a movement would have been successful. It is surely far more probable that during these few weeks General Baratieri was pursuing the only true course of action, namely, that of allowing the Abyssinians to exhaust their provisions, devastate the country, and then perforce retire,—probably to melt away into insignificance; and this is, I think, the view now most generally adopted. At all events it is known that Menelik, during that period, was in a state of daily anxiety; that he was even praying with the Abuna to the saints to make Baratieri attack him. For he too needed a victory, unless he was to lose all prestige amongst the warlike Ras whom he had collected for his great invasion; yet with all his 120,000 men he was too wise to rush on a fortified position.

These fortifications are a constant source of irritation to Captain Menarini, who declares that they were merely put up in order to keep the men employed; that what was erected on the first and second days was destroyed on the third: "while the provisions and necessaries were being used up, and,—let us tell the whole truth,—the moral was growing weaker and discipline was becoming slack."

Tiresome as this may have been, it can hardly explain why moral should have deteriorated, or discipline become slack. The troops only remained three weeks at Sauria, and at the most it was only about two and a half months since they had sailed from Naples. From this one is led to suppose that these men had landed in a state of great enthusiasm, which had somewhat died out in face of the realities of war—namely, the everyday prosaic drudgery, bad food, cold nights, and work that brought no immediate result. On the very next page he admits, I think, that the regiments were in a condition in which no general would care to lead them against the enemy. "The various units (except the native) were as yet not nearly amalgamated; constituted only a short time before, of elements new to one another, they were still without that mutual knowledge of each other which is so necessary,—even indispensable,—between officers, non-commissioned officers, and men."

It will be understood that no remarks in this chapter are intended to convey any reflection whatever on the Italian soldier. The faults that existed were due to the system,—or to the want of system,—whereby the nation first allowed itself to be defeated, and then endeavoured to retrieve its honour by launching on a wave of enthusiasm this hastily organised army,—insufficient to achieve success, and yet too numerous to be properly fed or equipped.

The equipment was bad. As has been already related, the uniforms were not suited to the climate and many of them were soon in rags. General Baratieri complains that, although he had called the attention of the Government to the point, the Italian regiments were sent out without suitable

Alpine boots,—and during the battle of Adowa some of the men were seen taking those that were on the feet of their dead comrades,[1] because their own were quite useless;—this in a campaign that lasted under three months. Moreover, it is related that before the works at Sauria were ended, most of the picks and shovels had been worn out. This was perhaps unavoidable, but when it is calmly related that almost all the sword-bayonets, and some of the rifles were in want of repair, or beyond repairing, then we may fairly ask why was this so? Neither rifles nor bayonets ought to have become unserviceable so soon, had proper precautions been taken; either they were so bad that no officer should have allowed them to leave Naples, or else they had not been sufficiently cared for.

Apropos of the rifles, we may note what General Baratieri says in his "Memorie," namely, that some of the regiments which had been trained to use those of the latest pattern, had Remingtons issued to them when they reached Adigrat, and were obliged to learn their different action. Why? Because the Government either had not a sufficient number of the new cartridges, or wished to use up the old ones. But such things, to say the least of it, are irritating to the soldier.

Captain Menarini's description of the headgear in which the men arrived at Sauria is amusing. "They varied from a fez without its blue tassel, and from the straw hat of the royal navy, from the Lobbia grey felt, pressed more or less out of shape according to the peasant taste of the soldier,

[1] Menarini, *ib.*

down to the most ridiculous forms of helmets.[1] To these were added the marks that the commanding officers had had designed in ink on the various head-gear, in order to recognise more easily the branch of the service of which the soldier was an effective; for few had arrived at learning the battalion and regiment of Africa to which they belonged, and almost all of them, if asked, replied by naming the regiment and battalion of Italy from which they came."

It was perhaps not surprising that the Ascari should, with derisive grins, have referred to the Italian battalions as "the Kitet of Italy."

During all this time constant instruction was given to the men in the methods of fighting they were to follow, the principal theme being, that the Abyssinian is not so formidable when attacked as when attacking. As for the officers, the following headings are those on which General Baratieri tells us that he laid special stress.

1.—The rules for protection of the troops are always to be most scrupulously observed against the enemy, who is especially clever as regards ambushes and surprises.

2.—No one is to allow himself to be influenced by turning movements whether on a big or a small scale.

3.—General reserves, and partial reserves (of provisions) are to be kept, and to be employed only in a moment of necessity.

4.—The bayonet is to be used on every possible occasion.

5.—The officers are to dismount when in the fire-zone.

6.—As soon as the fighting begins the reserved cartridges are to be distributed from the commissariat.

[1] The supply of helmets had entirely run short; many had to be bought, at the last moment, in Egypt and India.

7.—In the firing line a close formation is to be employed.[1]

8.—No firing is to be ordered at a greater distance than 500 metres, and, except in unusual cases, volleys are to be employed.

9.—The men with the commissariat columns are to take part in the action, as many of them as possible advancing into the lines.

10.—Notes are frequently to be sent off, giving information of the hour, the place, and the situation of affairs at that moment.

It will be seen that more than one of these maxims represents a very different view to that taken by Lord Roberts in the advice that he sent home to Aldershot during the Boer war; but Baratieri had not had the benefit of our latest experience against civilized weapons.

The food difficulty was of course the worst of all; and although it has sometimes been made the basis of attacks on Baratieri, it seems hard to hold him responsible for it, as he could not possibly have foreseen the subtle diplomacy of Ras Sebath and Agos Tafari, to whom the failure of his communications was chiefly due.

Nevertheless it was a very high trial for the troops that had but lately arrived from Italy, to find their rations at times reduced by half; and on several occasions even less. The wine, to which they were accustomed, was of course the first to give out; but when the ration of bread failed, the matter became more serious. Flour was served out to them, and they learnt from the natives to make themselves

[1] Presumably the thin firing line of men shoulder to shoulder; *vide*, pp. 46—47.

small unleavened cakes,—very small cakes it will be admitted, when we hear that on one occasion even the natives made complaints, and it was found that the amount served out would hardly have filled a cup. Their meat supply was also very uncertain.[1]

Yet it was not of their hardships that the Italian soldiers seem to have complained, so much as of their inaction, and while chronicling the numerous disadvantages under which they worked, some officers insist that, in spite of all things, the moral remained wonderfully high. There were many instances of the reserve rations (of which every man had two) being opened, but in most cases the soldier only consumed one of the two, trusting to his second ration to carry him through any unforeseen emergency, and it was noticed that the spirits of the troops seemed always to rise when there was a chance of fighting. It was the inaction in face of the enemy that told on them. Baratieri might indeed have had a better chance of success, had he decided to attack before these hardships began; but, on the other hand, of course he would have had to fight with absolutely raw battalions.

As to the reasons for the shortness of food, (apart from Sebath and Agos Tafari) the following quotation, which is absolutely reliable, will give, I think, a complete picture of the situation.

"We had always been short of transport animals, and especially at the present moment, as many camel

[1] To these short rations has been attributed the weariness that overcame many of the young soldiers during the latter hours of the battle of Adowa.

drivers fled with their camels in order to escape from this hard service, and from the danger of falling into the ambushes of the rebels. The animals that still remained were reduced, for the greater part, to a pitiable condition; and their proprietors and drivers, time after time with earnest prayers and protestations, demanded a rest for their beasts,—a rest that could hardly ever be allowed them. We did not know how we were to go on (tirar avanti). The arrivals from Massowah were continually decreasing, the stores were almost empty, the crisis was becoming more and more acute, and the situation caused more and more anxiety . . . . And things went from bad to worse. I (the writer) who had already been rendered apprehensive by this state of affairs, did not fail to inform the Commander-in-Chief, who on his part, guided by other conceptions and intent on his own projects, continued to ask for supplies; demanding them even with threats, and making a final appeal to the efforts of everyone, that the *corps of operations should not be compelled to beat a humiliating retreat!* But what could we do if the means of transport were absolutely lacking? The Commissariat could ask for them, but it had no way of obtaining its request. From the Vice-Governor,[1]—from Massowah alone,—could animals and supplies come, because the country could offer us nothing, or practically nothing, of what in ordinary times we might have expected to find. The Vice-Governor himself must have been short of means, for he had for some time been sending us a storm of protests, assuring us that if we did not return him the

[1] General Lamberti; he is said to have shown great ability in the discharge of his arduous duties.

transport animals he would be obliged to suspend the furnishing of supplies. And not only were we unable to send back even one animal, but those that were employed at the end of February from Adi Caje to the front were not sufficiently numerous to do the work. Many, in fact too many, were lacking of those required for the daily supply of the Corps of Operations . . . . there should have been (according to the numbers sent there) at the disposition of the Commissariat on its arrival in Adi Caje, about 5,000 camels. When on the 25th the general situation was reviewed, it was found that there were barely 2,300. Meanwhile, in order to assure the arrival of what was absolutely necessary for the corps of operations, at least 3,000 were required between Adi Caje and the front.

"Three days later these 2,300 had become 1,700! What had become of the others? Dead of hardships or fatigue, or vanished. Certainly the camel drivers seeing that their remonstrances, their entreaties, and their protests produced no effect, had betaken themselves to a more silent system and one that produced more certain results—namely, that of absconding."

This, then, was how the transport worked between Adi Caje and the front during the fortnight before Adowa. It might be supposed that my quotation is taken from the memoirs of some overworked and disappointed transport officer;—not at all. It is an extract from the official report of Colonel Ripamonti, who was in command at Adi Caje.

During this period, while many indefinite accusations are levelled at the General, there are only a few that are capable of being really pressed home. There appears, indeed, to have been a universal impression that things at the front were in a disorganised condition;—a want of confidence probably existed throughout the whole army, which was not lessened by the scarcely concealed antagonism between him and General Arimondi.[1] As regards the general laxity, it is said that owing to omissions, or to pointless orders, much purposeless labour was created for the men; that, for instance, no directions were sent out as to where the various regiments were to encamp until after they had actually made their arrangements, so that it often happened that the whole camp had to be altered at the last moment; and that then, so bad were the plans, that one brigade would sometimes be found drinking the water in which the men of another brigade had just been washing themselves. But whether these statements are true or not, there is one accusation of which one cannot acquit the Governor,—that is his laxity in the matter of outposts and the facility with which he allowed himself to be duped by the Shoan spies. I recollect having a long conversation with a British traveller who had spent many months in Abyssinia, shortly after the war, and who told me that the opinion there was that for some weeks before Adowa the Italian camp had been in a state of great disorganisation, and that to this fact their defeat was entirely attributable. On asking him for details, he singled out one above all others—namely, that there were so many natives of both sexes passing to and fro from the Italian camp that the Shoans could get their spies in without difficulty; and

[1] Captain Menarini relates (with approval!) that after the reconnaissance of February 24, General Arimondi openly characterized it as the onanism of the military art.

that on the night of the battle, some of the Italian guides were actually selected from among the followers of Menelik. Now the narrative of Captain Menarini coincides almost word for word with this statement. On page 17, for instance, it is stated: "He (the enemy) knows the ground thoroughly and has,—as we have since found out,—a splendid intelligence service composed of clever and faithful men, whose work was facilitated by our ill-arranged, and not very strict, system of outposts, through which there was a continual come and go of peasants, submissive and indifferent in appearance, but only more or less genuine.

"Having no maps or sketches we based our calculations solely on the information obtained from an ill-organised service of natives, of whom we knew little or nothing; and who in the opinion of most people were merely Abyssinian spies, munificently paid by us."

It is probably owing to the deficiency of reliable information as much as to several other causes, that during the last eight or ten days of February General Baratieri's orders are those of a man who does not know his own mind;—or perhaps we should rather say, of a man who knows his own mind but distrusts it, and has no longer the strength of character to follow, in the face of universal opposition, the course that he believes to be best.

On February 17th Menelik retired on to Adowa. "Why do we not attack?" was the cry amongst the Italian soldiers; but as Baratieri had, for the moment, little more than 13,000 men, he did not care to risk a battle even with the rear-guard of the Shoans.

On the other hand, to retire meant to destroy the moral

of his own army, and to raise open rebellion in all the country round. The only course left open was to remain in his entrenched position as long as his supplies held out: on February 22nd he could not rely on his provisions lasting for more than ten days.

Meanwhile news was brought in, daily, of the straits in which Menelik found himself for food,—and it was true. The two armies were in the position which Mr. Bloch believes to be the culminating point of all future wars; neither dared attack the other, and each was waiting until the lack of supplies should compel the other to make a move.

In Rome, as the prospects of a great victory grew less and the proposed "Rivincita" resolved itself into a series of small defeats, General Baratieri's prestige sank lower and lower. On the 22nd he was secretly superseded, General Baldissera being named Commander-in-Chief of the troops in Africa; but every precaution was taken to prevent Baratieri's hearing of this change, until his successor arrived.

On the 23rd Baratieri ordered a retirement to Adi Caje, but changed his mind owing to fresh information. So on the 24th the movement was stopped, and a reconnaissance was ordered under General Dabormida with Colonel Airaghi as second in command,—two men whose names are remembered above all others for their service in this campaign.

Meanwhile Menelik, in order to create a diversion and collect supplies, sent 12,000 men under Ras Gabeiu, "the lion of Amba Alagi," to devastate Serae, the province due north,—on the right of the Italian army. Baratieri at once sent Major Ameglio with a battalion to cut off Gabeiu, with the result that the Ras promptly retired. It was a success, but owing to a mistake in recalling Ameglio, that officer and his battalion did not return before the battle of Adowa.

On the 25th a retirement to Adi Caje was again thought of, but again abandoned. It was on this day that the following telegram was received by the Governor from Signor Crispi :

"This is a military phthisis not a war; small skirmishes in which we are always facing the enemy with inferior numbers; a waste of heroism, without any corresponding success. I have no advice to give you because I am not on the spot, but it is clear to me that there is no fundamental plan in this campaign, and I should like one to be formulated. We are ready for any sacrifice in order to save the honour of the army and the prestige of the monarchy."

This reproof ought not to have been sent off. Even though Signor Crispi and General Baratieri had always been on terms of friendship, it was not justifiable for the minister to interfere in such a manner at the critical point of the campaign. There was nothing definite in the telegram beyond the demand for a "plan of campaign," but its meaning was obvious. It meant "I want you to do something active;" "a military phthisis" was obviously directed at the inactivity of the army. Now it happened that this defensive attitude was that which Baratieri considered to be best,—but he must have seen how his measures were viewed at Rome.

He was able, however, to send to Italy on the same day news of a small Italian victory won by Colonel Stevani and his Bersaglieri. At Mai Maret that officer had met and defeated the rebels and Tigréan peasants of Ras Sebath and

Agos Tafari. The Italians lost 37 killed and wounded, but the enemy left about 50 dead on the field; and the action gave rise to a quarrel between the two Ras, for Agos Tafari complained that when this encounter was recognised to be of a serious nature, the agile Sebath left most of the fighting and the losses to his ally.

After this success the troops of both Stevani and Valli returned to the camp at Sauria, and the numbers were again brought up to over 20,000 men.[1] Baratieri had very nearly ordered a retirement on the 26th, but the spies had told him that the Shoans intended to attack him, so that he halted his army; but the attack never came, and the troops, impatient and tired of awaiting the enemy, were inclined to ridicule their general, as being the only man in the camp who believed what the spies said.

By this time Menelik also was becoming desperate. He too had only provisions for three or four days and, it is said by Italian writers, spent the time when he was not praying for his enemies to advance, in spreading reports of impending retreats, of stampedes, of rebellions and schisms in his own army, in order to entice and deceive Baratieri; even offering a reward, Lieutenant Melli tells us, to any man who could induce the Italians to attack; the situation had, in fact, almost an element of comedy.

On the 28th a fresh retirement was ordered through Mai Gabeta to Mai Maret, and the baggage started, but on that evening Baratieri called a meeting of his four generals, each

[1] This was one reason that influenced the Governor's decision in favour of giving battle. His numbers had now reached their highest possible limit; he could not have fed any more men.

commanding a brigade (it was the third that had been called during the three weeks at Sauria). He explained to them that the provisions would not last beyond the 2nd, or at the latest the 3rd of March, and that "therefore some precaution must necessarily be adopted, which might take the form of a retirement to the hollow of Senafè, or even to Adi Cajè, unless, in carrying out the retreat, it were found more convenient to go back as far as Asmara."[1]

This statement proves beyond all doubt that General Baratieri was not in favour of attacking the Shoans. He had obviously intended to stand on the defensive, as long as he could do so with safety, and would probably have retreated on several previous occasions had not his spies brought him false tidings of Menelik's similar intention.

"Retire? Never!" said General Dabormida who was the first of the four generals to reply.[2] He then gave his reasons; first, that in Italy they would prefer the loss of 2,000 or 3,000 men to a retreat which would seem dishonourable; secondly, that a retirement would depress the moral of the soldiers to a fatal extent; and thirdly, that as the enemy could always outmarch the Italians they would be able to overtake them and fight on ground of their own choosing. He ended by saying that it would be better to move out to the attack.

General Albertone agreed with Dabormida and added that

[1] General Ellena's evidence before the Military Tribunal at Rome. It was an informal meeting, not a real council of war.

[2] He was the junior, and would therefore reply first; the generals give their opinions in order beginning with the junior, so that no man's opinion may be influenced by that of his senior officer.

it was said amongst the natives that some of the enemy were away collecting food, that others were on their way back to Shoa, that two of their leaders would probably not fight, and that the Shoan camp was divided into two parts in the nearest of which there were only 14,000 or 15,000 men.

General Arimondi was also in favour of an attack, remarking that several opportunities had already been missed.

General Ellena was in favour of an attack, but, having only lately come from Italy, grounded his opinion simply on the information of his colleagues.

Finally, Baratieri closed the interview (for it was not a formal council of war) with the question:—"The Council is full of spirit; the enemy is brave and despises death; how is the moral of our soldiers?"

"Excellent," replied all four Brigadiers.

Then Baratieri dismissed them with the words:—"I am expecting further information from spies, who ought soon to arrive from the enemy's camp; when I have it I will *come to a decision.*"

On the following day, February 29th, 1896, at 5 o'clock in the evening, the Governor finally made up his mind to advance,—a decision momentous in the history of Italy, Erythrea, and Abyssinia. Had he been able to remain in his fortified position for another week,—perhaps even for another day,—Menelik might have been compelled to retire; possibly to disband his army; and then in the course of years we should have seen the ancient empire of Ethiopia, ruled over by a set of vassal Ras, gradually succumbing to the domination, and becoming imbued with the Latin civilization, of Italy. The warriors who fought at Adowa won a fresh lease of independence for their race,—whether this is a gain to the world and whether they or their descendants will take advantage of the chance thus obtained is a problem of the future. It may of course be possible, as a French writer has suggested, that they, with their Semitic blood, are destined to be the first of the African nations to make a successful revolt against domineering Europe; but if so, there still remains an enormous amount for them to learn.

As regards General Baratieri, one can only feel sorry that, after so many years of work, his name should in Europe be connected almost invariably with a great defeat. Kassala and Coatit are forgotten, Adowa is remembered. It seems a pity too, that having waited patiently until success was actually in the palm of his hand, he should have been persuaded to throw away the fruit of his labours and experience.

CHAPTER IX

BEFORE ADOWA

Plan of Baratieri's advance—Mistake about Kidane Meret—Order of the day, Feb. 28th, 1896—Tabular list of Italian forces—Their totals—Telegraphic errors—Totals of the Abyssinian army—Description of the country to be crossed.

The battle of Adowa was fought in a difficult country, and every event of that day was governed by topographical considerations, but their description is very simple.

The Italians were encamped at Sauria, and the Negûs's force round about Adowa, some sixteen miles to the South West. Between these two places, at a distance of nine miles from Sauria, there are three hills in a row, which form a barrier across all the direct paths leading from Sauria to Adowa;—they are called the Spur of Belah, the Hill of Belah, and Mount Belah. It was the line formed by them that Baratieri meant to occupy; there he intended to halt and offer battle to the Shoans.

On their left is another hill of which the name is not yet known for certain; Baratieri, on his map and in his orders, called it Kidané (Chidane) Meret. It was necessary, for the safety of his left flank, to occupy this rise, and it is owing to his having given it a name which belongs to quite a different place, that most of his misfortunes arose.

The hill appears in reality to have no very distinctive name, but about four miles further on there is one called "Enda[1] Kidane Meret," and near it a smaller height, which is the true "Hill of Kidane Meret," apparently the only one that would be understood by the natives if they were asked the way to that place. Hence Baratieri having ordered his left wing to occupy the hill of that name, found eventually that it was four miles in advance of the rest of his army, entirely unsupported and isolated. It will be seen also that the true hill,—next Enda Kidane Meret,—is one of those that actually overlook the plain of Adowa, where the Shoans were encamped. It is, in fact, one amongst several that almost commanded their position.

Now Baratieri's line, through the Spur of Belah to the hill *which he named* Kidane Meret is a good one; and immediately behind it is a second row of mountains,—Mt. Eshasho (Esciascio), the Hill of Rebbi Arienni and Mt. Raio—that forms, as it were, a buttress to the first line of defence.

His idea was to march during the night by the three paths indicated on the map; then having arrived unobserved behind the line of buttressing hills, to deploy and occupy a strong defensive position on the front slopes. Should the enemy attack him, he felt confident of success; should they not do so, he would at all events have raised the spirits of his more wavering supporters by showing that the Shoans dared not accept his proffered challenge. There was also a third possibility, that the enemy might beat a hurried retreat before his advance, as he understood their condition to be

[1] Enda merely means "the church."

much the reverse of prosperous. In that case he would re-enter Adowa, the capital of the province, as a conqueror.

a.—His right, under Dabormida, was to occupy the Spur of Belah and the Hill of Belah, or the ground thereabout.

b.—His centre, under Arimondi, was to occupy Mt. Belah.

c.—His left, under Albertone, was to occupy the hill which he called Kidane Meret, (but which was not in reality known by that name) and the slopes of Mt. Raio.

d.—The Reserve, under General Ellena, was to be posted at Rebbi Arienni.

The dispositions are not explicitly mentioned in the orders, a translation of which I give, because he did not decide on the exact position until after a careful selection on the day of the battle; but the orders, as will be seen, virtually foreshadow this scheme of distribution. The hills of Belah formed the inevitable front of the line that he had chosen.

Without going into details, it may be taken as a general rule that the country was very difficult, that the roads were simply mountain paths winding up and down precipices, and that it was impossible to move otherwise than extremely slowly or, owing to the hills and vegetation, to see far in any direction.

The orders that he issued on the day before the battle are as follow:

ORDERS OF THE DAY, FEBRUARY 29TH, N. 87.

To-night the Corps of Operations moves from the position of Sauria in the direction of Adowa, formed in three columns as follow.

The Right Column (General Dabormida): 2nd Infantry

Brigade,—battalion of Mobile Militia—Staff of the 2nd Battery Brigade,[1] with the 5th 6th and 7th Batteries.

The Central Column (General Arimondi): 1st Infantry Brigade,—1st Company of the 5th Native Battalion,—the 8th and 11th Batteries.

The Left Column (General Albertone): Four Native Battalions—the Staff of the 1st Battery Brigade with the 1st, 2nd, 3rd and 4th Batteries.

The Reserve (General Ellena): 3rd Infantry Brigade—3rd Native Battalion—2 quick-firing batteries, and a company of engineers.

The columns of Generals Dabormida, Arimondi, and Albertone will move from their respective camps at 21 o'clock;[2] the Reserve will move off an hour later in rear of the Central Column.

The Right Column will follow the road from Zahala (Zala) hill, through Guldam Hill to the hill of Rebbi Arienni. The Central Column and the Reserve will follow the road from Adi Dikki through Gundapta to the hill of Rebbi Arienni. The Left Column will follow the road from Sauria, Adi Cheiras to Kidane Meret; the General's Staff will march at the head of the Reserve.

First objective: the position formed by the hills Kidane Meret and Rebbi Arienni, between Mount Semajata and Mount Eshasho, the occupation of which will be carried out by General Albertone's column on the left, General Arimondi's column in the centre, General Dabormida's column

[1] The Italian word *brigata* means either the grouping of several regiments, as in England, or of several batteries.

[2] The usual Italian form; equivalent, of course, to 9 p.m.

on the right. Further—General Arimondi's column, if it finds itself on ground that can be held in sufficient force by the columns of Generals Albertone and Dabormida, will take up a waiting position in rear of these two brigades.

POINTS TO BE OBSERVED

Every soldier of the Italian troops will carry his proper allowance of cartridges (112), a reserve of two days' rations, his cape, water-bottle, and haversack. Following the troops, and in rear of each individual column, there will march two transport animals for each Italian battalion, carrying hospital requirements, and eight with the reserve ammunition. All the remaining baggage animals, with one soldier for every five beasts (besides the men leading them), one non-commissioned officer per battalion or battery, one subaltern officer per infantry regiment, one captain for all the commissariat (furnished by the 2nd Brigade of Infantry), will rendezvous at Entisho with the rations issued to-day (to be served out to-morrow), the thirty cartridges per soldier issued to-day from the park of artillery, the tents, the blankets, and the other materials not carried by the various corps. These baggage columns as well as the commissariat sections, the Servizi di Tappa, [1] and the park of artillery will remain halted at Entisho (Entiscio), ready to move when they receive the order from Headquarters, under the protection of a guard from the 7th Regiment of Infantry which will arrive to-night from Mai Gabeta. The brigades of artillery

[1] The Corps that prepares food at the end of the day's march; it is taken from each regiment in turn.

and the native battalions will regulate their baggage in a manner analogous to that ordered for the Italian battalions. No man is to pass the points and the flankers of the columns.

All persons arrested by the military police are to be sent at once to Headquarters.

The Directors of the Engineer Corps will see to the establishment of the telegraph, so that the General's Staff shall be put in communication as soon as possible with the columns on either flank and those in front, by means of the heliograph.

The commanders of the various columns will send frequent advices to the Headquarters and to the neighbouring columns.

O. Baratieri,
Lieutenant-General.

From these orders, then, the General's intention is plain: his columns were to march off at 9 p.m. on the night of February 29th (it being leap year). On the morning of March 1st they were to deploy behind Rebbi Arienni,—that is, hidden behind the second line of defence, formed by Rebbi Arienni and Mount Raio. They would thus arrive within about seven and a half miles of Adowa, unobserved, and within some three or four of the nearest Shoan camp, which would be on their right front. The line of defence was their first objective,—it would then remain to be seen what the General might be able to do; he might, for instance, be able to shell the Shoans out of their advanced camp at Mariam Shavitu, on his right front. In any case the conditions for him seemed absolutely safe, as his line of retreat teemed with strong defensive positions, each of them covering his communications. The paths back to Sauria ran almost straight; there were no sharp deviations to right or left, by means of which an active enemy might succeed in cutting him off from his base.

The forces were divided as follows:—

Column on the Left.

Native Brigade (Major-General Albertone).

Four Native battalions (1st Turitto, 6th Cossu, 7th Valli, 8th Gamerra)	about	3,700
Irregulars of Okule-Kusai and Gheralta (Sapelli and Luca)	„	376
One battery (1st Henri) and the 2nd section of the 2nd battery (Vibi) of Native mountain artillery,	guns	6
Two batteries of Italian mountain artillery, (3rd Bianchini and 4th Masotto)	„	8

Central Column.

1st Infantry Brigade (Major-General Arimondi).

One regiment of Bersaglieri (1st Stevani) of only 2 battalions (1st De Stefano, 2nd Compiano)[1]	about	773
One regiment of infantry (2nd Brusati), 3 battalions (2nd Viancini, 4th De Amicis, 9th Baudoin)	„	1,500
The 1st Company (Pavesi) of the 5th Native battalion	„	220
Two mountain batteries—Italian (8th Loffredo, 11th Franzini)[2]	guns	12

[1] Of these battalions, the 2nd Bersaglieri, under Colonel Compiano, was only 350 strong, having left 115 men with the baggage.

[2] Franzini's battery was at Mai Maret, and only arrived at mid-day; it fired only one shot before being captured.

Column on the Right.

2nd Infantry Brigade (Major-General Dabormida).

Two regiments of infantry of 3 battalions each—namely:		
3rd regiment (Ragni) consisting of battalions 5th (Giordano), 6th (Prato), 10th (De Fonseca)	about	1,310
6th Regiment (Airaghi) consisting of battalions 3rd (Branchi), 13th (Rayneri), 14th (Solaro) . . .	„	1,330
One battalion of native mobile militia (De Vito) .	„	950
One company of the Kitet of Asmara (Sermasi) .	„	210
Three Italian mountain batteries (Zola), namely: 5th (Motino), 6th (Regazzi), 7th (Gisla) . . .	guns	18

Reserve Column.

3rd Infantry Brigade (Major-General Ellena).

Two regiments of Infantry of 3 battalions each, namely:		
4th Regiment (Romero), consisting of battalions 7th (Montecchi), 8th (Violante), 11th (Manfredi)	about	1,380
5th Regiment (Nava), consisting of one Alpine battalion (Menini), the 15th (Ferraro) and the 16th (Vandiol) of infantry	„	1,550
The 3rd Native Battalion (Galliano)	„	1,150
A half company of Engineers	„	70
Two quick-firing batteries,—namely: 1st (Aragno) 2nd (Mangia).	guns	12

The forces of the Abyssinian Army are given by Melli as follows:

The Negus Menelik . .	25,000	rifles,	3,000	horses	and	32	guns.
„ Empress Taitu . .	3,000	„	600	„	„	4	„
Negus Tecla Aimanot. .	5,000	„	—			—	
Ras Maconnen	15,000	„	—			—	
„ Mangasha and Alula	12,000	„	—			6	„
„ Mangasha Atichim .	6,000	„	—			—	
„ Mikael	6,000	„	5,000	„		—	
„ Oliè and others . .	8,000	„	—			—	
Totals. . .	80,000	rifles,	8,600	horses	and	42	guns.

These figures, says Lieutenant Melli, agree with those of the Russian Elez, who, in order to exalt the Abyssinians, underrated rather than over-estimated their numbers. The firearms were nearly all breach-loaders, Gras, Martini, Lebel, and many of them Remington.[1]

In addition to these totals there were about 20,000 men carrying lances, and various bands of armed peasants, or of rebels such as Ras Sebath and Agos Tafari.

The number of Italians who actually took part in the battle amounted to a total of about 17,700 men in all, of whom 10,596 were white men, and the rest natives. 14,519 rifles, 56 guns, no cavalry.

In addition to these, 1,415 white men, 1,600 natives and 51 officers were left in camp.[2] There were also 900 unarmed natives to lead the mules, but they, I suppose, are not included in the totals, not being fighting men.

Three native companies, and the irregular bands from Serae, being still stationed near the Mareb, whither they had gone to counteract the Shoan raid under Ras Gabeiu, a telegram was despatched to Major Ameglio, the officer in command, to occupy Yeha (Jeha) on March 1st. This would have placed him within reach, and might, as matters turned out have proved very useful; but owing to a mistake in the telegram he marched towards Hoja. From Hoja he was recalled by a second telegram which, however, was also incorrect, so that the Italians were deprived of his 1,200 good

[1] Mr. Wylde, whose figures are gathered from Abyssinian sources, gives their total at 120,000.

[2] These figures are taken from Major Bourelly, who has made a careful study from both official and unofficial sources.

rifles. Lieutenant Melli remarks on these two telegraphic errors as being "a strange fatality," and it is impossible, of course, to say what difficulties may have been encountered to cause them. But there seems to have been a superabundance of such telegraphic fatalities on the Italian side; owing to these two errors, and that before Amla Alagi, the Governor lost the services of 3,000 men on the decisive day at Adowa.

With their 17,700 men and 56 guns, the Italians were about to offer battle to 80,000 Abyssinians armed with rifles; and at least 20,000 more armed with spears, who, when one of their comrades fell, stood ready to seize his weapon and ammunition, and take his place in the firing line.

As a specimen of the many Italian descriptions of the country between Sauria and Adowa, whose difficulties are continually adverted to by the European officers, we may quote Lieutenant Melli's vigorous and vivid picture. "The soil," he says, "upturned by ancient phenomena, offers the "same physical characteristics, and the same Alpine and wild "appearance, that is common to the whole of the Ethiopian "region; green valleys covered with rich tropical vegetation "in whose depths some muddy stream winds to and fro and "finally loses itself; rugged slopes, precipitous and broken, "abounding in ravines, gorges, and crevasses; narrow and "tortuous clefts in the hard rock; passes half closed, steep "and very difficult, and granite summits that rear themselves "to the sky in the most strange forms and dimensions. The "surface seems like a stormy sea moved by the anger of God.

"Few villages, but many huts are met at the moderate "altitudes; here and there cultivated and green pastures in "the declivities and on the low land; thick bushes and "trees in the forests; while scattered everywhere are many "euphorbias, mimosas, wild olives, junipers, and some giant "sycamores."

The only paths to be found are small beaten tracks winding in and out amongst the mountains, now in the depth of a valley, now on the summit of a hill,—sufficient, perhaps, for the natives who have known them from childhood, but very difficult for a column of European soldiers, especially at night. Such was the country over which the three brigadiers had to trace their path in the darkness, relying for information only on the native guides, and on the small incorrect sketch map supplied to them by Baratieri.

CHAPTER X

THE BATTLE OF ADOWA

The night march—Albertone's native brigade crosses Arimondi's path—Albertone's difficulty on Kidane Meret—Whose fault?—5.15 a.m., Dabormida in position—5.32, Albertone's advanced guard opens fire—6.45, Dabormida ordered to support Albertone—His divergence northwards—8.15, Baratieri perceives the critical position of Albertone's native brigade—Description of Albertone's action—Series of mishaps—Arimondi's left wing attacked—Spur of Belah seized on his right—Ellena's reserve brigade engaged—Italian centre pierced—Vain attempts to fill the gap—Retreat—The Governor's movements—Further misfortunes—The Governor's despatch—It can only apply to a comparatively small portion of his army.

At 9 o'clock on the evening before that fixed by General Baratieri for his fateful advance, a storm broke over the heights of Sauria,—a storm of which he must have carried the remembrance to his grave, for had it occurred twenty-four hours later the night march would have become impossible, and his name might perhaps never have been connected with disaster. From what he tells us, it appears to be a common occurrence in that part of the world, when the clouds are hanging about those mountain peaks, for them to burst at the same hour on several consecutive days; and as during the whole of the 29th the sky was overcast, it seemed, to the last, extremely probable that the expedition might, of necessity, be countermanded. At the appointed time, however, on the second evening, instead of the expected storm breaking, the sky suddenly cleared, and all gave promise of a splendid night for the march along the uncertain tracks that led westwards. The brigades were ready; at the head of each was a body of natives with a guide, under the command of an Italian officer; a short distance in rear of them came the advanced guard, which was but a small space in front of the main body.

As the columns moved off by the light of the African moon, no sound was to be heard except the tramp of men and the slight rattling of weapons. Smoking was forbidden lest the glow should be observed by the enemy, and the shadowy lines of the columns soon began to mingle with those of the heights in front of them, and were presently lost amongst the natural undulations of the ground. The native brigade was on the left under Albertone, Arimondi's brigade in the centre, and that of Dabormida on the right, according to the orders of the day. Both men and officers seemed in high spirits, their only fear being that, owing to some unforeseen circumstance, they might not after all succeed in bringing the Shoans to battle; everything appeared to promise success.

As soon as he had made a final inspection of the arrangements for the sick and wounded, who were to remain in the camp, the Governor mounted and proceeded to follow his army. After crossing the Mai Cherbara, he at once noticed that the last battalion of Dabormida's column had swerved to the left, and was now marching in rear of

Arimondi's brigade. He promptly sent an officer to order it back. But the fact that so important a mistake should have occurred at so early a period in the march, augured ill for the success of the Italians, and well illustrates the difficulty attending even the most simple movements in the dark. Nevertheless, starting at 9 p.m., the Governor had a full period of eight hours in which his army was to march a distance of little more than nine miles, so that he had allowed (as he says) for the occurrence of mistakes; and noticing on several occasions that the individual units were not sufficiently "closed up" to those in front of them, he sent messengers to the officers, ordering them to "sacrifice celerity of movement to the supreme advantages of good order." It is plain from his description, how each small incident had impressed itself on his mind, and one may see in his pages an almost pathetic antithesis, presented by the careless good humour of the soldiers who were marching to their death, and the anxiety of the commander who was unfortunate enough to survive the defeat.

The paths, though very difficult, were better than usual; and the men, in spite of their clumsy, hard boots, (Baratieri complains bitterly of the regulation boot, which he says hurts the feet when it is old, and damages them still more when it is new) marched well. The night was fresh and the air keen. The Governor as he rode with the regiments, noted a general appearance of cheerfulness, and heard whispered jokes passing from one man to another. Suddenly he came upon a battalion of Bersaglieri halted on each side of the path, some of the men being asleep. He at once sent for the commanding officer, Colonel Stevani, who, in explanation of the halt, handed to him the following note:

"Gundapta, 1st March, 1896. Hour 3.30.

"The advanced guard, having reached the height where the valley opens on to the plain of Gundapta, has been compelled to halt in order to allow Albertone's brigade, which is following the same path, to defile past them. I suppose that the cause of this unforeseen crossing is due to the fact that the two routes assigned to the brigade, have a stretch of ground which is common to both.

"I will follow in rear of them; but I shall not be able to start from this point before 4 a.m.

"I have not been able as yet to get connection with Dabormida's brigade.

"Arimondi,

"Major-General."

It was apparent that the native battalions had taken a wrong path, but the gravity of the mistake was not even suspected. Yet by this error the ensuing battle was already half lost; disaster had become unavoidable, owing to a chain of events which developed themselves in the following manner.

Albertone, having thus delayed the two other brigades for almost an hour and a half, naturally reached his post before either of them were within miles of their destination. In was, in fact, little after 3 a.m. when the head of his column arrived at the hill that, according to the Governor's sketch map, was named Kidane Meret, and which it was intended that he should occupy. The General quite understood this, and halted his men in order to await the arrival of the other brigades on his right; but unfortunately, as has been already explained, the hill on which he stood was not generally known by the name of Kidane Meret.

Albertone waited for perhaps half an hour, and then, finding that there were no signs of Arimondi's column on his right, began to think there was some mistake. He therefore consulted his guides, who told him that Kidane Meret was not the spot on which he stood, but was situated some four and a half miles further off from Sauria. This naturally added to his misgivings; moreover, if he had still four and a half miles to march, there was obviously little time to be lost. So after waiting in vain a full hour, for Arimondi's arrival, he decided to march on to the true Kidane Meret that overlooks the hollow of Adowa, and was not more than three miles from the Shoan camp. During the march, it is said that on several occasions he showed signs of irritation and anxiety, and, if so, one cannot but sympathise with him, for he had been driven into one of those terribly harassing situations in which there are two alternatives,—the one, for a man to pursue the strictly accurate and logical course which nevertheless he feels to be wrong; the other, to act contrary to the letter of his orders, but according to what he believes to be their true meaning. Albertone chose the former, distrusting his own judgment, and the results of his advance were fatal to the Italian army; for it was not very long before he was isolated and surrounded, which compelled the other brigades to fight all day with their left flank ill guarded, and to make futile efforts to relieve him,—efforts that finally disorganised their whole line of defence.

As regards this mistake there has been a great deal of enquiry. Baratieri urges strongly that the fault was not attributable to him, because—

Albertone, like all the other generals, had special orders to keep in touch with the column on his right; having lost it, he never sent any messengers to say where he was; hence he could never be supported.

That he knew the position which was to be held by the army, and that he was to guard the left flank; further that he knew of some ten or fifteen thousand Shoans, who were encamped in the hollow of Mariam Shavitu, and whose presence would have rendered his advance highly injudicious, and even have endangered his being cut off.

That even if the name Kidane Meret was a mistake, he could not fail to know where he was to go, as it was carefully marked on the map.

After considering these arguments, it is unfortunately impossible to acquit the Governor of all blame. One can only regret that so brave and able a man, who had not only spent his life in the service of Italy, but had even assisted in making her a nation, should ever be connected with such a disaster. At the same time it must be admitted that his error in writing the name Kidane Meret opposite the hill which lies to the South of Mount Raio, was largely responsible for that disaster.[1] General Albertone could

[1] The Governor did not draw the map himself; but he issued it to the brigadiers and is therefore responsible. In his memoirs

hardly have pursued any other course than that of marching on the position named in his orders; no man can be absolutely sure of his whereabouts at night, in a comparatively strange country, amidst a labyrinth of streams, cliffs, bushes and other natural obstacles. He was ordered to go to Kidane Meret, and he was provided with a native guide to show him the way; the guide showed him the way and he went there.[1]

On the other hand, the Governor is perhaps right in urging that no messengers were despatched to him by Albertone, and that the brigadier should have been more careful to keep the rest of the army informed of his whereabouts. There is also little doubt that had the native brigade not originally strayed out of their path the situation would never have arisen.

Whatever may be the truth as regards these disputed points, at three o'clock, when the Governor was receiving the note from General Arimondi, he attached no great importance to the matter. As soon as it became possible, the brigades of the centre and right moved forward, and by 5.15 a.m. the Governor received a note, brought to him by

he still maintains that the hill was called Kidane Meret, but the balance of testimony is against him. In any case his' map was far from clear.

[1] I see that Captain de la Jonquière, of the Etât Major, considers General Albertone to have been responsible for the mistake and not the Governor. It is a question on which military opinion is divided. He urges that whatever was the name written by the Governor, Albertone knew the position to be defended and should have conformed to that. But Baratieri's strongest supporter is Major Bourelly.

two Ascari, saying that General Dabormida had occupied the hill of Rebbi Arienni according to orders. At 5.30, as the sun was rising, Arimondi's brigade wound into its position on the eastern slopes of Rebbi Arienni, where they branch out towards the towering Mount Raio. The reserve column under Ellena was already in sight, in fact at 5.45 all seemed well, except that the native brigade of Albertone was missing.

Meanwhile the Abyssinians were awake and moving. So certain had the chiefs become that Baratieri intended to remain in his entrenchments that this sudden night-advance might conceivably have taken them by surprise, but that old Ras Alula was on the watch. Though he was stationed on the opposite flank, his spies brought him word of the Italian movements, and he sent to warn the other chiefs. The great chance had at last arrived. When provisions were exhausted and retreat seemed inevitable, the white men had suddenly left their fortified position and had thrown themselves into some of the deepest valleys of rugged Ethiopia. Menelik's whole army was to move out of its strong defensive position and envelop the invaders.

On the extreme right, to the South of Adowa, lay the troops of Gojjam under King Tecla Aimanot (in his youth known as Ras Adal, and celebrated for his battles with the Dervishes), with their cavalry thrown out in front. Adowa was occupied by the Harrarese under Ras Maconnen, who that day added greatly to his fame and position amongst the chiefs. On his left lay old Ras Mikael, the enforced convert from Mohammedanism, with his Wolo Galla mounted riflemen lined along the southern and south-western slopes of Mount Shelloda (Selado). On the North of that mountain was Ras Mangasha with his faithful Tigréans, while guarding the extreme left, as far back as Adi Abuna, lay the followers of Ras Alula. Ras Olié, Wagshum Guangul, Menelik himself and the Empress Taitu appear to have been in reserve behind Adowa, while the splendid Galla cavalry was encamped in some water meadows about eight miles off. The whole of this great host was now on the alert. A hundred and twenty thousand men thrown up from the unexplored depths of Africa were preparing to rush against the Europeans. The chiefs were issuing their commands, but each warrior knew the general plan of the battle and was accustomed to take his own course in a moment of difficulty. How extraordinary must the scene have appeared during those grey hours before dawn amongst the irregular and crowded tents! Thousands of lean fierce-looking Ethiopians in the cloak of brilliant colours that they wear on a day of battle; riflemen, spearmen from the hills, swordsmen buckling the curved blade on to their right side so as to give free play to the shield arm; wild riders from the plains, azmari, priests giving absolution, women and children even, and here and there some great feudal chief with black-leopard or lion skin on his horse, with gold embossed shield, silver bracelets and all magnificence of barbarian war. The sun had not yet risen when they moved out across the fertile plain of Adowa. Then the army of King Tecla Aimanot, Menelik's own followers, those of Ras Mikael and of Mangasha began the attack on Albertone's brigade, in which they were presently supported by Ras Maconnen and Ras Olié. It is said that when they opened fire Menelik entered the church of St. George, where he prayed with passionate earnestness for the success of his arms.

Presently, therefore, some very credible news of the missing battalions was brought to the ears of the Governor, in the form of a brisk though distant fusilade on his left, which sounded clear and unmistakable through the fresh morning air.

The first exchange of shots with the Shoans took place about 6 a.m. from off the true hill of Enda Kidane Meret, which Albertone's advance guard had just crossed. It was, as a matter of fact, due to another mistake, attributable entirely to General Albertone or to his subordinates. He had halted his men close to Addi Vetshi (Vecci), in order to try and gain connection with the brigade on his right, before proceeding to Enda Kidane Meret; but his advanced guard, consisting of the 1st Native Battalion under Colonel Turitto, continued its forward movement, and the Ascari threw themselves on the Shoan outposts, with whom they were soon hotly engaged.

Baratieri had reached the hill of Rebbi Arienni at 6 a.m. He had no suspicions as to Albertone's whereabouts, but assumed him to be at his post on the left. Even the sound of firing, so far in advance of the true position, did not alarm him; he concluded that it came from some scouts of the native brigade, who had probably run suddenly into one of the enemy's outposts; his whole anxiety appears to have been centred on the movements of Dabormida, for he knew that only about three miles in front of his right there was the large camp of ten or fifteen thousand Shoans at Mariam Shavitu. Between the hours of 6 a.m. and 7 a.m., therefore, he spent the time in reconnoitring the ground on the right and front. He appears to have imagined that Albertone had perhaps advanced a little beyond the line of defence, but he was confident of being able to find him when necessary. At 6.15 he did indeed send off two messengers to discover where that general might be, but they were not given any orders for him,—the Governor never for a moment suspecting that his left wing was already in danger of being cut off and annihilated; while Albertone, on his part, believed that the orders left him no choice but to defend Enda Kidane Meret. This mutual ignorance of each other's movements had already seriously imperilled the whole army.

At 6.45 the Governor ordered Dabormida's brigade to advance,—to occupy the Spur of Belah, and if possible to support Albertone. Another command that led to fatal misunderstandings! This is the order he tells us he gave, but nobody seems to have understood it as such, [1]—and it

[1] The whole matter is inexplicable and has given rise to continuous polemics; unfortunately it is one of the turning-points of the battle and cannot be neglected. What order did the Governor really give to Dabormida? He insists that he merely told that general to occupy the Spur of Belah and to support Albertone if possible, keeping connection with Arimondi all the time. But Dabormida obviously never understood this. Colonel Valenzano, chief of the Staff, was present and discussed the matter with both of them; it was he who first suggested the order. He says that what the Governor told Dabormida was, to post his artillery on a certain spur (that he pointed out) in order to protect his (Dabormida's) own advance up to Albertone, "with whom he was to join hands as quickly as possible. (Quoted in Baratieri's Memoirs, p. 407.) To me this seems most probably the order actually given, and when Dabormida reached the Spur in question he most likely perceived that Albertone

would have had very little meaning, for how could Albertone be reached by a brigade that still occupied the Spur?—What he probably intended was that, after occupying that height, Dabormida should continue to advance with some of his troops and join hands with Albertone, whom the Governor apparently believed to be within quite a short distance. But the results were in every way disastrous, for Dabormida thought it his duty to advance without any further delay to the assistance of Albertone, and owing (probably) to the paths being flanked by high cliffs he was eventually led away northwards, far from either Albertone or Arimondi; instead of inclining to the left he inclined to the right and became entirely isolated. But with his force,

being farther off than had been thought, his artillery would protect him better from a more advanced point. He would therefore have moved forward to help the Native Brigade, considering this the true gist of his orders, while Baratieri still believed him to be occupying the Spur.

The technico-military enquiry resulted in a verdict (by Colonel Corticelli) on this matter entirely in favour of the Governor; but the Tribunal at Asmara some weeks later decided that Baratieri "had abandoned his conception of awaiting the enemy and had ordered General Dabormida to advance towards the native brigade of Albertone and support it." One thing is certainly extraordinary—namely, that Colonel Valenzano says he quite realized the direction in which Dabormida was about to march, and also how far off Albertone had succeeded in placing himself. The Governor says he never supposed Dabormida would go beyond 800 metres distance, and did not know for certain of Albertone's whereabouts until 8.30 a.m.—an hour and three quarters later.

So much for polemics. As to results: Dabormida, though engulfed in the valley of Mariam Shavitu, succeeded after some which, like that of Albertone, fought a separate action, we shall deal later.

For the two hours between 6 a.m. and 8 a.m., the Governor remained on the right, reconnoitring the ground and giving orders according to the plan of battle already mentioned. Yet by eight o'clock the men were not in their positions; he says they were obliged to move in single file and marched slowly, and they must indeed have done so, but it should also be remembered that there being only one path, for part of the way before reaching Rebbi Arienni, Arimondi had been obliged to follow Dabormida, and consequently the rear of the first brigade was late in arriving at its destination.

At 8.15, the sun having now risen over the mountains and pierced the morning mists, Baratieri took up his stand on the precipitous side of Mount Eshasho (Esciascio) and

hot fighting in placing himself almost in line with Albertone; but there always remained a large gap between them. Dabormida could not join Albertone's right, because he was shut off from it by the wall of hills (Mounts Derar, Adi-Becci, Nasraui and Gusoso) that separates the Italian front into two parts; Nasraui ("Nazareth") was occupied by overwhelming numbers of Shoans, who kept the two brigades separated.

At 9.15 Dabormida sent a note to the Governor, saying: "I am holding out my hand (tendo la mano) to Albertone." He had ordered De Vito's Militia Battalion to move to the left, but they never effected the juncture, being repulsed and annihilated. The note misled the Governor, who thought that all had gone well; he never realized that, to reach Albertone, Dabormida would have to advance by the path of Mariam Shavitu that makes a wide detour to the right,—thereby leaving Arimondi's right flank entirely uncovered and allowing the Shoans to slip in and cut him off from the centre.

swept the horizon through his telescope. From that height he was able to see that the Shoans at Mariam Shavitu were aroused, and were beginning to run from tent to tent, calling on each other to arm. He therefore sent word to both his brigades to hasten their movements. On the left also he was now able to see for himself,—and for the first time,—that Albertone was very seriously engaged by the enemy. The situation was at last made plain to him, and yet he did not recall the native brigade,—for the following reasons, he says: (1) That he thought a retreat might be dangerous, down a slope commanded by the enemy. (2) That his own brigades not being as yet deployed were not in a position to support the retirement,—which they would presently be able to do. (3) That not having received any communication from Albertone, he did not suppose any serious emergency had arisen, for he trusted to the well-known shrewdness of that general.

These reasons seem, indeed, to have some weight, for it might very probably have been dangerous at 8.15 to order the retreat of a brigade that was almost enveloped by the enemy. But it must be remembered that he had now been on the field of operations for two and a quarter hours, and it is surely not hypercritical to say that, in so long a time, the officer in command should acquaint himself with the exact position of each of his brigades; it is true he had sent out two messengers at 6.15, but they had not returned.

At 9 a.m. two notes from General Albertone at length brought him certain tidings of how the native brigade had fared. One was dated 7.30, informing him that they had occupied Kidane Meret and that the 1st Battalion was hotly engaged; the second, brought back by one of his own messengers, was dated 8.15, and told him that the 1st Battalion was still seriously engaged, but that all the others were in position in rear, and that he (Albertone) was managing to disengage it; that the enemy were in great numbers, and that reinforcements "would be well received."

Up to 8.15 all had evidently gone well; the brigadier had not only all his regiments at his disposal after three-quarters of an hour's fighting, but even talked, without anxiety, of disengaging the reckless 1st Battalion. After reading these notes Baratieri galloped southwards to take up his post of observation on Mount Raio; but here a sight met him which, he tells us, went to his heart,—namely, a long line of wounded and fugitives streaming back from Enda Kidane Meret. Along the paths that led back to Sauria this melancholy procession wended its way, passing without heed directly under the eyes of the Governor and his Staff. Baratieri sent some of his officers to intercept them, but although they rode amongst the Ascari, endeavouring to rally them at the foot of Mount Raio, all efforts were vain; discipline had vanished amongst these unfortunates, and the Italians could hardly make themselves understood.

And here, for the present, we may leave the Governor endeavouring to halt his Ascari, and take our departure to the side of the unfortunate General Albertone, in order to appreciate the anxieties and mishaps that fell to his share during that disastrous morning. At 6 a.m. the 1st Battalion, having crossed[1] Enda Kidane Meret, had come into collision with the Shoans on the other side. Albertone, though he saw it hard-pressed, did not think it safe to advance the whole of his force against the enemy, but he sent an order to Colonel Turitto to retire, and prepared himself to support the retirement.

His brigade was disposed in the shape of a cross of which Turitto formed the front arm. The right (the 6th Native Battalion) rested on Mount Gusoso, which he considered inaccessible; the rest of the troops were in the broad undulating valley, the 7th Battalion being on the left, and the 8th some distance behind in reserve; in the centre of the cross were his three batteries and one section (14 guns); some irregulars were sprinkled on either flank. The point from which he expected attack was the long ridge connecting the all-important hills of Enda Kidane Meret and Lazata, about a mile in front of his centre,—particularly suitable for the enemy's artillery. All being thus prepared for the fray, he sent off a note at 7.30 to the Governor,—the first of the two which reached their destination at 9 a.m. as already described. It is not necessary to give the whole of it, but in it he informed him that he had occupied the position of Kidane Meret; that the 1st Battalion was engaged by the enemy; that he foresaw a serious action, and would

[1] According to Baratieri, and according to the official account; but Ximenes and others say that the 1st Battalion had not quite reached the height and that the Shoans were already waiting for them, having been warned by spies of their approach. Mr. Wylde was told by the Abyssinians that Ras Alula had gained information of the Italian advance and had warned the rest of the army.

be glad if Arimondi's brigade were advanced to support him; and "that it would be very advantageous" if Dabormida's brigade moved forward to create a diversion.

This message took an hour and a half to reach the Governor, though he was only five miles off. Had it been possible to use the heliograph the whole course of events would at once have been altered; but the sun had not yet risen and the heliograph does not appear to have been employed at any time during the day.

It was at about this hour that Turitto, who, by pushing on too far, had involved himself in a single-handed fight against the whole Abyssinian army, gave the order to retire; he had been under fire now for about seventy minutes and the enemy was getting very close to him. Leaving one company halted at the foot of the hill to cover the retirement, he endeavoured to lead the remainder back over the ridge, and the three and a half batteries (fourteen guns) opened fire from the main position with splendid effect (8.30). But the Abyssinians were too quick for them; the covering company was "rushed" and overwhelmed by numbers, and, in spite of the dropping shells, many Shoans succeeded in getting almost on to the heels of the unfortunate 1st Battalion, whose retreat became a flight. It was only when the pursuers came under the rifle fire of the main body that they were checked, and most of the fugitives were able to rally in the centre of the brigade; but even then, some of the Shoans, creeping round the flanks, fell upon the stream of wounded men who were making their way back to Sauria.[1]

[1] In Turitto's battalion fourteen Italian officers were killed, and three made prisoners. The remaining two escaped.

The action soon became general, and to make clear as shortly as possible its various phases, the following skeleton description may suffice. The Shoans advanced in the usual half-moon formation adopted by savage races, their right extending as far as Mt. Semaiata, and their left being soon ensconced on the thorny heights of Mt. Gusoso, which was a very serious mishap, as it prevented Dabormida's brigade from ever coming to the support of Albertone.[1] Their first two or three attacks were repulsed, but being reinforced, they presently opened with a quick-firing battery from the ridge of Kidane Meret, and sent 15,000 men to attack the 7th Battalion on Albertone's left. It was this overwhelming onslaught that proved fatal to the native brigade.

But no writer can hope to describe the scene with half the verve of one who was himself present. Major Gamerra, Commander of the 8th Native Infantry, gives an exceedingly spirited account of the fight,—and we may remark that although on more than one occasion, British officers have fought back to back to the end, (as, for instance, when

[1] This is an all-important point, for it explains Dabormida's subsequent note—"I am holding out my hand to Albertone." At 9.15 Colonel De Vito had been ordered by Dabormida to make the connection, and had actually reached the northern slopes of Gusoso while Albertone's men were still defending themselves on the South of it; but the Shoans held it too strongly ever to allow the two brigades to join hands. *It was this central division of the Abyssinians that decided the day: starting at Mount Gusoso they pushed Albertone to their right and Dabormida to their left,* and eventually seized the Spur of Belah, rendering Arimondi's position untenable. They consisted, according to Mr. Wylde, of men from the detachments of Maconnen, Mangasha, Ras Olié, and Wagshum Guangul.

Hicks Pasha's force was destroyed by the Mahdiists,) there have been few men in history who have seen, as he did, their whole battalion destroyed in hand-to-hand fight with the enemy, and who have lived to tell the tale. He describes the scene most graphically; after relating how he was placed in reserve at about 6 a.m., and how he remained there for some three hours with only one short move forward, he says:

"Meanwhile some firing began to be heard on our front, but few of us were taking much notice of it, when a powerful volley rang out like a thunder-clap, and woke us up. It was the 1st Battalion (Turitto) which had come in contact with the enemy. After a little the wounded began to fall back to the rear, and amongst these I saw our brave Menelik, eldest son of the Dedjazmatch Sabatu of Asmara, one of our really faithful chiefs. A bullet had struck him in the chest and had gone out near the right shoulder-blade. He was proceeding slowly on his mule, and a private of the irregulars was supporting him. That virile and handsome face was overspread[1] with pallor, the strange pallor of the black man. As soon as he saw and recognised me, he called out, 'Major, I am wounded ... but it is nothing.' 'Bravo, Menelik!' I replied. 'Honour to you and to your father!' Scarcely had they passed me when, as if to give the denial to his chief, the private pointed to the large bullet hole which the wounded man had in his back, and shook his head sadly. Other wounded men came by, and my adjutant-major,[2] a hero on whose breast shone a 'medaglia di prode,'[3]

[1] Lit. "shining."

[2] Corresponds to our "adjutant."

[3] "Medal of a brave man," an ordinary medal.

said to me, pointing to his forehead damp with sweat: 'It is a strange thing, is it not, Major, that the sight of blood makes me sick? .... And yet it is so.' I distracted him from this first ill effect by interesting him in the fight, which was developing under our eyes. The 1st Battalion, having no hopes of being supported because it had advanced too far, and feeling that it had on its hands the whole Shoan army, was retiring, decimated, but in very good order, and closely followed by enormous masses of the enemy. The four batteries of the brigade opened on them a murderous fire, cutting furrows through them with their projectiles; the irregulars and the battalions on the firing line followed the example of the batteries, but their firing was so violent that the General soon made them slacken it. It might have been about 8 o'clock, when the fight, now general along the whole front, became quite superb (superbamente bello). Seldom, even during manœuvres in time of peace, have I seen such discipline amongst the troops, such calmness amongst the officers, or such composure in the General. The Artillery was admirable, and General Albertone sprang from his horse to embrace the captains,—poor heroes who all four remained on the field of battle close to their guns. The white batteries, consisting of Sicilians, and who owing to this distinction were called by us 'the Sicilians,' renewed the glorious feats of their corps; the black batteries vied nobly with them.

"Nevertheless, the Shoans manœuvred with great skill; but suffering from the play of our guns and rifle fire, they were compelled to retire from their first attack. The sun of victory was shining on us! It is even said, I do not know on what grounds, that the Negûs, seeing this failure of one portion of the corps led by Maconnen, Ras Mikael and Ras Olié (22,000 to 25,000 men) gave the order for a general retirement,[1] but that on the entreaties of the Queen Taitu and of Ras Mangasha Joannes, he countermanded it, sending into the firing line the soldiers immediately under his command, who were for that reason known by the pompous name of the Royal Guard. Here was a new hurricane of 25,000 men who, together with the others, were let loose against us,—it was the hurricane which would presently overwhelm, disperse and annihilate the Native Brigade!

"The General, immovable on his horse near the batteries, gazed fearlessly at the whirlwind that was approaching. If any man saw General Albertone at Abba Garima without sincerely admiring him, one can only say that he had no heart in him, and no soldier-blood in his veins. The Artillery is on the verge of falling into the hands of the Shoans, but he shows no sign of perturbation; there is still one battalion in reserve.... Let the 8th therefore advance; and it proceeds resolutely into the hottest part of the fight, in order to give a moment to the batteries. The 7th will support it! The order to advance rings out for the battalion with the yellow facings, and immediately afterwards the other battle-cry which has sent its terrible notes over so many battle-fields.... the 'Avanti! Avanti!'[2]

[1] Ras Gabeju, "the lion of Amba Alagi," had fallen with many other chiefs. It was at this moment that Albertone, radiant with triumph, sent off his second note to the Governor.

[2] "Forward! forward!"

of the old Bersaglieri. The officers repeat it, and an avalanche of men hurls itself on the enemy. Loud, fierce cries break from them, and above all there rises triumphant, sublime, the fateful shout of 'Savoia! Savoia!'[1]

"The 7th Battalion, which is unable to advance, perhaps owing to the rocky ground in front of it, excites with its deafening shouts the 8th.... and the proud Royal Guard of the Shoans turns about. This is a moment of indescribable enthusiasm; but cold, inexorable as death, a storm of lead arrests the 8th Battalion in its headlong course. Three companies deploy, and one remains in reserve; a furious fire replies to that of the enemy, who again retires. One more effort, one only, and victory will be ours.... perhaps! Again the command to advance rings out, and again the battalion dashes furiously on to the Shoan hordes who, confounded by such boldness, do not await the shock, but fall back. But they soon return, and in such numbers that they seem to rise up out of the earth; the artillery is again threatened and the 8th hastens to cover it, until the last section of the native batteries has retired. 'Major, we are outflanked on the right,' says an officer, Lieutenant Mora of the 4th Company. The battalion then executes under a murderous fire a change of front in that direction, counting on still having on its left the 7th Battalion and the irregulars; but these troops have already been compelled to give ground and retire! The 8th is

[1] It was with this shout that the 34th Bersaglieri charged through the gap in the walls of Rome in 1870, completing on that day the unification of Italy.

henceforth alone, isolated,—and on it is being concentrated the fire of thousands and thousands of Shoans; it continues, nevertheless, to manœuvre fearlessly for some little while, but then its ranks break up and it disperses. Its commanding officer runs to the General begging him to retire, but the latter calls on the 8th Battalion for a last effort, one last stand. Then in the midst of the clamour of battle, a voice thunders: 'Ascari, halt! 8th Battalion, halt!'... Many other voices repeat these commands adding: 'Ascari, it is your Major,' and 300 Ascari halt and reopen a desperate fire on the enemy, who checks his advance against our front. But on the flanks?.... All is lost, all is lost, and the few survivors are trying to save their lives.

"The 8th Battalion no longer exists... it is destroyed! Twelve officers,—amongst them all the captains,—are dead, the commander has no longer a command and becomes simply a soldier. He follows, stupefied with grief, the remnants of his splendid battalion, but he deludes himself with the idea that at all events his General is in safety, and thinks that his task has been accomplished to the end. He stops, dismounts, and takes his revolver in his hand, facing round on the enemy. Four officers and a few Ascari follow his example and gather round him. The Adjutant-Major who had emerged from the melée disarmed, asks him for his sword and is given it. One by one these gallant men fall, first of all the Adjutant and Hassan. [1] Not until there remains only one on his feet,—the Major,—do the Amhara rush on to him, and while he defends himself desperately,

[1] Major Gamerra's faithful servant.

one Galla bends over the body of the Adjutant-Major, who, though mortally wounded, has the strength to recover himself and to continue his defence until he is despatched by a rain of sword cuts. Then, on that inanimate body, the brutal hatred and the savage fury of the cursed Galla is able to sate itself.

"Then the Major, surrounded and hemmed in by his assailants, after having killed one, and let fly a shot that misses the side of his chief opponent, and then another shot with the same result, receives in return a blow with the hilt of a sword on his right cheek-bone, and is thrown senseless to the ground, is closely bound with his hands behind his back, and dragged towards the enemy's camp."

Such is the narrative of Major Gamerra, who remained for ten months a prisoner in the hands of the Shoans, but has since returned in safety to his native land.

It was, as he describes, the enormous numbers of the Shoans breaking through the battered 7th Battalion on the left flank, which eventually sealed the fate of the Native Brigade. But, owing to the firm support of the 8th, it held out for another half-hour, and not until about 10.30 a.m. did General Albertone deem it necessary to give the order to retire; the Governor had already at 9.30 sent this order, but it does not appear to have reached its destination. Albertone therefore ordered a general retirement, except by the two white batteries, who were commanded "to continue firing to the last round and to sacrifice themselves where they stood" so as to cover the retreat. For a time the native regiments retired in good order, but the enemy had so far enveloped them that there was never much chance of their escaping. It was not long before the Shoans broke through the defence and captured a battery, but a company of the 7th Battalion rallied, charged them and recaptured three guns at the point of the bayonet. It was a futile effort, as half a mile farther on the three guns were again taken by the Shoans, but it must have been the work of a hero; for an officer whose battalion has borne the brunt of a disastrous attempt at defence during two or three hours, and then been broken through and hurled back in all the indescribable confusion of a bayonet struggle, to be able to keep in hand his company—of natives,—and to re-animate them to an almost hopeless attack is a feat to be remembered. It is not, I believe, known who the officer was—doubtless some junior captain or lieutenant,—but all honour to him and his Ascari.

At 10.15 the Governor had sent another order to Dabormida to move forward and support the left, but Dabormida was not to be found, having already begun the advance which eventually led him into the Mariam Shavitu valley.

Albertone's brigade, therefore, left to its own resources, struggled manfully. The 3rd and 4th black batteries fired their last round (they had ninety rounds per gun) before being finally captured; the two white batteries stood their ground according to orders, continuing to fire for an hour, until in fact the Shoans actually rushed in among the guns. A hand-to-hand struggle then ensued in which "the Sicilians" died gloriously, the two batteries being annihilated almost to a man.[1]

[1] Out of the four batteries only four officers escaped death, all of them seriously wounded and three of them sent to the rear before

The Governor meanwhile had been watching the progress of the fight, and as early as 9 a.m. he saw that matters were becoming serious; it was then that he decided to recall Albertone and to re-assemble all his forces on the original defensive position that he had intended to occupy. We now come to the series of mishaps that rendered it entirely impossible to retrieve matters; for the sake of conciseness we may number them.

I. At 9.15 he sent a note to Dabormida, ordering him to be ready to support Albertone's retirement, but this note never reached its destination, for the messenger meeting one from Dabormida, bringing word from that general that "he was holding out his hand to Albertone," thought it useless to proceed and returned to the Governor.

II. At 9.30 Baratieri sent to Albertone himself, ordering him to retire, but Captain Amendune, the officer who carried the message, was unable to reach his destination. He forced his way bravely through the crowds of fugitive Ascari and

the final rush. The following table shows well how the 3rd and 4th "Sicilian" batteries carried out their orders to sacrifice themselves.

IIIrd Battery.	Strength	Killed	Wounded or Prisoners	Escaped.
Officers	4	2	1	1
N. C. O.'s. . . .	4	3	1	
Corpls. and men	58	38	18	2
IVth Battery.	Strength	Killed	Wounded or Prisoners	Escaped.
Officers	4	4		
N. C. O.'s. . . .	2	2		
Corpls. and men	71	46	21	4

These figures are taken from "La Battaglia di Abba Garima" by Major Bourelly, whose work contains an analysis of the latest official returns. Out of 81 line officers in the brigade no less than 48 were killed, and almost all the others wounded or made prisoners.

advancing Shoans, only to hear that Albertone had fallen, and that the brigade was already retiring.

III. At 9.45 Baratieri sent to find out where Dabormida was, for it was becoming apparent that the right wing was now lost as well as the left. The messenger came back saying "that he saw them advancing just in front of the position." But what he probably saw in reality was the battalion of De Amicis, who had been ordered to follow in rear of Dabormida and preserve connection with the centre, (Armondi and Ellena); for the 2nd Brigade itself was now far away and already engaged by the enemy.

IV. At 10, and again at 10.15, he sent an order to Dabormida to advance and support Albertone, but neither order reached its destination.

The Governor had therefore entirely failed in his endeavour to concentrate the army on its original line of defence. And, which was worse, he had not even discovered the exact position of Dabormida, nor did he know that since 9.30 that general's brigade had been engaged by the enemy, who had very soon cut it off from the centre. He appears still to have believed that his right flank was in perfect safety; he tells us that he still supposed the Spur of Belah—a point on which everything depended—to be held by Dabormida, whereas it was now *occupied by no troops of any kind*; for that general was fighting his own action some three and a half miles away to the right, in the valley of Mariam Shavitu. This Spur of Belah, it may be well to note, commanded Arimondi's right flank and his line of retreat.

In the centre, under Arimondi's command, now that De Amicis' battalion had followed the right wing, there were only 1,773 rifles and two batteries; and the Governor, fancying himself secure on the right, turned his whole attention to the left, and lined these battalions along the slopes between Mounts Raio and Belah.[1] He reinforced them with two quick-firing batteries from Ellena's reserve brigade (still at Rebbi Arienni), and with the celebrated native battalion of Galliano, that had distinguished itself at Coatit, and had heroically defended Macalle. This native battalion, 1,200 strong, was placed on the extreme left, to guard the flank and rally fugitives; on the extreme right of the brigade were two battalions of Bersaglieri occupying the slopes of Mount Belah, and the Hill of Belah.

Before 10 a.m., while the Governor was still watching the stream of fugitives from Albertone's battalions (which had not then begun their organised retirement), the 8th Battery opened fire from Mount Raio on the pursuing mass of Shoans, but found it hard to avoid hitting the Italian Ascari, so closely were they pursued; some volleys were also fired, but with the same difficulty. By degrees, therefore, small parties of Shoans were able to creep up and lie down

[1] The slopes are called Mariam Cumbur; he had thus got his brigade facing almost due south, with no support for its right flank; the Shoans were eventually able to surround both its flanks and some groups of them seem even to have climbed Mount Raio (creeping upwards from the rear), and opened fire from the top of it before they were observed.

As regards the non-occupation of the Spur of Belah, the official account of the battle says it was not visible from the lower slopes of Mount Raio; so perhaps the Governor had a good reason for not knowing that the key of his position was unoccupied.

under cover,—within range of the Italians. Presently these hidden marksmen began to make such good practice that the battery was in danger, until the native battalion of Galliano arrived, from the reserve, and opened fire. But while the Governor was attending to his left, the real misfortune was coming upon him from the right. Out of a deep valley in front of the Spur of Belah, a huge mass of Shoans was suddenly seen to emerge, running upwards along the slopes and pressing on so boldy as even to attack the reserve regiments at Rebbi Arienni. In a moment they were on the Spur and all further communications between the Governor and Dabormida were at an end. The Shoans had now pierced the Italian centre, and had divided their line into two parts, each surrounded by a semi-barbarous horde almost as well armed, and six or seven times as numerous as itself. It was this great central column of Shoans that had in the morning brushed aside Albertone's right, and Dabormida's left, preventing their ever joining hands.

The time was only about 10.15 to 10.30 when this important height fell into the hands of the enemy, and Col. Stevani of the Bersaglieri at once sent two companies to retake it. A regiment was also despatched from the reserve, but the attack was a failure. So rapid was the advance of the Shoans that only 40 of the Bersaglieri, (under Col. Compiano [1] and Captain Fabbroni) succeeded in

[1] Col. Compiano had been wounded in the leg, but he refused to retire; and when the Shoans came to close quarters he was last seen "with his left hand and knee on the ground defending himself heroically with his sword until a blow from a lance laid him low."

establishing themselves on the sides of the Spur; of this handful of brave men hardly one returned.

The regiments on the Hill and on Mount Belah itself were now outflanked by the Shoans on the Spur, and they soon began to give ground. Baratieri sent order after order to them to hold the mountain, while he despatched a battalion from the reserve to their support. For a moment the Bersaglieri rallied and held their ground, but the reserve was already engaged in firing volleys at the Shoans advancing from under the cover of the Spur, and also on others in rear who had swept right round the Italian left,—mingling with the refugees of the native brigade,—and had established themselves in the hollow of Gundapta, threatening the line of retreat: the Italians, in fact, were almost surrounded.

It was while the right of Arimondi's brigade was thus at its most critical moment, that (on their left) the native battalion of Galliano,—1,200 strong and relied upon above all others in the colonial army,—suddenly wavered, broke, and fled. This flight was as unexpected as it was disastrous, for the Ascari had only been under fire some twenty minutes,—and so suddenly did their nerve fail that the idea ran through the Italian ranks that treachery was at work. It is very hard to assign a cause for this sudden stampede; it has been insinuated that during the march from Macalle to Adagamus, Maconnen's men succeeded in seducing them from their allegiance to Italy. Whatever the cause, only a few of them remained with their officers, most of whom, including Colonel Galliano, lost their lives. [1]

[1] Colonel Galliano was taken prisoner wounded in the face. After his captors had led him for some distance, his weakness

"Up to this period," (*i.e.* midday) says Baratieri, "it must be confessed that the losses were not serious. The bullets whistled high in the air, but did practically no damage, being fired recklessly from the lower ground."[1] Nevertheless, his men could not remain in their positions, for both flanks were turned, some of the enemy were in rear of them, and their reserves were engaged. The Governor decided, therefore, on a general retirement which he supposed would be safely conducted under cover of Dabormida's brigade.

"Having given the order on the left, he started to ride over to Rebbi Arienni on the right, but the confusion was already dreadful; the mules belonging to General Arimondi and his Adjutant-Major were carried off in the tumult,—an accident which afterwards cost those officers their lives.[2] As he rode past Mount Belah he saw the enemy crown its

and exhaustion became too great, so he sat down, refusing to move another step; he was at once shot.

[1] The losses were heavier than he supposed. When, some months later, a party of Italians were permitted to visit the field of battle and bury their dead, they found 776 corpses on Mt. Raio and the adjacent ground; as many of the bodies had been burnt, we may assume that the losses round Mt. Raio were not far short of a thousand killed,—and the wounded would probably be as numerous.

Of course many of these casualties would occur when the men rose to retire,—perhaps more than half, but even so it is scarcely justifiable of the Governor to say that the "losses had not been serious," and that it was "not until the retirement that the true losses began."

[2] General Arimondi was shortly afterwards brought to the ground with a bullet in the knee, but died sword in hand, together with almost all his officers, defending himself against a horde of Shoans.

heights, firing downwards on the confused mass of Bersaglieri who were now crowded into the valley below. Here he met the last reserves available,[1]—the 16th Battalion and two companies of the Alpini,—still in good order; it was attempted to throw them across the gap in the centre of the position, a gap which was rapidly widening, but these unfortunate companies never even had a chance of stemming the torrent. Before they could deploy (they must have been still in fours, or possibly in file, along the mountain path), the horde of fugitives broke through their line, accompanied by some of the more active Shoans who caught them up, and mingled with them, springing from rock to rock or creeping along the paths and the clefts in the ground, while their companions on Mount Belah had a splendid opportunity for some careful and deadly shooting,—and the Abyssinian does not, as a rule, waste his powder or bullets.

[1] Ellena's Brigade (the reserve) had been gradually used up. It consisted of the following units.

The 7th, 8th, and 11th Battalions (Col. Romero) which were already fully employed in defending Rebbi Arienni, though Baratieri did not suspect that the Shoans had penetrated so far.

The 3rd Natives (Galliano) and two companies of Alpini, that had gone to reinforce the extreme left of Arimondi.

Two quick firing batteries that had gone to reinforce Arimondi's artillery.

The 15th Battalion that had gone to reinforce the 1st Bersaglieri on Mt. Belah, but had arrived too late, and had been cut off and overwhelmed.

The 16th Battalion and two companies of Alpini. Theseal one remained in hand. Their disaster is described in the text.

Romero's battalions (7th, 8th and 11th) endeavoured to cover the Italian retirement and lost very heavily in the unequal struggle.

"By this time some of the battalions had become separated one from another,—the front having been rather too much extended for their numbers owing to the absence of Albertone's brigade,—but they were still resisting to the best of their power. In many parts of the field 'the retire' was being sounded on the bugles, but it was not until about mid-day that the retreat became general; then the Shoans made a wild rush and in a moment had seized all the principal positions. Captain Franzini, for instance, who brought his battery into action at this moment,[1] had only time to fire one shot before he was killed, and his men swept away with the rest,—artillery being the arm on which the Italians chiefly relied!

"It was then, that Captain Benucci of Galliano's battalion, who had succeeded in keeping in hand a small band of Ascari, brought word to the Governor that the enemy had occupied a rise between Mt. Belah and Mt. Raio; General Arimondi was not to be found. The Shoans were already advancing up the slopes of Mt. Raio itself, and some were creeping up amongst the Italians 'taking advantage of their own likeness to the Ascari.' From this time our troops were broken and the soldiers fired haphazard, except a few groups who, kept in hand by energetic officers, halted from time to time and formed for defence in rear of the retiring battalions."

There we get from Baratieri's narrative a powerful picture of the beaten army retiring after its line of defence had been broken. He tells us of his last attempt at rallying his men to form a rear-guard, before he joined the retiring columns.

[1] He had only just arrived, after a march of thirty miles.

"But the disorder was at its height in these narrow paths, and on that difficult ground.—I halted for some time on a small ridge, and was surrounded, for my defence against the on-rushing enemy, by a group of Bersaglieri. And thus, separated from the Staff, I remained with the orderly officer Lieutenant Chigi, and with a few Carbineers and Zaptié. . . . The fire continued from the height, on the flanks, and in rear; and already, the ranks being broken, the tail of the retiring column became a confused mass of white men and black men, Ascari of Galliano, and Ascari of the other units, together with the Shoans, who dashed themselves into the middle of them, leaping as if possessed by a madness to kill or to be killed. [1]

"In the midst of this turmoil I was retiring with Lieutenant Chigi alone of the Staff, surrounded by a few groups of brave men who were still kept in hand by their officers.

"On a spur that extends downwards from Mount Raio towards Rebbi Arienni, opposite Mount Belah which was swarming like an ant-hill with the enemy. I noticed a walled-in enclosure, perhaps the ancient cemetery of a ruined

[1] This madness has been explained to me by a traveller who was in Abyssinia soon after the war. He said that before the battle of Adowa, many of the Shoans were sensible enough of their shortcomings to dread the Italians; that although they had defeated Ascari and others of their own race they were doubtful of success against the European battalions. But when they found that they were beginning to press back the formidable white men, then their enthusiasm rose to madness. It was then that they began to dash up to within ten or fifteen yards of their enemy before firing, so that not a bullet should be wasted. This sentiment appears to me to explain with some vividness the scene described by General Baratieri.

20

church. I endeavoured to renew some kind of resistance in order to protect the retreat,—and I collected Alpini, Bersaglieri, and other white soldiers, with some officers among them. And in that pitiable situation, face to face with acts of individual heroism, my distress was lightened by the transitory hope of saving us by means of a flank movement. 'Viva l'Italia' I called out, grasping my revolver; and this shout was repeated by perhaps a hundred mouths, parched with thirst and bloodstained! But, on the inside, the wall did not permit of firing, because it was higher than the shoulders of a man. An instant later the Amhara gained a position overlooking the spur; and every moment the confusion kept increasing owing to the waves of men sweeping by the hail of the bullets, the sight of the dead and dying,—while one's heart was being torn in, two with the despair of ever being able to give an order or of getting it carried out.

"And we continued along our path of sorrow."

It was indeed a path of sorrow on which General Baratieri followed the retreating army. When he reached Rebbi Arienni after giving up the hopeless defence of the cemetery, he had only two carbineers and two or three Zaptié with him, and his faithful native servant; it was a moment of respite, and he was soon joined by some of the rallying Bersaglieri and Alpini. [1]

[1] In this rout, as in most others, there were many brave men who preferred to sell their lives dearly to seeking a disgraceful safety in flight,—men whose names are amongst the "missing" and whose fate will probably never be known to their friends. On Mt. Raio, for instance, the sound of rifle-firing was heard

Presently he met General Ellena, who told him that Col. Valenzano and Major Salsa of his staff, believing him dead, had gone on to select the next line of defence. Before anything could be done, the Shoans were on them again, and the Governor had only time to collect about a hundred volunteers to form a rear-guard. With this little band of heroes he opened fire, and even repulsed the leading Shoans at the point of the bayonet; but so small a body of men could only delay the enemy for a few minutes.

The Galla cavalry were already cantering in large bodies along the road to Sauria, so that the retreating column was obliged to keep further north,—and Major Salsa, who rode at their head, directed his course towards Yeha. By this time the moral of the troops had sunk practically to the vanishing-point. In his memoirs General Baratieri says: "They were almost unconscious of their surroundings, and careless of everything except of their individual defence. The officers had lost authority over the soldiers, who looked in a bewildered and stupefied manner at those who gave an order or attempted to halt them." The Governor himself, though his uniform made him a distinctive mark for the enemy, rode calmly in rear of the column, refusing to hasten the pace of his mule, and still trying to form a rear-guard under cover of which he might organize some plan of retirement. General Ellena and some other officers remained with him, all of them bravely risking their lives in these

until four o'clock, proceeding, it is said, from a handful of Italians about 140 in number, who ensconced themselves between the folds in the ground and fought to the end;—probably until their ammunition was exhausted.

vain endeavours, while the Shoans became so bold that some of them galloped even within revolver range before firing.

Between the hours of 2.30 and 3 p.m. the Governor met Colonels Brusati and Stevani (afterwards the conqueror of the Dervishes), and it seemed to him a good opportunity for making a last attempt at resistance. He halted on a small hill between Yeha and Cocma, and calling around him the officers, drew his sword with a shout of "Viva l'Italia!" in order to rally the men. "A few soldiers," he says, "despising their lives obeyed the call, and for a moment crowned the height." "We were able to form a strong nucleus," says Colonel Brusati, "of Alpini and mixed drafts, but no one opened fire for fear of hitting their own companions, who were retiring hotly pursued; and only one squad on the extreme left, by my orders, fired a volley against the Galla horsemen who were flying about at a distance of perhaps 400 metres from that part. At this point his Excellency the Governor, raising his sword high and turning back to face the enemy, shouted 'Viva l'Italia!' to which the soldiers who were retiring further off in the plain replied 'Viva il Generale Baratieri!' just as if they were unconsciously taking part in a demonstration. From that moment (about 3 p.m.) the retreat continued uninterrupted in various columns and in various directions, by difficult paths, always under the fire of the Shoans, at whom, from time to time, one of our men would fire a single shot in reply."

Resistance was at an end and discipline remained alive only amongst a few heroes. But Colonel Stevani, in a short and unpremeditated sentence, lays his finger on the true causes that overwhelmed the unfortunate raw Italian regiments: "*All vigour*," he says, "*being lost owing to the extreme weariness and thirst*, each man sought the road to safety on his own legs, and by relieving himself of every weight." From these words one can picture the miserable column of men, who had been marching all night and bungled with all day, who were now trudging onward down that fatal valley of Yeha, so stupefied by weariness, disaster, and thirst, that they cared little even when the Galla horsemen halted to take deliberate aim at them within a short range.

It would be easy to prolong the details of the retreat over many pages, but sufficient has surely been said to give a true idea of it; the rest may be related very shortly. The Shoans did not continue their pursuit for more than some six to nine miles,[1] but they lit bonfires on all the hill-tops in order to arouse the native population to rebellion. At sunset the battered column reached a small village on the East of Mount Amba Beesa. There the Governor halted his men and allowed them an hour and a half's repose. Then, under cover of night, the column resumed its march, this time in good order; the natives in front, as guides, unarmed men in the centre, armed men in the rear, each portion being accompanied by several officers.

But even now the ill fortune of the Governor did not forsake him. Owing to a very natural mistake in the dark, the front portion of the column, with the guides, became

[1] Melli.

separated from the main body which had halted, and General Baratieri was left in command of this large nucleus of soldiers, many of them without provisions, many others wounded, in a strange country and without an efficient guide. As was to be expected, he had some difficulty in finding his way; no less than three times did that column go astray amongst the mountains. "A terrible destiny," says the unfortunate general, "weighed on my head; it was the third time that I had lost the way during the retreat, and my heart was breaking at the long hours during which it had been impossible to give my orders or to receive information."

Finally, at 9 o'clock on March 3rd, he arrived at the fort of Adi Caje, from whence he sent off the celebrated telegram to the Italian Government, announcing the disaster; a telegram written at a moment of such extreme depression that those about him feared that his reason was departing; and one which has earned him great unpopularity amongst his fellow-countrymen. It is, perhaps, not surprising that they should take exception to certain portions of it,—to his description, for instance, of the fight in the centre of the the line of defence.

"Albertone retired under the position occupied by Arimondi, which descends, steep and rugged, under the hill, in order to reinforce which, Galliano's battalion was already assigned as reserve. But, although the fire of the enemy was not particularly efficacious, although our positions were good and commanding, the troops soon allowed themselves to be affected by groups of the enemy, who, profiting by the dead angles, were collecting and trying to surround us. One group of these, which had ensconced itself on a mountain, caused the rapid retirement of two battalions of Bersaglieri, while the battalions of Colonel Brusati's regiment also abandoned their positions. Besides this, the Alpini battalions of the reserve were not prepared to offer any resistance; they were broken by fugitives as soon as they advanced. The enemy, meanwhile, with great boldness, were mounting upwards to our position and were penetrating our files, firing almost point-blank at our officers. Then all control was at an end and no orderly retirement could be organized. It was in vain that the officers tried to halt the soldiers on any of the successive positions, because the enemy bursting in on them, and a few Shoan horsemen dashing about below, were sufficient to throw everything into disorder. It was then that the real losses began; the soldiers, as if mad, threw away their rifles and ammunition, with the idea that if they were taken without arms they would not be emasculated, and almost all of them threw away their rations and cloaks. In vain I and General Ellena, etc., etc." [1]

Such a description, proceeding from a general whose dispositions had certainly not been faultless, requires a strong justification. It is evident that he feels this, for in his

[1] These, and the following statements about the behaviour of the Italian troops have been denied by the united testimony, verbal and written, of the officers who have returned from the battle. (Printed as a footnote in the Green Book, N. XXIII, Bis.)

It is pleasing to read in Mr. Wylde's book, "Modern Abyssinia," that the Abyssinians themselves bear witness to the courage displayed by the Italian soldiers; they say also that from the moment that Baratieri left his fortified position, his defeat was certain owing to their great superiority in numbers.

memoirs he devotes several pages to remarks on it; he insists, with reason, that it was his duty to convey his exact impression to the Government, and admits that after undergoing "the mortal torture" of those three terrible days he may have taken too black a view; he owns that he did not make enough distinctions throughout his somewhat sweeping statements; beyond this, however, he withdraws nothing.

The one powerful argument which he pleads,—and justly pleads, I think,—is that, though he felt it his duty to convey his inmost thoughts to the Government, he took every precaution to prevent their becoming, in any way whatsoever known to the outside world. He wrote in cypher, —a secret official despatch of which the Government alone could discover the meaning; they, he says, thought right to publish it, and the responsibility remains with them. This surely is a valid plea; a general can hardly be limited in what he is to say to his government, nor can he be blamed for making public that which he intended should remain private. The government is not in any way bound to publish his despatches, though it may sometimes find it necessary to do so in order to explain its own decisions: but, as far as an outsider may judge, there was no object to be gained by printing this report verbatim. It would have been more judicious, and more patriotic, to keep such a document securely hidden; writing it in cypher would have done no harm to anyone, but disseminating it abroad in ordinary type was indefensible.

There is one point on which, oddly enough, the Italian writers have never laid much stress—namely, the fact that, at the most, Baratieri was only qualified to speak about two brigades out of the four. There was one force that he had not even seen since 6.30 a.m. that morning; this was Dabormida's brigade, who by their gallant resistance in the valley of Mariam Shavitu were able, if not to restore the fortunes of the day, at all events to retrieve the honour of the Italian army.

CHAPTER XI

THE BATTLE OF ADOWA—DABORMIDA'S BRIGADE

General Dabormida—Start of the brigade from Rebbi Arienni 6.45 a.m.—Troops on its right flank, left flank and rear—The halt at 9 a.m.—Dabormida's note at 9.15—De Vito's militia battalion attacked—Colonel Ragni and Colonel Airaghi advance—The position of their battalions—Attacked by Abyssinians—The Galla cavalry—De Amicis—After mid-day the Italians take the offensive—Successful bayonet charges—Attacked in rear—Attack repulsed—Shoans reinforced—Dabormida's difficulties—The last counter-attack—Retreat in the evening—Guns lost—Thunderstorm rises after sunset.

The name of General Dabormida is one that every patriotic Italian pronounces with a mingled sense of pride and sadness, for it sheds a gleam of glory over the darkness of their disaster. Like Baratieri and many other of the leaders amongst the war party, like Crispi himself, he had in his youth taken part in the great work of unifying Italy. His father, to whom he bore a striking resemblance, had been Minister of War in 1848 when the small nation of Piedmont, defeated but not discouraged, was preparing to strike another blow against Austria; and in 1866 young Dabormida himself was present as a subaltern of Artillery at the battle of Custozza, where he was noticed for his coolness under fire; but courage, which alone is no guarantee of a good officer—the man whose duty it is to think for others,—was by no means his only qualification: he had seriously studied his profession; he had thought. And an index to his character may be found in the following sentences from a private letter written to his family, which, since his death, has become known to the outer world. "Age quod agis: Do your duty, come what will: I repeat this old motto to myself continually, and I hope always to be able to conform my conduct to it... anyhow I will do my duty,—all my duty to the end." This was the man who, unlike most of his type, appears to have been exceedingly popular among his equals; among the officers and men of his brigade he had aroused an *esprit de corps*, an enthusiasm in fact, which so far from being destroyed seems only to have been strengthened and perpetuated by defeat.

It was at 6.45 on March 1st that the Governor ordered Dabormida to advance from the hill of Rebbi Arienni, and himself stood near, together with his Staff, while the brigade moved off, headed by the native battalion of De Vito, into a narrow tortuous valley, through the centre of which ran a small stream. Hardly had Baratieri moved away than Colonel Stevani of the Bersaglieri galloped up to the group of officers standing round General Arimondi, who had also been present, and asked: "But are those heights occupied?" pointing to some dark sharply defined cliffs on the right of the path along which they were moving. "On my own account I've given orders to occupy that summit," he added, pointing to one still higher and nearer. The officers at once turned their field-glasses on to it, and after a little, General Arimondi, nodding his head with a bitter smile, said to Colonel Airaghi: "My dear Airaghi, it seems impossible that we should go on for ever with this same system!"

"If you approve of the idea," interrupted Colonel Airaghi, "I can send one of my battalions over there to guard the flank of our advance."

"Yes, yes, you make good what has been forgotten, and do it quickly," answered the General. [1]

A small incident in itself this seems, but such a remark from the second-in-command has a peculiar ring, especially on the field of battle; it is significant of the state of feeling amongst the officers immediately surrounding the Governor. It is noticeable, however, that Colonel Airaghi interrupted his general almost before the words were out of his mouth. This whole anecdote is recorded by an admirer of Arimondi, who was present and heard the conversation.

A battalion was at once despatched from the left to occupy these heights on the right, but, owing to the path being covered by a long line of artillery etc., it was unable to cross, had to make a large detour, and eventually was ordered back to its original position. Meanwhile it was noticed that the heights in question were in fact occupied by natives. Who could these natives be?

They were a company under Captain Pavesi and belonged in reality to Arimondi's advanced guard, but they never rejoined their own brigade; they continued during the whole day to protect the right flank of Dabormida, being joined by a company of the Kitet under Captain Sermasi. These two companies of natives, though suffering very heavy losses, were successful in repulsing all attempts of the enemy to turn Dabormida's right flank.

[1] Menarini: *La brigata Dabormida a la Battaglia d'Adua.*

As regards the left flank,—it ought of course to have been protected by joining hands with Albertone's brigade, but this was never successfully accomplished. The advanced guard, however, (De Vito's natives) having been ordered to move towards the South, covered the left front before any actual collision occurred with the enemy. [1]

In rear of the brigade, connection was in the end maintained with Arimondi by the battalion of De Amicis (posted on the extreme right of that General) who at about 10.30 a.m. advanced to join Dabormida's reserve. This battalion naturally bore the whole brunt of the Shoan attack when they tried to cut off Dabormida from Arimondi; but as that great struggle did not begin until about 11 o'clock we may for the moment leave it, and return to the advance of the 2nd Brigade which, as has been already noticed, started from Rebbi Arienni as early as 6.45 a.m.

The foregoing has merely been written because, in order to understand the important points in this action, it was

[1] De Vito having seen (during the march between 7 and 9 a. m.) a strong body of the enemy on his left advancing towards the ground where he believed Albertone to be, sent word of it to Dabormida, who at once ordered him to move to his left and effect a junction with Albertone. It was then that Dabormida sent off his famous note to the Governor "9.15 . . . . extensive encampments of Shoans are to be seen to the N. of Adowa; a strong column is advancing from them towards the native brigade; I am holding out my hand to it, while keeping a strong body of troops massed near the road that leads from Rebbi Arienni to Adowa, and watching the heights on the right."

The unfortunate results of this note have been already described pp. 282—284.

necessary to begin by examining the troops posted on the right flank, the left flank and in rear.

* * *

For over an hour the brigade wound its way along the depth of the valley beside a small and filthy water-course, but then the path branched to the right, on the side of the hills, and became a little less broken, though still disagreeable owing to being covered here and there with traces of the Abyssinian camp,—small circular huts built of branches, beds of straw, remains of fires—"a veritable collection of rotten things," says Captain Menarini, "which compelled us to advance with our handkerchiefs to our noses."

Presently the column took a path to the right,—presumably that which branches off towards Mariam Shavitu,—and entered a long valley, some 3½ miles from Rebbi Arienni, Here it halted at about 9 a. m., and the officers began to make observations. The valley in which they found themselves is perhaps 2 miles long, and between 700 and 800 yards broad. On the South the cliffs rise rugged and abrupt, dotted with thorny shrubs; but on the North it is bounded by hills whose slopes are less steep; while the centre is a plain that shelves downwards, covered with high grasses, dried and burnt by the sun, but still standing almost as high as a man,—giving rather the appearance of a field of ripe corn. In the far distance, at the other end of the plain, was visible a great Shoan encampment on a hill, (a portion of Mount Shelloda).

No sooner was the column halted, than the men, wearied after their long march and almost sleepless night, threw themselves on the ground, and, while resting, began to eat any light provisions that they had brought with them for immediate use. The officers, too, formed small circles and at once set about their breakfast.

Close beside them ran a stream which Colonel Airaghi, after careful inspection, decided to be unfit for drinking, as he had found putrid carcases lying here and there in the water. But so great was the thirst of the soldiers, that no power in the world could keep them away from it; in vain the Colonel went about shouting furiously: "Boys, don't drink that water; it will do you harm, and give you typhus." [1] The men ran and filled their water bottles in secret, and when sentries were posted, they were soon discovered to be merely the suppliers-in-chief of water to their respective companies.

While here, Captain Menarini tells us, the whole scene wore so peaceful an aspect, the thousand and one little episodes occurring as they do at a halt on a big field-day, seemed to be so familiar, that the idea of fighting had for the moment almost vanished from their minds. The men joking about the stream, and the officers sitting at their meal, little suspected the tragedy that would fall upon them before sunset.

It was during this halt that Major De Vito, in command of the advanced guard, sent to inform the General that a large body of the enemy were visible on his left; and that the General, ordering him to move to the left, despatched his message to the Governor to apprise him of the fact. [2]

[1] Figliuoli non bevete di quell' aqua; vi fara male, vi verra it tifo."

[2] V. note on p. 317.

At the same time the company of Kitet, under Captain Sermasi, was sent to join Pavesi on the right flank; both these forces at once started down the valley.

General Dabormida himself was standing on a rise, talking to some of his officers, when the rattle of far-off rifle fire from the direction of the Shoan encampment fell on their ears. It was received with some laughter, without, in fact, much attention being paid to it, until suddenly one of the officers, Major Bolla, was struck in the right elbow by a spent bullet.

The engagement had begun.

THE BATTLE UP TO MID-DAY.

The front on which the brigade was about to fight may be divided into three parts, the heights on the left, the valley in the centre, and the heights on the right. In obedience to the General's orders, Major De Vito's native battalion of Militia had begun its march towards the left, while the Kitet Company of Sermasi was still in the valley, directing itself towards the right, when contrary to all expectation they sighted some Galla horsemen advancing. Neither unit had reached its true position, but Sermasi at once extended his men across the little plain, while De Vito led his regiment up the steep ascent on their left, prepared to dispute the enemy's further progress in order to gain time for the main body,—as is the duty of an advanced guard.

The heights are rocky and covered with thorny shrubs, but De Vito's brave natives dashed up them rapidly; for it was all important that they should gain the steep ridge in front of them before the Shoans could reach it. As they came nearer and nearer all seemed well, and presently, with a final effort, they rushed on to the crest triumphant,—only to meet with bitter disappointment; opposite them was a deep cleft with another ridge rising on the far side almost as high as that on which they stood. Breathless as they were, a fresh dash forward was at once decided on, and, "like a black wave," the three leading companies,—some 700 men,—hurled themselves into the valley and then struggled up the opposite height, with the fourth company following in reserve. This supreme effort was successful; they reached the summit just in time to prevent the enemy from seizing it, and throwing themselves on the ground, opened along the whole line a rapid fire, that soon extended to the Kitet company on their right, down in the plain below. The time of day was now hardly later than nine o'clock, and the rest of the brigade was still halted at the entrance of the valley.

But they soon found their position was untenable; they had run into a body of Abyssinians about 15,000 strong,[1] who where already coming to close quarters. It was not long before the Kitet company, though fighting gamely, was compelled to give ground, and their retirement exposed

[1] The men of Ras Mikael, and of Ras Mangasha who was also in command of a detachment of Ras Maconnen's men. They did not wait to complete the destruction of Albertone's brigade, but seeing that it was inevitable, turned at once against Dabormida. He was also opposed by a detachment of Ras Alula's, who was engaged until the afternoon in guarding a pass at Adi Abuna.

the right flank of De Vito's men on the high level. Here was a moment that required some decided action on the part of the commander,—but what had become of Major De Vito? No one knew; he seemed to have vanished as soon as the firing began. Captain Tola took it upon himself to send a hundred men[1] to reinforce Sermasi, and ordered Captain Ferraro with his company to strengthen the right of his (Tola's) men, so as to prevent a gap occurring between them and the plain; already the losses were severe, and his whole line was becoming thin.

The natives stood well by their white leaders, but a feeling of anxiety was running through the ranks, for they felt themselves to be hopelessly outnumbered, and they knew the fate that was in store for them if captured by Abyssinians. "Are the white troops coming?" was a constant question as the officers passed along the line, and these few young Italians, calm and smiling, "but with death in their heart" re-assured them: "they are just coming... Corragio!"—looking, as they spoke, anxiously to the far-off hill, but seeing no signs of their brigade.

The enemy were being constantly reinforced, and the shower of lead was rapidly thickening. It was a gallant effort of this isolated battalion of native Militia to hold out against the thousands of Abyssinians, but many of its officers were lying dead or wounded on the ground, and the black men, who followed their captains and lieutenants with much the same personal feeling that they had formerly entertained for their own chief, were beginning to waver. The extreme

[1] Captain Nobis with his centuria.

left of the line was visibly shuffling backwards towards safety, when suddenly Lieutenant Gaslini, with a handful of devoted men, dashed forward against the enemy,—he fell, but the company reoccupied its position. Yet this act of heroism was unfortunately useless, for the right flank was already being enveloped; Sermasi had found it impossible to hold out on the plain, and was retreating to the opposite heights on the right of the valley, where, with the remainder of his company, he fought successfully for the rest of the day. Captain Tola was thus compelled to give the order for the whole battalion to retire down the precipice behind it and up on to the ridge that it had first crossed, where he hoped to make a stand. But even this was soon seen to be hopeless, for his men could no longer hold their ground, although the white reinforcements were now at last visible,—the 3rd Regiment under Colonel Ragni to reinforce the heights, and the 6th under Colonel Airaghi with artillery to hold the valley. His natives continued to withdraw, still firing, but in disorder, as might well be expected, seeing that in the whole battalion there were only two white officers left alive out of the fourteen who marched into action. Amidst the confusion Tola happened to meet Major Zola of the artillery, and at once asked him where his (Tola's) commanding officer De Vito had gone to; "Your Major will never again leave the position," replied Zola,—and it was true. De Vito had been hit, one of the very first, while directing the extreme left of the line, and his fate had never been known on the right.

A few moments later Tola, who was one of the only two remaining officers, and who, though wounded, had been the last to leave the ridge, was caught up by the enemy and made prisoner.

Such was the end of the native Mobile Militia battalion whose fate is peculiar in some respects. The whole affair had taken only twenty minutes, and the destruction of these four isolated companies was accomplished at no great distance from the main body of the brigade, yet they could never be supported,—for such are the results of fighting on mountainous and unreconnoitred ground, especially against an agile, half-savage enemy. They appear also to have had extremely few white officers,—why there should not be more than 14 of them in a native battalion 950 strong, is a question hard to answer.

* * *

In spite of the rout of these two native units, the scene of operations remains practically the same,—Colonel Ragni at the head of the 3rd Regiment (in all 1,310 strong, but two of its companies were elsewhere) occupies the heights, while Colonel Airaghi in command of the 6th Regiment (1,330 strong) takes up a position in the valley; on both grounds their advance is barred by a line of the enemy.

At the first moment Colonel Ragni's regiment (the 3rd) was almost swept away by the torrent of native fugitives, amongst whom were mingled many of the charging Shoans; and his two leading Italian companies, having advanced at the very top of their speed to succour the unfortunate Militia battalion, were quickly thrown into disorder. "There was a moment of such panic," says Captain Menarini, who was at that time not far off, "that the officers were obliged to draw swords, and to threaten the men with their pistols in order to keep them at their posts." But this lasted only for a moment; hardly had the fugitives cleared the front of the companies than the line of Shoans became visible within a short distance of them, and Colonel Ragni at once gave the command to charge. Twice his men "got in" with the bayonet, and then, emptying their magazines, drove the enemy back over the first ridge. It had been a rough baptism of fire, but successful; they lost two officers killed and two wounded in these charges; the number of men is not known. But the most noticeable point about the affair, is the peculiarly advantageous nature of the ground for the active Shoans, who, if attacked and put to flight, could always find fresh cover, and when reinforced renew the onset.

The battalions were now well deployed. A long line of men could be seen, beginning on the high crest of the hill far away to the left (the 10th Battalion of the 3rd Regiment), and stretching from thence right on to the edge of the valley, one unit being carefully thrown back to guard the far-off outer flank. On the right of the 10th Battalion was the 6th of the same regiment, and still nearer on the right, the string of men was continued by the 5th, until it reached half way down the dark coloured cliffs. These three battalions of the 3rd Regiment were all under command of Colonel Ragni.

In the centre of the valley stands a solitary sycamore, some distance in front of which Colonel Airaghi posted a company of his 14th Battalion. Under cover of this advanced company, his mountain battery came forward and took up its position on the right of the plain; then the rest of the

14th Battalion lined itself across the shelving ground from the northern slopes to the southern precipice.

The other two battalions of the 6th Regiment—namely, the 3rd and the 13th, were kept in reserve by Airaghi, and remained at the head of the valley. In this manner we get Ragni with three battalions on the left,—the high ground,—and Airaghi with three battalions on the right,—in the valley,—but two of Airaghi's battalions are kept back and form the reserve of the brigade; on the hills to the extreme right are Sermasi's natives.

Hardly had the Italian regiments completed their deployment, than the enemy who had been creeping towards them under cover of the high grasses, dashed forward to the attack with furious yells, and some hundreds of Galla horsemen raising their battle-cry of "Ebalgumè! Ebalgumè!"[1] made a wild charge in the direction of the batteries. It was a magnificent effort, as we can tell from the descriptions of those who saw it: "How fine, how superb was that charge of the Gallas, with their strange and rich trappings glancing in the sunlight, bending low over the small horses that dashed headlong forward, and coming stoically onward to be massacred by our guns!"[2]

But the Italian infantry were equal to the occasion; calm and silent, the companies rose to their feet so as to bring each rifle above the thick stem of yellow grass, and then poured in a murderous magazine fire at a short range, the

[1] Ebalgumè—From a word meaning to mow or reap. The idea is that of sweeping their enemies down like grass in a hayfield.

[2] Menarini: *ib.*

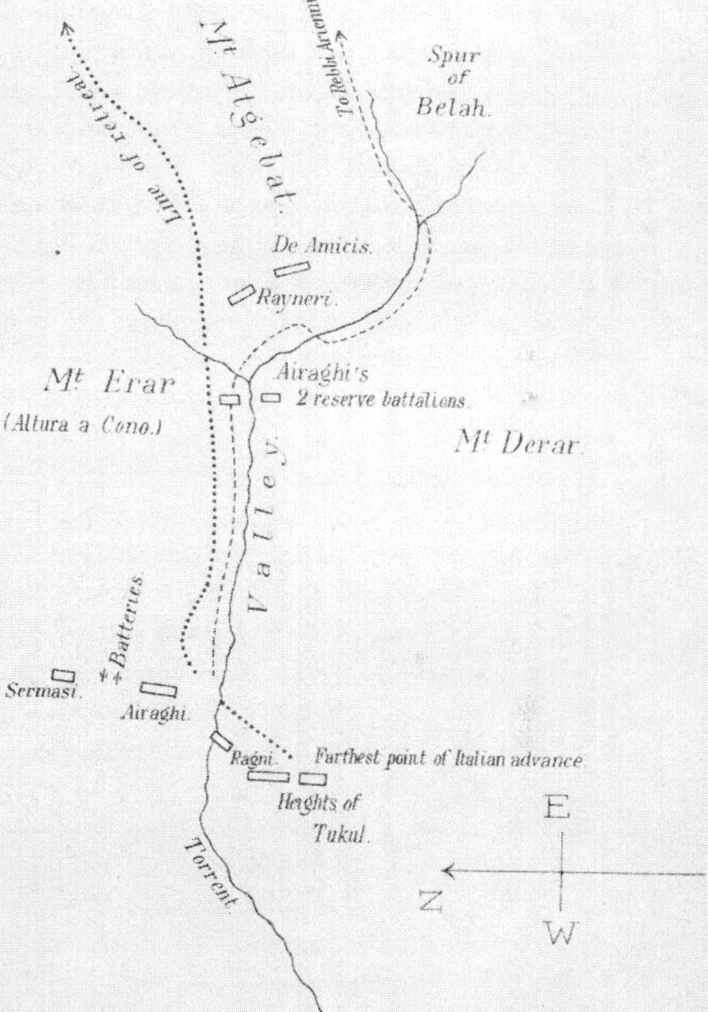
Mt Atgebat.
Line of retreat.
To Belah Arconi.
Spur of Belah.
De Amicis.
Rayneri.
Mt Erar
(Altura a Cono.)
Airaghi's
2 reserve battalions.
Mt Derar.
Valley.
Batteries.
Sermasi.
Airaghi.
Ragni.
Farthest point of Italian advance.
Heights of Tukul.
Torrent.
E
N
W

Face p. 326.

artillery supporting them by firing battery volleys on the right. It was splendidly done; the charge was repulsed and the enemy retired decimated and in disorder.

After this failure the Shoans' fire seemed to grow weaker, and finally became so slack that towards midday General Dabormida considered it a good opportunity for taking the offensive, and driving them off their position on the heights crowned by the tucul, which endangered his own men in the valley. He ordered up the 3rd Battalion of Airaghi's regiment from the reserve, and sent it to reinforce his firing line in the plain. No other alterations were necessary; hitherto everything had been carried out with entire success. The disaster to De Vito had been retrieved, and the remnants of his battalion had been rallied. Every company was posted to the best advantage, and every man was working as if part of a great automatic killing-machine. The men were firing coolly, picking off each individual that shewed himself in the hostile ranks. One eye-witness relates how he saw lying on the rocky ground a batch of Venetians, "more cheery and talkative than the rest" who pointed to where the dead bodies lay, and shouted to him in the old dialect of the lagoons "So sta mi"—"That's my work."[1] The General himself smiled cheerfully as he gave his orders or conversed with Colonel Airaghi, having no anxiety in the world except the slight cloud caused by his not having received, as yet, any communication from General Arimondi or the Governor. But this occasioned him no real disquietude

[1] Account telegraphed by l'onorevole Ferrucio Macola to the "Corriero della Sera" of Milan.

for he saw on the heights in his rear a battalion belonging to Arimondi's brigade (namely, that of De Amicis), so that he felt confident that all was going well in that direction.

The presence of this force under De Amicis, to which we have already adverted (p. 317), requires some explanation. It had been ordered forward, very early in the day, to form the connecting link between the brigades of Arimondi and Dabormida; it had occupied the hill (Mount Atgebat it is called on some maps) on the right of the junction where the paths from Enda Chidane Meret and from Mariam Shavitu meet; here, after an hour or two of uncertainty, it was assailed by the bodies of Shoans who were trying to surround the 2nd Brigade. De Amicis, seeing the importance of holding the hill on which he stood, inasmuch as it commanded Dabormida's line of retreat, gave up all idea of rejoining his own brigade, and entrenched himself as well as he could, turning to good account an old wall that he discovered on the side of the mountain. This was a most wise disposition, for it was solely due to his efforts that the 2nd Brigade was not surrounded and crushed, like General Albertone's men, by an overwhelming attack in the rear. Even as matters stood, so determined was the Shoan onslaught that they broke in upon the Sezione Sanita, killing and wounding doctors and attendants, and dispersing its mules with the medical provisions. De Amicis, hard pressed, sent to the reserve at the head of the valley for reinforcement, and General Dabormida, who was passing at the moment, promptly despatched the 13th Battalion (Major Rayneri) to his assistance: this occurred between eleven and twelve, at the time when the brigade was also engaged on its front. But so successful were Rayneri and De Amicis, that on this side also the Shoans were repulsed, and by twelve o'clock their fire had become as slack here as it was on the front. Hence Dabormida felt doubly safe, for he knew that the enemy had suffered severely during their endeavour to surround him; he believed that in that quarter he had no cause for anxiety. And he was indeed so far right that the two battalions continued to hold their position to the very end of the day, although furiously assailed by the thousands of Shoans who, after dispersing Arimondi's brigade, were let loose against the sole remaining column.

THE BATTLE FROM MIDDAY TO 4.30 P.M.

The Shoans had by this time brought into action several pieces of artillery, and opened fire from the heights of the tucul, but without much effect; they served their guns slowly, and each shot sent out a cloud of smoke, but, as far as could be seen, without doing any damage whatsoever. The Italian artillery, on the other hand, was making splendid shooting. On the height of the tucul, which was the main object of attack, their shrapnel was bursting right over the Abyssinians, some of whom could be seen running for safety after each discharge; while on the plain their shots cut long furrows through the tall grass amidst which the enemy was posted. So good, indeed, did the chance seem of dislodging them from their stronghold, that Colonel Airaghi led two assaults and drove back the Shoans in the valley, but Colonel Ragni, who directed simultaneous attacks along the higher level, could make no impression on the defenders of the tucul, so that Airaghi was obliged to retire almost to his original line. The only result of his success was, that the artillery had seized the opportunity to dash forward and take up a position from which their fire told even more heavily than heretofore; whilst the medical staff advanced to the post near the sycamore tree, hitherto occupied by the batteries. Several of the companies then attempted to gain ground by individual rushes, but they were quickly obliged to return to their cover, and in this manner the opposing lines swayed to and fro without any definite result, but with the advantage inclining, on the whole, slightly to the Italians.

"Till now," says Captain Menarini, "the losses had not been very great amongst the men, but were numerous amongst the officers, who became a special mark for the enemy; and who through a *mistaken sense of pride* remained on their feet even when the troops were lying down."

The great difficulty of the two colonels was timing their attacks so as to be exactly simultaneous. Ragni on the high ground could not hear the orders given on the plain,—even though the "advance" "halt" and "fire" were directed by bugle call,—but he succeeded in managing matters so well that throughout the whole day the officers below believed that their bugles reached his ear.

Presently a fresh supply of cartridges was served out to the infantry, who were ordered to open magazine fire, which they did, splendidly seconded by the artillery,—then, rising to their feet, they dashed forward in two short rushes of about thirty yards each, amidst a tornado of bullets from the enemy, who remained stubbornly on their ground, refusing to give way a foot. Italian and Ethiopian were now facing each other, hardly more than a hundred yards apart, and at this short range the rifles were crackling furiously, while the air was filled with the crash of artillery. The supports had already reinforced the firing line, Ragni had moved forward on the heights, and every man felt, with a wild sense of elation, that the decisive moment had arrived:—the moment when he is torn in one direction by the thirst for victory, and in the other by his human fondness for life.

"And at last the bugle shrieked out harsh and strident (as the Italian bugles are) "Prepare to charge." Our beloved General and Colonel Airaghi ride out in front of the firing line, followed by the officers of the Staff, and of the 6th Regiment. Down the long white front of the battalions, which extends from one height to the other, there runs a thrill, and then a tremendous shout goes up: "Savoia! Savoia!" After that continuous cries of "Viva il nostro Generale! Viva il Colonello Airaghi!" and every man there is carried away by the fury of the assault; with fierce eyes, and clenched teeth, and with our weapons convulsively clutched in our hands, we threw ourselves on the enemy." [1]

The Shoans did not remain to try their heavy swords against the Italian bayonets, but fled at the top of their speed; so the wave of white men halted amidst the high grasses and opened fire on those of their enemies who were trying to rally. Five minutes later came a fresh charge with the bayonet, and this time some of the Abyssinians

[1] Menarini, *ib.*

were caught up and killed; before the halt was sounded the enemy had abandoned every one of their positions, and were running back, decimated and in confusion, towards their camp on the far-off hill that towers upwards by the plain of Adowa. The young Italian soldiers were wild with enthusiasm; cries of "Vittoria! Vittoria!" burst from the ranks, mingled with "Viva il Re!" and the men of one company, who had charged through the Shoans, raised their helmets high on the blood-stained bayonets, while all around them there arose the great shout of "Viva l'Italia,"—that historic battle-cry that recalls the glorious days of Palestro, of Villafranca, and of many a reckless dash under Garibaldi.

"Sublime moments which it will never be given to any man to describe true to the life,—at the memory of which the eyes become dim and the heart beats more rapidly."[1]

Short-lived indeed was the triumph of the brave brigade, for it cannot have been later than one o'clock when Captain Menarini's native servant suddenly seized him by the arm, and, pointing back at the hill that they had crossed that morning, exclaimed in alarm: "Sir, there come the enemy! Look!" Menarini looked, and so did the General. It was true. There, on the southern edge of the valley and moving rapidly northwards, was a body of Shoans, accompanied by guns and headed by Galla horsemen, already descending the hill to attack them in their rear and cut them off from De Amicis. Dabormida's decision was at once taken, to maintain the position he had conquered without attempting

[1] Menarini.

any further advance, and to reinforce his rear; at the same time to reinforce his right flank which appeared also to be in difficulty.

Amongst the troops around him there was perfect order and discipline, but they were suffering from the inevitable results of four hours' fighting after an all-night march; namely, weariness, thirst, hunger, and the lack of officers (most of whom had been killed). Also from the unavoidable difficulty which often occurs when one section reinforces another, namely, that the men of two separate companies become mixed, and that many of them have to fight under an officer and non-commissioned officers who, perhaps, do not even belong to their battalion.

Beyond this, however, there was no confusion, and, on receiving the General's order, the 3rd Battalion at once moved away to the rear; having just ended a victorious charge, the men were called off, and ordered to turn about for a fresh attack in a diametrically opposite direction. This new effort was a rough trial for young soldiers knowing themselves, as they did, to be surrounded; nevertheless, supported by two batteries, they were presently advancing up the southern slopes of Mt. Erar, and with such success that the Shoans beat a hasty retreat, their right flank being already threatened by the indefatigable battalions of Rayneri and De Amicis.[1] To the troops of these two commanders the 3rd Battalion at once joined itself, carrying on the right of their line, taking post along the eastern slopes of Mt. Erar, while Rayneri continued to

[1] The tired gunners especially made splendid practice, driving the three Abyssinian pieces off the field in a few shots.

defend the outlying spur of Eshasho.[1] The gap between the two mountains was filled by the company of Lieutenant de Bonis. This successful piece of work kept open the line of retreat, and these three battalions may fairly be said to have saved the brigade from annihilation.

It was of course natural that owing to the continued advances of General Dabormida, who knew nothing of Arimondi's and Albertone's disasters, the space he covered in rear had become longer and longer, until De Amicis and Rayneri were unable to guard the whole of it; especially as the Shoans were now swarming back in great numbers after having completed the defeat of Generals Arimondi and Ellena. So numerous were they that soon Rayneri and his three battalions were again hard-pressed, while fresh groups of assailants began climbing up the long spur of the tucul from every point of the southern compass, and threatening the left flank of Ragni, who had hitherto held undisputed mastery of the heights. Soon the scattered groups became one long chain of assailants, and Ragni was obliged to bend back his left flank along the ridge; the Shoans were for the moment checked, but not defeated.

The net result of all these movements was that the brigade was now fighting on three different fronts: one (the original front) in the valley, under Airaghi; another, along the ridge of the tucul, under Ragni; and a third, guarding the rear, under Rayneri and De Amicis. Sermasi on the original right flank was also threatened, but not by any very overwhelm-

[1] It is named Mt. Atgebat on some maps: Mt. Erar is the height to West of it, and must not be confused with Mt. Derar which is to the South.

ing attack;—nevertheless, Airaghi was obliged to spare a company to reinforce him. It was now about two o'clock, the men had been on their feet for seventeen hours, the reserves were used up, the last of the cartridges were being served out, and the soldiers had begun to fill their pouches from those of their dead comrades, some of them also taking the boots off their feet, for in many cases their own were "absolutely unserviceable." But their lines of defence were still unbroken, and their courage was still high.

It was not long before they were called upon to give proof of it, for the Abyssinians could now hurl the whole of their army on to the solitary, isolated brigade. On all three fronts, thousands of Shoans were collecting, literally pounding the positions with a hail of lead, under cover of which they began a series of furious assaults; it was soon evident that the Italians would be obliged to abandon the ground they had conquered in the morning.

Captain Menarini gives a somewhat pathetic picture of their situation. "I seem still to see our General walking up and down near the sycamore tree where the artillery had taken up their position in the morning; it is the first time that he seems preoccupied and nervous: 'It is a serious thing, a serious thing!' he murmurs to himself. 'No message, no order, no reinforcement—nothing!...' and while the hail of bullets whirled round him, with a thousand different sounds and whinings, the General, having regained his calm demeanour, would turn, with his accustomed smile, from time to time to Colonel Airaghi and to us officers of the brigade staff of the 6th Regiment, telling us how since morning he had had no information from headquarters: 'It seems to have vanished; up to now it has given no sign of life.' And his manly face clouded again for a fleeting instant, since he, like all of us, could no longer deceive himself as to the desperate position in which the brigade was placed.

"And, in truth, we felt that we were approaching *the beginning of the end;* weary, thirsty, hungry as we were, in rags, and without shoes on a rocky ground covered with thorny bushes, facing an enemy three or four times as numerous as ourselves."

It was indeed impossible for them to hold their advanced positions any longer. Ragni could still protect the extreme left, but those of his troops who faced the orginal front were compelled to retire; and consequently Airaghi's men, threatened on both flanks, also withdrew slowly as far back as the ground they had occupied at the beginning of the action. Sermasi's natives, on the right, presently followed suit, for they had suffered more heavily perhaps than any other corps. From this time forth, the distinctions between companies and sections were in many places lost, but the positions were held by one continuous ring of determined men, who defied every effort of the Shoans.

At this moment the General, casting a glance all round him, called to Colonel Airaghi: "I want," he said, "to try one last general attack; who knows that in the meanwhile reinforcements may not reach me?" And seeing Colonel Airaghi smile with an incredulous air, he continued "and if reinforcements should not arrive, the assault will enable me to begin a retreat."

The news of a fresh attack spread like a lightning-flash all along the line, and the rifles at once redoubled their activity, seconded by the artillery, which was firing almost its last round; in a few minutes the advance began.

In front of the 6th Regiment rode General Dabormida himself, encouraging the men to a last charge, and waving them forward with his helmet in his right hand; close behind him was Colonel Airaghi with sword raised high. "One yell, one desperate effort, and the troops hurl themselves on the enemy who does not move a foot, but continues his fire; there is a hand-to-hand struggle, fierce and dogged, but only for a few instants, then the black mass once again is obliged to retreat wavering and confused...."

"We have gained the space necessary for beginning our retirement across the narrowing valley; but what numbers of men we have left on the ground behind us, and how thick are the enemy around us!

"Ah! if reinforcements had arrived even at that last moment, the day would not have been lost."

Then, at length, the General, turning sadly to Colonel Airaghi, said to him: "Airaghi, we must begin our retreat; you will cover it with your regiment!"

"Yes, General," replied the Colonel, and departed. They never met again.

* * *

The retirement was begun by the 3rd Regiment under command of Colonel Ragni. His six companies filed silently down into the valley in as many columns, exposed in some places to a heavy fire from the Shoans, who, the very moment they saw the white men withdrawing, dashed forward with triumphant yells on every side; trying especially to wedge themselves into the gap (now left unguarded by the retirement of the 3rd Regiment) on the left flank of Airaghi's men. To prevent the Shoans from breaking in at this point, Airaghi gave the command to retreat,—which was done as quickly as possible and in some disorder,—until his left had closed the gap by joining Rayneri's right. Here his men rallied and formed a firm barrier across the valley, covering the withdrawal of the 3rd Regiment.

Meanwhile the General had ridden off to give his last orders to De Amicis and Rayneri on the extreme left, accompanied by his A.D.C., Captain Bellavita. The hill on which they fought was steep, and presently the General's horse could go no further. Being too weary to climb the slopes on foot, and being anxious, moreover, to direct the gradual retirement of the battalions still engaged, he sent Bellavita forward to find Major Rayneri and order him "to stand firm as long as he could on the heights which he was occupying." Having despatched this message he remounted, and turned his horse's head towards the valley. Bellavita soon reached the top of the hill, and found Major De Amicis, to whom he gave the order, asking him to communicate it to Major Rayneri (who was near), and then returned to the valley; but nowhere could he find his General, although he searched for him in many parts of the field. This episode of his carrying the order to De Amicis, small in itself, has one great interest attaching to it,—namely, that it is the last that is authentically known of General Dabormida. Some indeed said that they saw him after this "on the accursed hill, with sad eyes, but calm and resolute as one who awaits death; others relate that, having met him there, they begged him in vain to retire, and then saw him fall, struck by a bullet while in the act of mounting . . . but then these stories are denied."[1]

Meanwhile the brigade was making its final stand across the mouth of the valley, while Ragni's columns were ascending the steep and thorny path on the North of Mt. Atgebat, still covered by De Amicis' battalion. As they got higher and higher, the men often stopped in groups to fire downwards, for as the view opened out, they could see all around them a circle of Shoans pouring lead into the lines of Italians; and far away there were visible great masses of the enemy in reserve, waiting for gaps to occur. This ground was visited some months after the battle, and in almost every little nook and corner of the rocks there lay the body of some brave fellow who had turned to fire on his pursuers;—almost all of them killed by bullets that hit them on one side or the other, showing how hopeless was their position with enemies on both flanks.

[1] When, some months later, the Italians were permitted to bury their dead, they discovered amongst thousands of others, a corpse, which Colonel Arimondi (brother of the General) believed he recognised as that of General Dabormida. This belief was confirmed by an old woman, who told them, with many gestures, that this was the General; "a chief, a great man," she said, "with the spectacles, and the watch, and the golden stars; he asked me for water and said that he was the General." This corpse was therefore buried at Adi Shun Cohena, with a cross and wreath over the grave. Some doubt has been thrown on its identity, but it seems likely enough that the General waited amongst the last as has been described, and was perhaps wounded; he may then have succeeded in dragging himself as far as Adi Shun Cohena, and there have found that he could go no farther. This is merely hypothesis, but it would combine all the stories of those who think they saw him.

Ras Alula was now pressing forward on their right, and Sermasi's natives, though making a magnificent defence, were by this time too few in number to keep him off.[1]

Soon it came to the turn of Airaghi's men (the 6th Regiment) to retire, and the Abyssinians, wild with enthusiasm at seeing them go, redoubled their fire, and then rushed in upon them, reckless of losses or death. Sword and bayonet crossed, and here and there the Italian column began to show signs of unsteadiness before this endless torrent of assailants. Then, Colonel Airaghi, seeing that resistance was giving way, sent Captain Menarini to stop the retiring artillery, and give orders "to bring some guns into action at any cost"; so two of the guns halted, and opened fire, although their position was hopeless. The enemy was surprised; the warriors drew back for a moment and Airaghi seized the opportunity to organize a defence on the crest. "Captain," he said to Menarini, "run and order the first battalion that you find to take up a position on the hill, to protect the retreat of our regiment. Run!" Before Captain Menarini could get there, he fell wounded in the shoulder, but, rising again, succeeded in finding on the hill Colonel De Amicis, who was sitting calmly on his mule, "with his two hands one over the other, leaning on the pommel of his saddle with his eye fixed on the enemy breaking in on all sides; listening intently to the remains of the brigade, which, though still fighting on his flank and in rear, was now retiring ragged and blood-stained." To him Menarini confided his order, but then so deadly a faintness came upon him that

[1] "That old Alula is always fatal to us." Ximenes, *Sul Campo di Adua.*

he could do nothing further. That he should have ever escaped and lived to write his absorbingly interesting account of the engagement, was a piece of extraordinary good luck, due primarily to the fact that Col. Rayneri, passing at that moment, gave up to him his own mule,—an action which for its supreme generosity deserves to become historical.

By slow degrees the 6th Regiment was formed up into column and retired, following the 3rd; then it came to the turn of the 4th Battalion,—that of De Amicis. For these rearmost companies it was a matter of great difficulty; all day long they had kept the enemy at bay, from the shelter of their trenches, but it was evident that as soon as they abandoned these defences, their advantage would be gone. Nevertheless, it could not be avoided; already they had won the honour of being the last to go, and heavy clouds were gliding across the red rays of the setting sun when De Amicis' men moved from the position, out of which no efforts and no weight of numbers of the enemy had been able to drive them. Hardly had they got clear of the trenches than the Shoans dashed forward with furious yells, and rushing on to the poor wounded men, who, after defending themselves for so many hours, had been unavoidably left behind, butchered every one of them, with swords and lances; revelling in a carnival of bloodshed and mutilation so thorough as to stay their pursuit for some minutes.

Meanwhile the two guns that had been halted by order of Colonel Airaghi had fired their last round and had no mules left, so the men fell in where they were, and, when the Shoans dashed on to them, each man defended his piece to the best of his ability. It is said to have been some of these men who were found and buried months later, still grasping their assailants.

The rest of the artillery was winding its way slowly up the hill when it too was caught up by the Shoans, but here they had to deal with the remains of De Amicis' battalion, who opened a furious fire on them from the crest above. Round these guns an awful struggle took place; the gunners were between two fires; on the one side the Italian bullets were whistling by them, on the other the Shoans, though checked, had taken cover behind every rock and bush, and were picking off men and animals right and left. Very soon some of them running forward, took cover behind the mules themselves, where of course the Italians could not aim, and having fired their shots, began to slaughter with knives and lances the unfortunate beasts, "that were soon piled up in a shapeless mass at the foot of the ascent leading to the topmost height of the hill. Only two mules made their escape with the cases for ammunition."

"Let us save the artillery, they will have it all!" Colonel Airaghi's shout was clearly heard above all the noise, as he spurred his pony forward towards the enemy; it must have been a good beast, for it had been wounded early in the morning, and though bleeding at the nostrils had carried him all day. This is the last that is known of either man or pony,—this supreme effort of Colonel Airaghi to retrieve a few small spars from the universal wreck. In him Italy lost a brave man and, what is more, a valuable officer; of apparently no great physique, with the thin face and high forehead of a man of learning rather than a soldier, he was beloved by his brother officers and he has left behind him the memory of a hero.[1]

And De Amicis? He remained directing the last defence of his battalion until it was finally pierced by the enemy; then he was seen with drawn sword to cut his way through the Tigréans and Shoans, and disappear amongst the groups of men struggling hand-to-hand in rear of the retreating column.

And then the thunder began to crash, and the rain came down in torrents, while the survivors wound their way up the rugged hills; flashes and rattling of rifle fire continued all round them, but in spite of the storm and darkness the enemy dared not press his attacks to close quarters.

But far behind, on the battlefield that they had left, rose

[1] The following is a detailed description of his death, taken from the narrative of Lieutenant Roppa, mentioned by Ximenes, "Sul Campo di Adua". "After having fearlessly led his regiment six times to the attack, each time on horse-back, which made him a continuous mark for the enemy, and after having had two horses killed under him, he was hit in the left side while he was trying to mount a mule, together with a wounded soldier. The bullet passed through his body. The Colonel made them prop him up against that cursed sycamore, ordering the soldiers who ran up to help him, to let him die facing the enemy, and telling them to retire. 'I am old,' he said, 'let me die here; you who are young save yourselves.'

"Soon after that he bowed himself forward and died."

In the text I have followed Captain Menarini's description, who obviously had not heard this story. But Lieut. Roppa, being presumably the officer of that name in the 14th Battalion of the 6th Regiment, was present at the battle; his narrative is doubtless perfectly reliable.

the Amhara song of triumph: "Mow, mow down the tender grass, Ebalgumè! Ebalgumè!

"The corn of Italy that was sown in Tigré has been reaped by Abba Dagnò, and he has given it to the birds."[1]

[1] Abba Dagnò means Menelik, because the name of the horse he rode was Dagnò. Ximenes, "Sul campo di Adua," p. 278.

CHAPTER XII

THE CLOSE OF THE CAMPAIGN

ITALIAN losses at Adowa—The number of prisoners taken—Their treatment in Abyssinia—Anxiety for their release—General Baldissera's plan of action—His five objects—Reorganizes the remnants of Baratieri's army—Retirement of Menelik, March 20th, 1896—Negotiations—Salsa imprisoned—Nerazzini negotiates a peace—Prisoners released—Operations for relief of Kassala—Convoy gets through Ahmed Fadil's lines—Defence of Sabderat—Battle of Mount Mocram, April 1st, 1896—Kassala relieved by Stevani—Battle of Tucruf—Governor advances to relieve Adigrat—Sebath defeated—May 4th, 1896, Adigrat relieved—Proclamation—Mangasha releases the prisoners in Tigré—The Italians retire from Adigrat—Conclusion.

AT Adowa the Italians lost 2,918 white non-commissioned officers and men killed, 954 permanently missing, about 2,000 Ascari and 261 officers, giving a total of 6,133 deaths; this is, of course, a heavy total out a force 17,700 strong, (10,596 Italians and about 7,100 natives), but even if it had not been so great, the victory would be no less complete, for the Italian army under Baratieri had for the time being ceased to exist as a fighting unit. Of wounded men there were 470 Italians (including 31 officers) and 958 Ascari,—in all 1,428, a total whose smallness speaks ill for the Abyssinians, as it points to the fact that many of the wounded must have been massacred; but this is merely a rule in the wars of most eastern nations; the European fights in order to win the day, the Oriental fights to kill.

The Italian casualties, then, not counting prisoners, amounted to over 7,560 or nearly 43 per cent of the force engaged, while those of the Abyssinians are said to have amounted to 7,000 killed and 10,000 wounded, a number which is hardly excessive when one considers that, advancing in close masses, they "rushed" three separate positions each defended by artillery and magazine rifles. In addition to their killed and wounded, there were, according to calculations, 1,865 Italians taken prisoners, of whom 14 officers and 92 men are known to have died; also many Ascari—at the least estimate 1,000 of the latter were missing. [1] Of the Italian

[1] De la Jonquière estimates the whole number of prisoners at between three and four thousand; the exact numbers are impossible to discover. On June 23rd, 1896, Werszowitz, the priest who went to Shoa to try and liberate them, says that there were "2,864 Italian prisoners in Shoa"; 120 afterwards turned up from Tigré. The one point of certainty is that only 1,759 (including 54 officers) ever returned from Abyssinia to Italy. It is impossible to suppose that 1,200 died in eight or ten months; one can only believe that Werszowitz included some of the Ascari in his total. Of course many Italians died of the hardships they underwent, a large number being wounded men, and some, it is said, committed suicide; others were massacred. Mr. Wylde, who was in Addis Abeba some months after the campaign, says that Menelik had "taken about 4,000 prisoners, Italian and native in about equal numbers." Others say that there were only about 1,500 native prisoners in all, and that nearly 1,000 of these died from the results of mutilation, etc.

In the text I follow the figures of Major Bourelly, who is the latest and the chief authority on the subject. See *La Battaglia di Abba Garima* by G. Bourelly.

prisoners 30 returned to Italy mutilated in the barbarous manner that has been customary from the earliest times amongst the Abyssinian warriors, who are said to justify it by asserting that David inflicted it (emasculation) on the Philistines. This was contrary to the expressed orders of Menelik; but of the Ascari, 406 were turned loose after having had their right hand and left foot cut off by his command, or at all events with his consent,—a fact that will live in history to his disgrace. Major Gamerra relates how he was obliged to pass down a long double line of these unfortunates, many of whom had been in his battalion and had been taken prisoners because they stood firm to the end rather than turn their back on him;—they called him by name as he went by, and waved the handless arm. Also how one of them kept him awake all night, crying out with the cold, and yet he would not accept the rug that the Major offered him, for it was the only one they had. The sufferings of the wounded were terrible, but this particular Ascaro fared better than the rest, as Major Gamerra succeeded in sending him back into the Colony in safety.

The position of the prisoners soon became one of the chief difficulties with which the Roman Government had to deal. Menelik had reopened negotiations soon after his victory, and intended to hold his captives as pledges that the Italians would observe the terms of peace, or at all events to make of their return a concession for which he should get some equivalent by treaty. In the meanwhile the plight of these unfortunate men was exciting pity all over Italy, and arousing fearful anxiety amongst their relatives, which was in no wise lessened by the bitter outcries of the press;

it became a question of the day, and a text for vituperation against the Abyssinians. And their lot was indeed a sad one, though, speaking with all reserve, I have as yet found no very good reason for accusing the Negûs[1] or his chief Ras of deliberate cruelty to the white men; the Italians were probably better treated than would have been prisoners of any native race. But they led, literally speaking, "a dog's life"; *i. e.*, when those amongst whom they fell were endowed by nature with any kindliness they were well treated, but the great mass of the people did not care whether they lived or died, and there were, as there are in every nation, a few despicable scoundrels who took a pleasure in increasing their sufferings. Major Gamerra, for instance, relates how one of his captors struck him on the head, but adds that his complaint to the Negûs produced a rapid change in demeanour on the part of this chief; how another poured insults on him, which he returned with impunity; and how the boy who was at first appointed to show him the way, thought it a splendid opportunity for tyrannizing over a wounded white man by shouting commands at him and ordering him to run when he deemed it advisable: "however," says the Major, "a good kick, given at the right moment, persuaded him not to bother any more about me."

[1] I omit all the more absurd grievances cited against the Negus, such as that of making Italian soldiers sing "Funiculi! funicula!" and "Bella Napoli" before him, which has been quoted as an intentional insult. But Mr. Wylde says that 80 Italian prisoners were massacred in Adowa alone, by the infuriated soldiery. This, of course, was contrary to Menelik's wishes.

It must be remembered that an officer of his rank would probably receive far more consideration than the private soldiers.

But the everyday inconveniences of living amongst barbarians are in themselves terrible to a white man; the filth of the camps, the disgusting crawling insects, the lack of water, lack of money, lack of boots and clothing, the cold nights,—all these things brought on deadly fevers and sickness for which there were no remedies to be got, and fearfully increased the sufferings of the wounded. The best-natured of their captors fed them just as they fed themselves,—which meant (except in the case of the greater chieftains), that they lived on small portions of Angera (a kind of flour made from native grains, mixed with water and then roasted) and sour milk; sometimes roasted beans, sometimes meat; sometimes Tegg (the native beverage) to drink, or Mar (honey and water). Such being the best food, it was not surprising that European soldiers should stray into the tucul, while on the march, in order to buy eggs, fowls, or even kids for their dinner. Their guards, perhaps naturally, resented these lengthy delays and did not hesitate to use their sticks on the laggards, who would sometimes retort. One of these crises is related by Major Gamerra: "Amongst these (the Italians) there were some so much affected by ophthalmia that they could not longer see at all, but, nevertheless, guided by their companions, marched for whole days along paths on which, even with perfect sight, there would always have been a danger of breaking one's neck. Atanafi and his dependents did not understand that a long column of European soldiers could not march hour after hour without a little time to breathe, or without a few minutes' rest; and once our movements began they continued to the end of the day's march! When I remonstrated with Atanafi, he appeared to be persuaded; he agreed with me, and promised that I should regulate the next march; but then all continued as usual, and I was powerless to remedy it. Things came to such a pitch that one day, after having remonstrated energetically at the ill treatment of the soldiers by the Ascari of Atanafi, I told him that I would no longer make myself responsible for anything and would for my part close my eyes to any act of disorder committed by my soldiers. This declaration of mine, coupled with the fact that a non-commissioned officer having been ill-treated by a sub-chief, had broken his head with some heavy blows of a stick, and that I had not thought fit to search out the striker of the blows, somewhat impressed Atanafi, and for some days things went much better."

He goes on to say that these disagreements were partly due to the men themselves, who, being worn out with hardships, were inclined to become insubordinate and quarrelsome. The condition of the officers was not quite so bad, as they were often entertained by chiefs, and this, of course, made an enormous difference.

Ligg Ilma, son of Maconnen, the Dejazmatchs Imar and Gugsa, and several of the other leaders, especially those educated in Europe or at civilized towns like Cairo, showed them the greatest kindness. Yet in ten months many had died, and the others were so much weakened for want of nourishing food that they were not in a physical condition to make their escape. "During these marches it happened only too often that I had to be present at the agony of some prisoner who, worn out by physical exertion, by loss of blood from his wounds, or by hunger, fell on the road not to rise again, and no one took any notice of him. Five officers died of sickness or fatigue, but who can tell the number of non-commissioned officers, of corporals, or of soldiers who died from the same causes?"

Such being the conditions under which they were known to be living, it is not surprising that their release was placed by General Baldissera in the fore-front of his program of operations; although, of course, it added a fresh complication to the many already existing, and one that was entirely uncommon. In no other modern war would the lives of the prisoners have become jeopardized by the continuance of hostilities.

When the new Governor arrived at Asmara on March 6th, to take command of the troops in the Italian Colony, he found that General Baratieri had already reached that town, and at once went up to his room to visit him. The interview between the present and former Governors must have been an ordeal for both; Baratieri says: "It was a meeting the remembrance of which still affects me. I placed myself at the disposal of the new Commander-in-Chief for service of any kind; and he had words of great comfort for me. He said (and not in confidence) what he had already said to others on the road from Massowah to Asmara, namely, that when he was appointed to supersede me in command, his first idea was to move out in face of the Abyssinians, with the purpose of inducing them either to attack us, or to retire."

It was a kindly thought of the new General to say openly that, had he been in his predecessor's place, he would have pursued the same course of action that had been followed.

The necessities for which General Baldissera tells us he felt himself bound to provide were five, which he arranges under the following headings: [1]

a Reorganize the Army Corps that had fought at Adowa.

b To defend the Colony from the advance of the Negûs.

c To enter into peace negotiations in order to gain time and obtain the release of the prisoners.

d Relieve Kassala, blockaded by 5,000 Dervishes:

e Liberate the garrison of Adigrat, where there were 2,000 soldiers.

To realize the gigantic work that lay before him, one must first realize the situation of affairs in the Colony when he landed. All over a vast expanse of territory were scattered small bands of soldiers, the remnants of the beaten army from Adowa, some of them counting their numbers by hundreds, others not more numerous than, for instance, the six men who reached Adigrat under command of Corporal Baldi after losing five comrades in the fighting by the way. The whole of the newly conquered provinces had risen; almost every ridge on the sixty or seventy miles between Sauria and Adi Caje was defended by armed peasants. The detached groups of survivors spent days and nights wandering without guides or food, struggling against superior numbers, sometimes firing on each other in the dark, and often deceived by the enemy into marching peacefully up to a hostile camp fire,—

[1] Guerra d'Africa—Relazione sulle operazione Militari nel secondo periodo della campagna d'Africa, 1895—6.

finally reaching a post on the lines of communication only to meet the bitter disappointment of finding it evacuated and destroyed. The survivors of Arimondi's and Ellena's brigades had become divided into three or four separate bodies of men,—those of Dabormida into several more, but, besides these, there were countless small groups of stragglers.

Meanwhile the Shoans were advancing through Entisho (Entiscio) towards Gura; there was no time to be lost and Baldissera at once settled down to his work. He burnt his fine supply of provisions at Adi Caje and abandoned that place, making Asmara the headquarters and occupying the line from Asmara to Ghindi. By thus shortening his communications he released a large number of troops for immediate requirements, at the same time gaining for himself a breathing space, and a safer line of defence. In a few days he had succeeded in gathering together no less than 3,260 white men, and 3,041 natives from the army of Adowa.[1] Weary, disheartened, and almost naked as they were, he formed them into four battalions, and being reinforced from Italy could thus, before the enemy was even near enough to threaten him, place in the field an army of about 18,000 men, for whom he had prepared a strong defensive position. The first of his five tasks had therefore been brought to a successful conclusion.

[1] This would include nearly all the survivors of Baratieri's force. Most of those who had not reported themselves by March 5th were not seen again: a large number were killed by Sebath, Agos Tafari or by the insurgent peasantry. In all, 222 officers (out of 551) and 4,376 white men (out of 10,045) made their escape from the field, many of them wounded.

The second, namely, the repulse of the Negûs, was very soon found, in a most unexpected manner, to have accomplished itself. On March 12th Menelik was encamped in Faras Mai, apparently showing every intention of advancing on Gura; on March 20th he had already begun his retreat towards Shoa, sending on his guns before him. It was a singular stroke of good fortune for Baldissera, whose position in face of that formidable monarch was by no means to be envied. It has been accounted for in more ways than one, but the Negûs's own words put his position most concisely before us. Speaking afterwards to a priest who lived in Serae, (on the way to Gura) he remarked: "We were very near to your country and intended to go there. I was not able to do so,—first of all, owing to the lack of water, and secondly, because many new enemies had arrived, and, as you know, I do not love spilling blood."

These, then, were his reasons,—the arrival of the reinforcements and the want of water. The latter cause was probably exaggerated to him by the chiefs whom he sent to reconnoitre, as many of them were tired of the war; they had suffered during four months some severe hardships, and did not feel equal to another effort as great, or probably greater, than that of Adowa. But it must not be thought that Menelik's retreat left the conquered provinces unoccupied; it simply meant that the Shoans had retired from Tigrè. The forces of Mangasha and Alula remained round Adigrat, while Sebath and Agos Tafari continued the campaign in the hope of gaining something that might turn out to be of value to them; the alliance with the Dervishes was also renewed by Mangasha, who wrote to incite them to further effort against Kassala. However, the question of an invasion of Erythrea was at an end; the utmost that the Tigréans could hope for was the capture of Adigrat.

As regards the third end in view, General Baldissera was not so speedily successful. Major Salsa had been despatched to the Negûs's camp on the 6th, but the terms offered by Menelik were not acceptable; he insisted on the abolition of the Treaty of Uccialli, the evacuation of Adigrat, and a return to the old boundary of the Mareb—Belesa—Muna. To these the Government would have agreed, but the release of the prisoners was not conceded, and Maconnen actually demanded that the Italians should erect no fortifications even on their own territory.[1] Such terms, naturally, could not be accepted, and Salsa had to move to and fro until, finally, on the third visit to the Negûs, he was made prisoner and kept as a hostage.

The question of the peace and prisoners may be dealt with at once. To relieve the sufferings of the latter the sum of 1,752,181 lire was collected and about 30,000 lire worth of goods, which were by degrees sent out to them. Meanwhile the Marchesa di Santafiora, lady-in-waiting to the Queen of Italy, had started another public subscription, the proceeds of which, on May 25th, she sent out to Addis Abeba by means of a priest named Werszowitz-Rey together with Père Oudin; but Maconnen kept this expedition waiting for many weeks, and during the delay Père Oudin died. Then the Pope himself, entirely of his own initiative, sent a special mission under command of Monsignore Macario,

[1] Melli: *La Colonia Eritrea.*

who reached the Negûs's capital on August 14th, 1896, and was there received with great honours. As an act of respect to the head of the Roman Catholic religion, Menelik returned two prisoners through Macario, and by his means the rest were able to obtain letters and presents, which these unfortunates received with an almost inconceivable gratitude.[1] But the Italian Government itself was not idle; on October 6th their plenipotentiary, Dr. Nerazzini, arrived in Addis Abeba, and in fifteen days he and the Negûs had succeeded in coming to terms. In the first place a convention was to be signed between the two nations, by which

I Peace was declared.

II The Treaty of Uccialli was abolished.

III Ethiopia became absolutely independent.

IV Until final arrangements had been made, the boundary of the Mareb—Belesa—Muna was to be observed; meanwhile Italy was not to cede Ethiopian territory to any other Power.[2]

Secondly, as regards the prisoners, Italy was to pay whatever sum she considered sufficient to cover their maintenance in the past, and then they were to be sent back to her. She eventually paid about ten million lire, which must have been at least twice the amount of their actual expenses, but the captives were promptly despatched to the coast, by way of Harrar, preceded by a small advanced detachment of fifty, whom the Negûs sent on before Dr. Nerazzini's treaty,

[1] Especially boots and linen, and such necessaries as sponges brushes, pipes, watches, soap, etc. It is related that even General Albertone was reduced to washing his linen without soap.

[2] Melli, *ib.*

to arrive as a graceful concession on the birthday of the Queen of Italy. By the end of March 1897, or thirteen months after the disaster of Adowa, all the prisoners from Addis Abeba had returned to Italy.

This disquisition on their fate has led us, perhaps, rather too far away from the main thread of events passing in the colony. Their restitution was the third of the five objects that General Baldissera had set himself to accomplish; but two more remained—namely, the relief of Kassala and of Adigrat. To understand these operations we must for the moment return to March 20th, 1896,—the date when the Negûs retired from Tigré, only three weeks after the battle of Adowa.

Baldissera was not, like Baratieri, hampered at every turn by false economy. The Crispi Government had fallen, amidst almost universal execration, on March 15, and had been succeeded by a new ministry under the presidency of the Marquis of Rudini, its leading spirit being perhaps General Ricotti. The colonial policy of these men may be roughly expressed by saying, that, having been called to office at a time when Italy was deeply involved in a difficulty, they meant first to get her out of it, and then to keep her from approaching it in future. 140 million lire, or about 5 million sterling, was voted for this purpose and it proved more than enough for the immediate wants. The whole war, in fact, from first to last, is estimated to have cost the Italians only about 200 million lire (say $7\frac{3}{4}$ millions sterling).

The first operation undertaken by the Governor was the relief of Kassala. Within this fort there was a garrison of

1,327 men under the command of Major Hidalgo,—20 officers, 82 Italian privates, and 1,225 Ascari of the 2nd Native Battalion; while outside it were entrenched 5,000 Dervishes armed with rifles, and 1,000 armed with spears. On February 22nd, while Baratieri was still at Sauria, struggling with the difficulties of his communications, the Dervishes, as already related, had made an unsuccessful attack on the cultivated land outside the town. But when the well-known Emir, Ahmed Fadil, took command on February 25th, matters became more serious. On March 8th, a week after Adowa, he succeeded in burning some of the stores at Sabderat (an important place with a good water supply East of the town), which Hidalgo was fortunately able to re-victual by night. Then, under Ahmed Fadil's direction the trenches were quickly completed, after which he wrote to Lieutenant Pajolo, an officer of the garrison whom he imagined to be the commandant of the fort, one of the most insolent letters that has ever been indicted in the history of war, summoning him to surrender, to come out with his men, to renounce Christianity, and turn Mohammedan.

After this ebullition, the siege was for a time turned into a blockade. It became evident that if Major Hidalgo could be furnished with a supply of provisions sufficient to last until the middle of May, when the Dervishes would be compelled to retire owing to the rise of the River Atbara, no further cause of anxiety need exist. So a caravan of 600 camels was prepared at Agordat, for the double purpose of provisioning the fort and of bringing back the sick and wounded and some of the civil population;—for there were 4,047 people in Kassala, of whom only 1,327 were combatants. On the night of March 15th it succeeded in slipping into the town without mishap,—a well-planned exploit on the part of the Italians that does not speak highly for the discipline maintained by Ahmed Fadil.

Roused, perhaps, by the news of this event, he again attacked (on March 18th) the Sabderat trenches, but without success. This day's defence was a feat highly honourable to the small garrison of the village, for they consisted of only 125 men,—a Jus-bashi, 4 telegraph operators, and 120 natives of whom only 20 were regulars. Yet they repulsed a force of 1,200 infantry and 300 cavalry, killing 43 of them; their own losses were only 3 dead and 10 wounded.

In spite of these failures the Dervishes were still powerful enough to prevent the caravan from accomplishing its second purpose, namely, that of carrying the sick and wounded out of the fort. In fact, all communication with the Colony was still cut off, so the Governor determined to send a force to relieve the garrison once and for all, and it was well that he so decided, because Ahmed Fadil, seeing that a blockade was now useless, had renewed his operations and had succeeded in entrenching himself strongly within five furlongs of the town. The relieving force consisted of the reorganized 3rd, 6th, 7th and 8th Native Battalions, (they were considered better suited to the climate of the Kassala region at that time of year than Italian troops) the same that had fought at Adowa; its artillery consisted of one mountain battery, and the expedition was entrusted to Colonel Stevani, who had commanded the 1st Bersaglieri at Adowa, and who had remained with the Governor to the end, endeavouring to organize a defence in rear of the retiring column.

On the East of the town stands Mount Mocram, beneath the southern slope of which runs the road from Kassala that passes through Sabderat to the Colony. This road had naturally been occupied by the Dervishes, who expected that Stevani would try and force it; but a letter of instructions having got through to Major Hidalgo, Ahmed Fadil found himself attacked in the rear, on the night of April 1st, by a sortie of the garrison; and while he was occupied with them, Stevani passed round the North of the mountain and made his way into the town.

Thus far all had gone well, except that the 6th Battalion had apparently become retarded, and had not reached Kassala. In half an hour's time, however, the sound of firing was heard, and news was brought that it was attacking the Dervish front. Stevani at once marched out with the whole of the garrison and relieving force, and owing to the night being fortunately clear and moonlit, he was able to distinguish his own battalion from the enemy, whom he promptly attacked. His success was complete; the Dervishes fled, leaving the road open. During this action, the battle of Mocram, the Italians lost 100 killed and wounded, but in a few hours the caravan started for the Colony and the blockade was at an end.

At Tucruf, on the North of Kassala, Ahmed Fadil rallied his men, who were still more numerous than the whole force of Stevani, and prepared himself for the final battle that was evidently about to take plaee. It was in this well-contested action that the Dervish leader gave undoubted proof of his skill, which during the former engagements had not been conspicuous.

On April 3rd, Stevani advanced from the fort with his 4 battalions forming a square, within which were his 4 guns. Having arrived at a distance of about two kilometres (2,200 yards) from the enemy, he began to shell their trenches. Then, as they gave no sign of life, he continued to move towards them by short advances of 200 metres, until he arrived within a kilometre of their line; at that point two large bodies suddenly rose from the trenches and, rushing out, endeavoured to turn his right flank. After some rapid firing on both sides the Dervishes were put to flight, and Stevani ordered out his cavalry who, after passing quite close to the trenches, sent word back that they were entirely evacuated. A company was therefore detached from the square to occupy them, but hardly had it advanced 300 metres than a furious fire broke out from the trenches that had been thought deserted. To support the advanced company, Stevani was obliged to lead his whole force to the attack, and, as the position was strong and his own men in the open, soon found the losses were becoming serious; at the same moment he became aware that his rear was threatened by a detachment of cavalry about 300 strong. Under the double peril he was obliged to retreat on to a better position, from which he succeeded in silencing the fire of the trenches and in dispersing the cavalry. He then slowly retired into Kassala, without being followed.

So ended the battle of Tucruf, in which the Italian native regiments lost about 300 killed and wounded. On news of it being brought to the Governor, he ordered Stevani to make no further attacks on this strong position of the Dervishes, knowing that in a few weeks they would probably be compelled to retire without further fighting. As a matter of fact, they were already beaten; a few patrols accompanied by artillery, who were sent to threaten them, on the 4th and 5th instants, caused so hasty a retirement that the wounded Dervishes and their baggage animals fell into the hands of the native brigade. Kassala was now entirely freed from its enemies.

The end of the war was at length approaching; only one last operation remained to be accomplished—namely, the relief of Adigrat, around which were encamped the forces of Ras Mangasha, Ras Alula, Ras Sebath, and Agos Tafari. This undertaking may be shortly detailed, for it led to no great historical results, and to no important battle; the chief points of interest are those that concern the final arrangements between the various chiefs.

The Governor advanced with great caution; he even made a reconnoitring expedition, with 140 natives, as far as Adi Caje. And here we may remark that although the forward movement did not begin for more than a month after the battle of Adowa, he found the greatest difficulty in organizing the lines of communication; his force consisted of only 16,717 men, but he could get no water for them. Starting on April 4th, he occupied Adi Caje on April 12th and was obliged to remain there until the end of the month.

The first of the four chieftains who barred his way was Ras Sebath. This able diplomatist had been left in almost undisputed power in Tigré since the destruction of Baratieri's army, and he had made the best use of his opportunity. On March 5th he had proposed to the commandant of Adigrat that he should abandon that fort, leaving everything within it as it stood ;—Sebath undertaking to guarantee his safe retirement. To this offer no answer was returned.

The regal tone of the above suggestion was perhaps due to the fact that he had lately, at the request of the Negûs himself, become reconciled to Agos Tafari, and had moreover made a private arrangement with that chief whereby they were to divide Agamé into halves, Sebath taking one and Agos the other.[1] But it seems likely that in reality he expected no great result from his demand for the surrender of Adigrat, as five days later the reports stated him to be at Surropo, securing a smaller but more certain profit by picking up Italian rifles. On April 4th he had again rejoined Agos Tafari before Adigrat, where we find him permitting some twenty Greek and Italian civilians to quit the fortress unmolested, on the payment of twenty-five Thalers apiece: for a man of his rank he displayed at times a singular lack of dignity.

Before proceeding on his final advance from Adi Caje, the Governor despatched Colonel Pagannini with 2,000 men towards Adowa, and Lieutenant Sapelli with irregulars in the direction of Coatit and Debra Damo, thereby threatening both flanks of the enemy. These movements had the desired effect: the Tigréans divided their forces, one body going to Debra Damo, and another, 2,000 strong under Alula, marching westward to defend Adowa. Meanwhile the Governor pushed on with his main body and Mangasha retreated before him, for Menelik had wisely forbidden the Ras to risk a battle. On May 2nd General Baldissera

[1] Diary of the Commandant of Adigrat.

easily discomfited Sebath at Guna Guna, killing 9 of his men and wounding 21,—the Italians losing 3 killed, 12 wounded and 1 prisoner,—and on May 4th Adigrat was relieved, without any further fighting. This, then, was the end of the program that the Government had set itself to accomplish, and they refused to attempt anything further.

Before retiring the Governor made the most of his strong position, both as regards obtaining the release of the prisoners that were in Tigré, and indirectly endeavouring to influence the peace negotiations of the Shoans at Addis Abeba. He published a proclamation to the Tigréan population,—which at that moment was looking forward with terror to an Italian revenge,—calling on the chiefs to give up their prisoners and threatening them with severe reprisals in case of non-compliance.

On reading this announcement Sebath at once saw a fresh opening for his peculiarly commercial talents. By way of proving his unwillingness to surrender them, he promptly sent to the Governor to say he had no prisoners and that he didn't care in the least if they burnt the whole country. But the Italians, knowing for certain that one, at least, (an officer) was in his hands, replied by despatching four battalions and a battery under Colonel Stevani, who stormed Sebath's rocky stronghold of Debra Matzo, and hunted him from hill to hill, killing twelve of his men, taking three hundred head of his cattle, and burning four of his villages: [1] shortly after these events Agos Tafari sent in all the prisoners that he had, both his own and those of Sebath.

[1] The Italians had been fired on from these villages.

Mangasha also hesitated to comply; but with him the case was very different, for he was, after all, the lawful ruler of Tigré, the acknowledged son of the Emperor John. He naturally wanted to see the Italians depart before giving up his hostages. For a fortnight he remained uncertain, but then, being convinced that the Government really intended to withdraw the troops, he had all the prisoners in Tigré, including Major Salsa, released on May 18th, and on the same date the tricolor of Italy ceased to fly over Adigrat.

* * *

At this point we reach the end of great events in the history of Erythrea [1] and perhaps the true beginning of her prosperity;—for as everyone knows, "happy is the land that has no history." But there remain a few isolated details to be recorded, more especially about those men who have played leading parts in the many conflicts of the past seven or eight years;—nothing perhaps is more remarkable than the incredibly short space of time into which these incidents have been crowded.

In 1897 the Dervishes once again crossed the River Gash in great numbers, but did not venture to attack General Vigano, who was in command of the Italian troops. The armies faced one another for a few days and then the Dervishes retired, the only result of their raid being that the Italian Government, considering the defence of their widely extended western frontier too expensive, determined to cede Kassala to the British: a cession which, after some months,

[1] For present condition of Erythrea see Appendix C.

was finally accomplished on December 19th, 1897. This hasty step has since been regretted by many Italians; for within nine months of the day when Colonel Parsons hoisted the British flag over Kassala, the Sirdar had marched down the Nile and had destroyed the Dervish power, once and for all, at the battle of Omdurman.

In the meanwhile several events of importance had occurred in Tigré. Ras Alula had fought his last fight; in 1897 he had attacked old Ras Agos of Shirè; Agos was killed and Alula received a wound of which he afterwards died. In the following year Mangasha rebelled against Menelik, but Maconnen, who was sent against him, easily subdued Tigré, which province he was then granted by Menelik as a reward for his services. It seems more than ever likely that he will succeed the Negûs on the imperial throne.

The death of Ras Alula brings to mind the man against whom he plotted and warred for so many years, and in whose downfall he was largely instrumental—namely, General Baratieri.

On March 21st, 1896, the order was issued that the ex-Governor should be tried on a criminal charge. It was barely six months since the day when, as he entered the Chamber of Deputies at Rome, every man there had risen to his feet, and the President had greeted him with such marks of honour and respect as no other Italian has ever received, except Garibaldi. He was to be brought to trial for having (i) decided on an attack (on March 1st, 1896,) from motives that were inexcusable, and under conditions that rendered defeat inevitable; (ii) for having abandoned his command from 12.30 p.m. on March 1st, 1896, until 9 a.m. on March 3rd, (*i.e.* during the retreat) and having thus omitted to give orders, or take measures, such as the circumstances required, etc., etc.

After going through the evidence at great length, the Court expressed a definite decision against Baratieri on six important points, [1] but qualified them by adding five considerations that formed some excuse for his conduct, and finally acquitted him. The following two considerations (the first and the last) together with the verdict, will show the state of feeling that prevailed amongst his judges.

"Considering, nevertheless, that the imputation cast on General Baratieri, of having been led to attack the enemy by motives other than those arising out of military considerations, has not been confirmed by the results of the enquiry; and that, although the vague indications collected about this subject were sufficient to justify suspicion and admitted of an accusation being made, yet they do not carry that serious conviction which is necessary to justify a condemnation....

"Considering, finally, that in the face of the above mentioned facts, the omissions for which General Baratieri is to blame are not provided for by the law; for although these omissions at first sight resemble a criminal derogation of duty they no longer have this appearance after the public

[1] It has been insinuated by several writers, amongst them Mr. Wylde, that Baratieri showed a lack of personal courage at Adowa,—an idea scarcely credible of the victor of Coatit. Apropos of this point, we may note the following passage in the finding of the Court: "Considering that General Baratieri, after having remained in the firing line, and having been amongst the last to retire from the field of battle," etc., etc.

enquiry, which has deprived them of the character of intentional guilt and wilful negligence that is essential for a condemnation.

"For these considerations the tribunal acquits General Baratieri of all criminality, but it cannot help deploring that the conduct of affairs, in so unequal a struggle and in circumstances so difficult, should have been entrusted to a general who has shown himself so entirely unfitted to cope with the exigencies of the situation."

APPENDIX A

OPERATIONS AGAINST THE DERVISHES

Part I, Chapter IV

THE first, of the series of dangers that fell one after another upon the young Colony of Erythrea, came from the North West; it was now seven years since the fall of Khartum, and during that period] a gigantic empire had been formed by the Dervishes, reaching roughly as far south as the fourth degree northern latitude, and as far north as the second cataract of the Nile; westward it stretched away as far as Wadai, and eastwards to the Anglo-Egyptian territory of Suakim.

Countries and tribes the very names of which are scarcely known in Europe, had been subdued to the ruler at Omdurman, who bade his followers carry the true religion to the ends of the earth.

In 1885 after triumphing over Egypt, England, and every other nation that opposed him, while his movement was still at the height of its power, the Mahdi died. For a time, however, the successes continued; masses of warriors would move about from one border to another of their empire, and then, at a sudden inspiration of God, would dash over the frontier and reduce the neighbouring province to a desert. In central Africa they were the terror of the surrounding peoples; in Abyssinia, even, their approach was dreaded; and in our own army has not the soldiers' poet recorded of "Fuzzy Wuzzy," that he was "a pore benighted 'eathen but a first class fightin' man," and that he "cut our sentries up at Suakim." But, apart from poetry, there is more than one regiment in the service that remembers how the Dervishes stalked these sentries during the night and how sometimes the bodies were found gashed and mutilated in the morning; or how the young soldiers would be brought back to camp nervous and feverish after the long strain during the hours of darkness, when any moment might bring a bullet from a hidden enemy.

But such movements as Mahdiism are of course doomed to a quick rise and an equally rapid fall, because no portion of the world can live on enthusiasm, whether religious or political, for more than a few years. Mahdiism was entirely unproductive; war was necessary for its existence; it could destroy, but could not create.

It followed, therefore, in the natural order of things, that within five or six years of the death of their prophet, the triumphant Mahdiist armies, which in case of need could place almost 100,000 warriors in line, should have sunk into the snarling Dervish hordes that lived largely on an organized system of raids, and received with a certain sprinkling of cynicism the religious exhortations of the Khalifa Abdullahi.

In some places the Dervish sank so low as to earn an honest living by doing business even with the unbeliever. In Kassala, for instance, the Emir Musaed Gaidum presided over a small but growing trade between that town and the sea coast of Erythrea, which might in time have aroused the rivalry and the resentment of the British in Suakim; but these developments were too often interrupted by wars to attain to any great results.

In 1890 the first collision took place between the Dervish raiders and the Italians. In the northern portion of the Colony there is a large tract of land occupied by the tribes of the Beni-Amer,—a race of mixed origin, being in part Abyssinian and in part Arab. Coming from such stock one might naturally suppose them to inherit some of the hottest fighting blood in the world, but, on the contrary, they are said to be unwarlike[1] cultivators of the soil. Such a peaceful and prosperous race were certain to excite the cupidity and contempt of the Dervishes.

In June 1890 Major Cortese, the commander of the garrison at Keren heard that a thousand of the enemy, many of them armed with rifles taken from the Egyptians, were ravaging among the Beni Amer. He at once ordered Captain Fara, with two native companies, to march westwards as far as Bisha (about two days' march). A few days later he heard that the Dervishes were threatening Dega (the capital of Beni Amer—situated at about one-third of the way from Agordat to Asmara), so he himself started to attack them in rear. The enemy had thus penetrated into the Colony unmolested, but both officers were waiting to cut off his retreat. After successfully ravaging Dega, the invaders began their homeward march; though laden with booty they managed to evade Major Cortese, who only succeeded in

[1] Baratieri: *Memorie d'Africa.*

catching up and hastening the movements of their rear-guard; but as they passed Agordat, Captain Fara suddenly attacked them with the bayonet, driving them off into headlong flight almost before they had time to organize any resistance; they lost all their booty, and prisoners, and left some 250 dead on the field.

In June 1892, another attempt at a raid was made in the same direction, but it was met at Serobeti and defeated by Captain Hidalgo, who with 300 natives brilliantly repulsed 900 Dervishes including 100 mounted men. This small engagement is chiefly remarkable as being the first success of an officer who afterwards made a name for himself. It was after this defeat that the trade from Kassala reached its highest pitch of prosperity; it seemed, indeed, as if the Dervishes meant to give up their inroads on the Italian territory.

Throughout the year 1893 the whole country was in a condition of profound peace; there was little movement in the Dervish world. In the territory of Gallabat between Lake Tsana and the Blue Nile, some 10,000 men were being drilled and subjected to the severe discipline by which the Khalifa prepared his followers for battle; a few small raids had been directed towards Suakim by order of Osman Digna; some ravaging had been done near the wells on the road to Korosco, and Mahmud Ahmed was occupied in suffocating a new religion in Kordofan; but no danger was apprehended in the Colony; the Governor had been called away to Rome, and Colonel Arimondi was in command.[1]

[1] Melli.

The system of defence had been carefully thought out by the Italians; spies selected as far as possible from the tribes that had a blood-feud with the Dervishes, were living in Kassala, the "advanced sentinel" of the Khalifa, and in the smaller towns Carcabat, Bitame and Elit, which are slightly to the East of it: an officer of whose ability the Governor had a high opinion was in command of the intelligence department.[1] In addition to these precautions, most of the chiefs around Agordat had been won over to the Italian interest, for they naturally disliked the Dervish raids. The fort of Agordat itself though not completed, was sufficiently strong to cope with uncivilized weapons; its position was a good one, commanding the point where the roads meet from Keren and Asmara; troops from Keren could reach Agordat in about a day and a half, from Asmara in about two and a half or three.

In November (1893) General Arimondi was informed that 3,000 men had been recalled from Gallabat to Khartum, but such movements were too common to excite any alarm; soon afterwards, however, he heard that the whole army from Gallabat had been moved to Ghedaref—viz., half way to Kassala, which was always the base of operations against the Colony. At the same time war preparations were being pushed forward at Omdurman; on December 14th (1893) their forward movement began.

The Italian troops were rapidly collected at Agordat; they amounted in all to 42 officers and 33 men, Italians; of the

[1] This account is taken from General Baratieri himself; but the opinion of Signor Mantegazza, who deals at some length with the subject, is that the intelligence department was a failure.

natives there were 2,106; Arimondi had also 8 guns and 212 cavalry horses—a total of 2,402 men including irregulars. The Dervishes were about 10,000 strong. Arimondi was therefore greatly outnumbered, but he had with him several officers who afterwards became celebrated in the colonial wars of Italy; in the following account which (except the narrative of Mohammed Idris, the Ascaro) is based solely on the general's official report, only the names of those who reappear will be mentioned.

It will be seen that the Fort of Agordat lies in an obtuse angle formed between the great river Barca, flowing from East to West, and its tributary the Damtai, flowing into it from the South East. Arimondi had aligned his army on the left of the Damtai facing northwards, with its left flank resting on Agordat; he intended to defend the Barca. But he had also made preparations for taking up a fresh position facing to either flank,—whether to East or West,—in case of the Dervishes declining to make a frontal attack and endeavouring to cut his lines of communication.

This was exactly the plan they had formed; crossing the Barca lower down (where it bends northwards) they appeared on the opposite bank to that on which Arimondi stood, but instead of making a frontal attack on him they passed by, leaving him on their right, crossed the Barca again, (taking no notice of a few shots from the guns of the fort), and occupied the small villages of Sabderat[1] and Algheden, due east of his position,—thereby turning his right flank and threatening his communications with Keren. Arimondi had

[1] This village of Sabderat must not be confused with the larger Sabderat which is just outside Kassala.

obtained full knowledge of their movements by means of the Asmara squadron of cavalry which he had sent out to keep in touch with them; he understood therefore at once the object of their march, and promptly changed front to his right, in the hope that they might attack him. His small force was disposed as follows. On its right was Colonel Cortese (already mentioned) in command of a composite battalion of infantry (two companies of the 2nd and two of the 4th Natives with the afterwards celebrated Captain Galliano) and the 1st Battery; in the centre was one company and one battery within the fort, on the left (next the Barca) was another company. Slightly in rear of his left flank was the reserve, consisting of two companies, two squadrons and some irregulars.

Perceiving that his enemies had no intention of attacking him, Arimondi decided, in spite of his small numbers, to take the offensive, being afraid that they would either cut him off from Keren, or attack him during the night when the superior accuracy of his manœuvring and fire would no longer be of any avail: it must of course be remembered that to a force like that of the Dervishes their own communications were of little importance.

At 11.30 a.m. on December 21st, 1893, the battle of Agordat began; the Italian batteries opened fire on the two villages, but without any great result; at 12.15 Arimondi ordered Cortese (on the right) to advance with his battalion and battery[1] and then, as soon as the

[1] Captain Giraud's company was ordered to occupy the ground on which Cortese's men had been posted,—after the first attack it reinforced the firing line.

movement was begun, directed the two companies forming the centre and left to make a simultaneous forward movement. Cortese's four companies in échelon quickly crossed the Damtai river, and ascended on to the high ground on the opposite bank; one company had even crossed the Inchierai stream when it suddenly came in sight of the Dervishes, between 800 and 900 yards distant. It at once opened fire, as did the battery some 300 yards in rear; at the same moment the companies forming the centre (Major Fadda) and the left (Captain Oddone), having advanced amongst the palm trees beside the river, also came in contact with the enemy. The Dervishes at first returned the fire without moving, but soon they brought their banners to the front and began to advance against the Italian right, endeavouring to outflank it, especially by means of their cavalry; they had no reserves, but simply advanced in the half-moon formation of savage races,—the first line being composed of men who carried rifles, and the second of rifles and lances intermingled. The fighting shortly became serious; it is described in the following terms by one of the Ascari in Galliano's battalion,—who, we may remark, was a Mohammedan and regarded the Dervishes as brothers, though he was ready to fight against them like a loyal Buluk-bashi: "I had," he says, "only to choose between doing injury to the Dervishes and, if necessary, slaughtering some of them, or being myself injured or, indeed, slaughtered by them: of the two alternatives I far preferred the former. Besides, they were guilty of such rapine and so many cruelties that it could not be displeasing to Allah that his faithful servant Mohammed Idris should fight against them and punish them." Animated by these pious sentiments, Mohammed Idris fought like a hero. He continues:

"From the moment when Lieutenant-Colonel Cortese ordered us to advance we may say that the battle began; but from that moment I can no longer tell you exactly what happened. I know that my company, with Captain Verdelli in front, was checked in its course by a furious counter-attack of the Dervishes, and thrown back, together with the others on to the 1st Battery. I know that Captain Forno's Company made a desperate defence of the battery itself, which was trying to get its guns strapped on to the mules and retire, but without success, because the poor brutes one by one fell dead or wounded, and the artillery remained in the hands of the Dervishes. I know that in this furious melée there fell Captain Forno, Lieutenants Pennazzi and Colmia-Piassotto, Furiere[1] Prófili of the battery, and a hundred Ascari. And, finally, I know that as for myself I got a good sword cut on the left shoulder. Still I admit that while we were retiring I was glad to have found out how well my fellow-countrymen fought,—far more bravely than the Abyssinians; but when I saw Captain Giraud's company, which had been posted elsewhere and was now coming to help us, and the cavalry dismounting and advancing into the firing line, I was still more glad, because I was an Italian Buluk-bashi and wanted the Italians to win."

This is a very good description of what happened. Cortese was compelled to retire (at 12.50) leaving his guns in the

[1] The highest rank of N.C.O.: there is no exactly corresponding rank in the British army.

hands of the enemy, but he succeeded in restoring order amongst his men, and retreated slowly. Owing to this repulse of the right, the centre and left were obliged to follow suit, although their attack had been more or less successful. But the Dervish losses had been very heavy, especially amongst the chiefs; the Buluk-bashi, who knew his compatriots, tells us that "amongst their dead they counted Ahmed-Ali and two other Emirs of great repute; and, in short, the Mahdiist hordes, remaining without their chief, lost heart, and their attack became less furious.

Observing this unsteadiness on the part of the enemy, Arimondi decided (at one o'clock) to reinforce his right wing by sending forward Lieutenant Giraud and two dismounted squadrons, (as detailed by the Buluk-Bashi). The attack was then renewed and, after one failure, the Italian troops succeeded in again crossing the Damtai and recapturing their guns. The centre and left were also reinforced, and the whole line began to gain ground. Soon the companies on the Italian right were able to press back the enemy opposite them, so far as almost to hem in the whole Dervish army between themselves and the river Barca. Then the flight began: by 2.20 p.m. the victory was complete. The Dervishes left 1,000 dead, 72 banners, a machine gun and over 700 rifles on the field; their total losses amounted to about 2,000. Some attempts at pursuit were made, but without success.

The Italian losses in the battle of Agordat were 4 white men killed and 3 wounded, 104 natives killed and 121 wounded, total 232. The news of the victory was received, as was natural, with the greatest rejoicing in Italy. Colonel Arimondi was promoted to the rank of general and most of the other officers were decorated,—with almost too lavish a hand one is inclined to think. Arimondi, however, deserves all praise for his mode of conducting these operations: in the first place for the rapidity of his concentration at Agordat; then for his decision to attack although he knew that by waiting ten or twelve hours his numbers would be increased,—Captain Persico's company being on the way; and, finally, for his altered tactics, to suit the broken ground. It was here that he first employed the formation known to the Italian writers as that of the "thin lines."[1]

It undoubtedly was a brilliant success on the part of the Italian officers, and produced a definite narrowing in the political horizon of the Khalifa. That potentate was beginning to discover that the conquests of war are barren unless supplemented by those of peace; it is said that he had launched these 10,000 men eastward, in the hopes of establishing under his authority a definite trade route to one of the ports of the Red Sea, and such a scheme might undoubtedly have prolonged the life of his Empire, as a similar opening has prolonged that of Abyssinia; but after the battle of Agordat there is no further question of his reaching the sea.

On the day that the news of the victory reached Rome General Baratieri hastened to return to the Colony; he felt that his absence during a time of war might create an unfavourable impression, although it had occurred through no fault of his own. He had arrived in Italy to find the Giolitti ministry about to resign, and had tendered his own resig-

[1] *Vide* Chapter III, Baratieri's Reforms. Also Luzeux, p. 33, Etudes critiques sur la guerre entre l'Italie et l'Abyssinie. Mantegazza, p. 191, La Guerra in Africa.

nation; but the new ministry of Signor Crispi refused to accept it, so that he could now return to the colony with full confidence of their support.

No sooner had he landed in Africa than he began to think of turning Arimondi's victory to some account, and preventing the Dervishes from attempting a fresh invasion. The enterprise that to him seemed most advantageous was a raid on Kassala, as the capture of that stronghold,—in its very existence a menace to the Colony,—would paralyze their attacks, which he felt might become dangerous "if they coincided, for instance, in December (1894) or in January (1895), with a raising of shields in Ethiopia."[1] These words of his prove that he quite understood the uncertainty of affairs in Abyssinia, and wished to strike his enemies singly, in which aim he was undoubtedly right.

There were still six months to wait before the moment for the expedition could arrive, as he did not intend to move until the end of June (1894), or the beginning of July, so that the River Atbara being flooded should cut off the Dervishes from the heart of their empire, and thereby prevent their receiving any assistance from either Ghedaref or Khartum. His preparations, however, began at once and with great secrecy; until July 11th, he says, "the operation was a mystery to everyone," and on the following day he received a telegram from the Government, who had till then demurred at his scheme, giving him "carte blanche" to act as he thought fit.

[1] Baratieri's letter of June 8th, 1894. He says elsewhere that it was the news of Mangasha's reconciliation with Menelik that finally decided him to dispose of the Dervishes at once.

The operations that led to the fall of Kassala are a remarkable instance of rapid and able management. The whole expedition presents to a great extent the appearance of a leap in the dark, for the country was of course unknown to the Italians, and its inhabitants were probably hostile. The corps of operations consisted of 56 white officers, 41 white men, 16 jus-bashi (native lieutenants) 2,510 Ascari, 146 horses, 250 mules and 183 camels; the line of march, starting from Agordat, was by Dunguaz, Anasciait, Uacait, Sabderat,—a slightly northern detour about 125 miles long, but well supplied with water; in only four days this distance was accomplished without the slightest mishap and the whole corps halted at Sabderat.

At 1 a.m. on the following night (of the 16th to 17th), it moved off, headed by Hidalgo's battalion, and advanced steadily through the mist until, at 6 a.m., the presence of some Baggara cavalry was signalled; the battalions were therefore formed into two squares, and then the advance continued. At 7 a.m. the advanced guard opened fire at the enemy's cavalry who had chanced upon it,—for the force was now very near to Kassala,—and Captain Carchidio led his squadron out of the square to charge them; this charge was not altogether successful, as he was killed, with eighteen of his men, eight more of them being wounded.

The Dervishes, however, were completely surprised; not until the Italians were within 400 metres (440 yards) of the enemy's camp was it found necessary to form line. Hidalgo then led his men to the attack; at 8 a.m., being reinforced by the main body, he ordered a charge, and with a shout of "Savoia!" the enemy's camp was entered at the point of the bayonet. By 9 o'clock Generals Baratieri and Arimondi were in the market place; from 10 to 11 the troops rested, and then a battalion under Colonel Turitto was sent in pursuit of the flying enemy.

In the town were found many slaves; some of them white men, a hundred of them Egyptian soldiers,—the remains of the brave garrison of Kassala,—others from the surrounding tribes of Beni Amer etc. The Governor proceeded at once to complete his work. He had to provide for the return to their various countries of all the captives; to protect the peaceful cultivators; to burn the corpses; to collect the spoils of war and destroy the supplies that could not be used by the Italians.

The losses were 1 officer and 27 soldiers killed, 2 chiefs and 39 Ascari wounded,—those of the Dervishes do not seem to be known. But they fled leaving behind them 600 rifles, 700 lances, 100 swords, 52 banners, and 2 mountain guns, besides a store of supplies, ammunition etc. together with a large number of horses, cattle, camels etc. Their numbers before the battle amounted to about 2,000 infantry and 600 cavalry.

This operation, the capture of Kassala, was probably the most brilliant performance of Baratieri's life; as almost every detail was foreseen by him and provided for. He carried 2,500 men over 125 miles in four days without the enemy even suspecting his proximity, and then captured one of their most important towns in less than three hours. The actual fighting was of course not to be compared to that at Agordat, but one can hardly help thinking that for a commander the task required more skill.

Having taken the town, what was to be done with it? The Italians[1] determined to place a garrison there as an outpost against the Dervishes. On July 23rd he departed, leaving 1,000 infantry and two guns under command of Colonel Turitto and returned to Massowah; before he went, a small fort was built, named by order of the Government, Fort Baratieri.

As for the value of this conquest, it has been often decried by Italian writers, especially those of the Anti-African party. They assert that Kassala was too far from Massowah to be of any practical use, that to garrison it even temporarily meant withdrawing over a thousand men who were badly wanted elsewhere, while a permanent occupation was out of the question owing to the clause relating to it in the treaty with England of 1891. They even go so far as to say that Baratieri planned this expedition merely to win a personal success that would counterbalance Arimondi's triumph at Agordat.

As regards the uselessness to their colony of Kassala, they may perhaps be right, for it has since been ceded to England, but there can be no doubt that as a blow directed against the Dervish power this raid was efficacious; and, further, that it immensely increased the prestige of Italy,—a very tangible gain when dealing with savage races. These, after all, are the only two advantages that were ever claimed for it by the Governor.[2]

[1] General Baratieri says that it was the Italian Government who suggested this course of action, which has since been adversely criticised.

[2] The Governor urged, that if the Anglo-Egyptians had supplemented his success by advancing as far as Berber, or towards the lower Atbara, all danger of a fresh Dervish advance would have been removed.

APPENDIX B

THE GOVERNOR'S INTELLIGENCE SYSTEM

Part II, Chapter VIII

The Governor himself details his spy-system; he divides the spies into three classes: first, there were the Zaptié, or native carbineers in disguise; secondly, Ascari who had fought against Mangasha in the war of Debra Aila, and were therefore trusted; thirdly, the native peasants in the pay of Italy, who hated the Shoans for their ravages.

These men were not supposed, according to the system, to know each other. Some of them came in every night to report progress, others came in only when some special move of the enemy or other important event was beginning, others were permanently attached to a particular division of the army. Captain Amendune, as head of the department, questioned each man personally, but the Governor also interviewed most of them himself.

Theoretically this system ought to have produced good results, but, practically speaking, Menelik was master of Baratieri in secret intelligence matters—as indeed was natural. Signor Eduardo Ximenes tells a story very much to the point, of how Colonel Brusati of Arimondi's brigade, when returning to camp (Feb. 18th) after a small reconnoitring expedition on his own account, suddenly perceived two men hiding in a bush beside the path. Being accompanied by five other men, he went up to the place where they lay and captured—two of the Italian spies! Their excuse for hiding was that they had mistaken him for an Abyssinian—this to an Italian officer with a helmet on his head! Colonel Brusati returned to camp with the firm conviction that they had concealed themselves, either because they had some good reason for fearing discovery, or (more probably) because they meant to take news of his proximity to the Shoans and have him made prisoner.

APPENDIX C

PRESENT CONDITION OF ERYTHREA

Part II, Chapter XII

By a royal decree of February 11th, 1900, the Colony was placed under the rule of a civil government, established at Asmara and within the department of the Minister for Foreign affairs. It now costs Italy eight million lire annually (over £300,000) and is administered by 90 colonial officials and employés of various kinds. Its military force consists of 187 officers, 1,196 men (Italians), and 57 officers with 5,400 natives; the whole being divided into 3 companies of Chasseurs, 6 native battalions, 1 company of Carbineers, 1 squadron and 2 batteries (native) and a company of Engineers.

The Colony includes about 100,000 square kilometres (about the size of Portugal), but its population only amounts to 327,502 natives,—about one-fifth of that which Münzinger found some 30 years ago; this is due to the constant wars and the resulting famines. In 1898 there were 1,741 Europeans in Erythrea, (not including the soldiers) of whom 1,356 were Italians; this was a considerable increase in numbers, as compared with former years, for in 1894 there were only 623 Italians in the Colony. Of other nationalities the Greeks are the most numerous; oddly enough there does not seem to be a single British subject in the Colony of our ally.

As regards commerce: Erythrea exports coffee (chiefly to Italy), gum (to Trieste), hides (to Marseilles and Italy), wax (to Trieste), pearls and mother-of-pearl (to Trieste, Bombay and America), ivory (to Bombay),—also tortoise-shell, civet-cats and various animals; the whole value of her exports amount to about two million lire annually, which is about a quarter of her imports. The chief of these items is undoubtedly the pearl and mother-of-pearl trade which is now being systematized by the "Societa perlifera italiana" to whom its monopoly has been granted.

During the three years 1897, '98, and '99, these exports have shown no increase: on the contrary they have even diminished owing to temporary causes,—Mangasha's rebellion which interrupted the coffee trade from Gojjam, and the re-organisation of the pearl and mother-of-pearl industry which reduced the export of pearls from 612,500 lire in 1898 to 180,000 lire in 1899, and the mother-of-pearl from 906,000 lire in 1898 to 508,000 in 1899. (The coffee had sunk from 310,000 lire to 28,000.) On the other hand, apart from these temporary diminutions, there are indubitable signs of rising prosperity—every other product shows a notable increase. A convention has also been signed with the Egyptian Government relative to the trade of the Sudan.

Of the imports, the chief is the rapidly growing trade in cotton goods—(in 1897, Lire 2,370,000; in 1898, Lire 2,489,000; in 1899, Lire 3,231,000).[1] About a quarter of the Erythrean imports come from Italy.

[1] In addition to this, Italy has imported cotton goods to the value of 33,000 lire in 1897, 48,000 lire in 1898, and 90,000 lire in 1899; her returns are kept on a separate list.

The Government steadily encourages colonization: it makes a gratuitous offer of plots of land not more than one hundred hectares (a hectar is over two acres) in extent, and for a period not exceeding thirty years, to those who undertake to cultivate it in the European way, and not to sublet to natives. Twelve Italians availed themselves of this offer during the year 1899. In various parts of the Colony the agricultural and other experiments still continue; in Hamacen there is hope of discovering gold.

Perhaps the most conclusive sign of increased prosperity under Italian rule is that offered by the "tributes" exacted from the natives: these taxes amount to two or three per cent on their cattle and grain, and hitherto they have shown a marked increase during each year since the end of the war. At the end of 1896 they amounted to only 312,190 lire, in 1897 to 353,475 lire, in 1898 to 446,981 lire, and in 1899 to 587,650 lire.

There is therefore good ground for hoping that some day Italy may find in Erythrea a reward for all her past sacrifices, and enjoy those benefits, to win which for their native land, so many thousands of brave men have given their lives.

INDEX

A

B

C

D

E

F

G

H

I

J

K

L

M

N

O

P

R

S

T

U

V

W

Y

Z

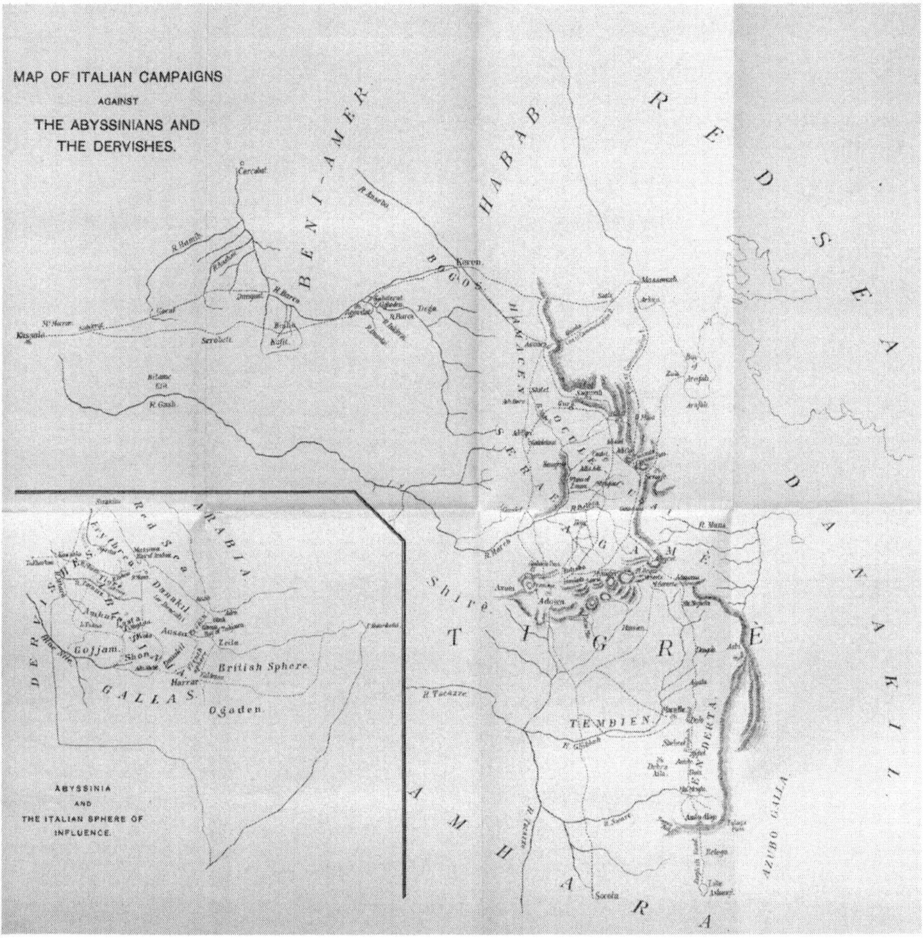
MAP OF ITALIAN CAMPAIGNS
AGAINST
THE ABYSSINIANS AND
THE DERVISHES.
ABYSSINIA
AND
THE ITALIAN SPHERE OF
INFLUENCE.
RED SEA
DANAKIL
BENI-AMER
HABAB
TIGRÉ
AMHARA
TEMBIEN
Shirè
AZUBO GALLA
Keren
Massowah
Adowa
British Sphere
Ogaden
GALLAS
Gojjam
Red Sea
ARABIA
Harrar
Zeila
R. Tacazze
R. Gash

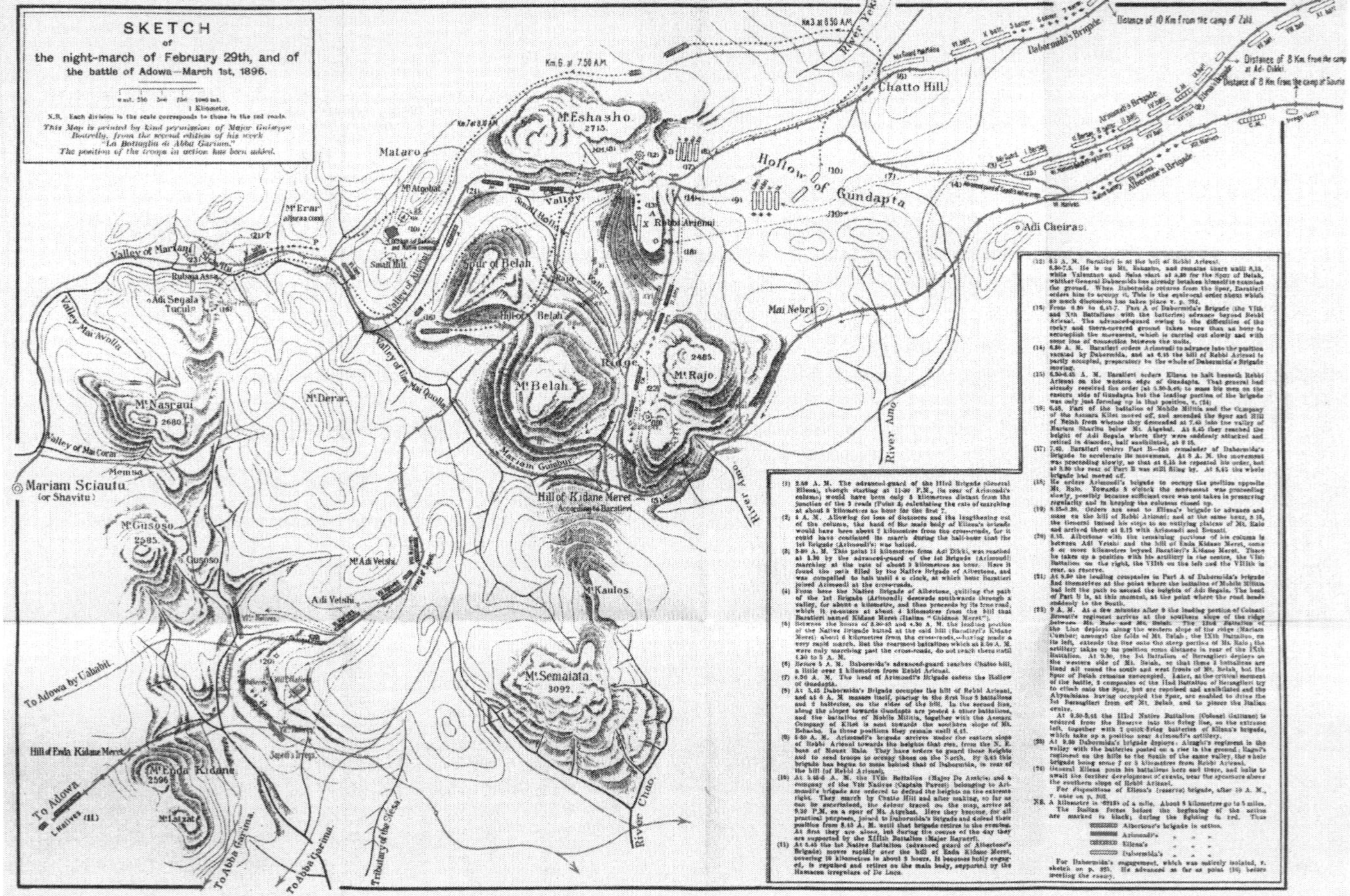
SKETCH
of
the night-march of February 29th, and of
the battle of Adowa—March 1st, 1896.
1 Kilometre.
This Map is printed by kind permission of Major Guiseppe Bourelly, from the second edition of his work "La Battaglia di Abba Garima."
The position of the troops in action has been added.
Mt. Eshasho
2715
Chatto Hill
River Yeka
Dabormida's Brigade
Distance of 10 Km from the camp of Zala
Distance of 8 Km from the camp at Adi Dikki
Arimondi's Brigade
Albertone's Brigade
Hollow of Gundapta
Adi Cheiras
Mataro
Mt. Atgobat
Mt. Erar
Valley of Mariam
Valley Mai Avolia
Adi Segala
Mt. Nasraui
2680
Valley of Mai Coram
Memsa
Mariam Sciautu
(or Shavitu)
Mt. Gusoso
2585
Gusoso
Mt. Adi Vetshi
Adi Vetshi
Mt. Derar
Valley of Atgobat
Small Hill
Spur of Belah
Belah
Ridge
Mt. Belah
Mt. Rajo
2485
Rebbi Arienni
Mai Nebri
River Amo
Mariam Gusbur
Hill of Kidane Meret
According to Baratieri
Mt. Kaulos
Mt. Semaiata
3092
River Chao
To Adowa by Uahabit
Hill of Enda Kidane Meret
Mt. Enda Kidane
2596
To Adowa
To Abba Garima
To Abba Garima
Tributary of the Mesa